P9-DBJ-064

Pesto-Spinach Dip . . . Salsa Chowder . . . Warm Scallop-Rice Salad . . . Quesadillas with Three Cheeses . . . Lamb Kabobs . . . Fettuccine Alfredo . . . Apple Strudel . . . Black Forest Pie . . . Baklava . . . Gazpacho Cooler

You'll find easy-to-follow recipes for these and many other sumptuous, guilt-free dishes in *Weight Watchers Simply Light Cooking*. Now delicious, healthful eating without changing your individual lifestyle is simpler than ever. Created with the health-conscious cook in mind, these quick, nutritious recipes will enable you to indulge in savory foods you thought would never pass your lips again!

Weight Watchers®
Simply Light Cooking

Simply Light Cooking

OVER 250 RECIPES

FROM THE KITCHENS

OF WEIGHT WATCHERS®

BASED ON THE

PERSONAL CHOICE®

PROGRAM

Photography by Matthew Klein

A PLUME BOOK

PLUME
Published by the Penguin Group
Penguin Books USA Inc., 375 Hudson Street, New York, New York 10014, U.S.A.
Penguin Books Ltd, 27 Wrights Lane, London W8 5TZ, England
Penguin Books Australia Ltd, Ringwood, Victoria, Australia
Penguin Books Canada Ltd, 10 Alcorn Avenue, Toronto, Ontario, Canada M4V 3B2
Penguin Books (N.Z.) Ltd, 182–190 Wairau Road, Auckland 10, New Zealand

Penguin Books Ltd, Registered Offices: Harmondsworth, Middlesex, England

Published by Plume, an imprint of New American Library, a division of Penguin Books USA Inc.
Previously published in an NAL Books edition.

First Plume Printing, September, 1993
10 9 8 7 6 5 4 3 2 1

Weight Watchers is a registered trademark of Weight Watchers International, Inc.

 REGISTERED TRADEMARK—MARCA REGISTRADA

LIBRARY OF CONGRESS CATALOGING-IN-PUBLICATION DATA
Simply light cooking : over 250 recipes from the kitchens of Weight
    Watchers : based on the personal Choice program / photography by
    Matthew Klein.
        p.   cm.
    Includes index.
    ISBN 0-452-26875-3
    1. Reducing diets—Recipes.   I. Weight Watchers International.
RM222.2.S5544   1993
613.2'5—dc20   93–13628
                                                   CIP

Printed in the United States of America
Set in Fournier
Designed by Signet M Design, Inc.
Photographer: Matthew Klein
Food Stylist: AJ Battifarano
Prop Stylist: Judy Singer
Introduction by Diana Morris

. . . .

We salute the thousands of Leaders and the meeting-room staffs whose dedication, patience, support and understanding have brought the Weight Watchers program alive to millions of members. With cheerful words and encouraging smiles, these wonderful men and women warmly greet their members and consistently demonstrate their commitment to helping each member succeed. Their special skills, learned through personal experience and professional training, smooth each member's path as they offer wise counsel to all who need it and congratulations for every small and large success.

We dedicate this book to Weight Watchers Leaders and the meeting-room staffs everywhere because we know that in many ways, these pages are a result of their efforts.

Contents

NTRODUCTION

Time was when plain meat and potatoes would satisfy just about everyone. Today, we demand much more. We want balanced nutrition and flexibility. Our hectic life-styles leave us little time to spend in the kitchen. We look for appetizing recipes and practical cooking techniques that fit easily into our family lives, careers, and personal goals.

For almost thirty years, Weight Watchers has meant sensible weight control through delicious, nutritious eating. We believe that healthy living should be easy and fun and that a food plan should fit your life-style—not the other way around.

This is the experience and commitment behind this very special cookbook from Weight Watchers, *Simply Light Cooking*. Inside you'll find exciting ideas for more than 250 mouth-watering dishes, a wealth of helpful cooking tips, an easy-to-understand glossary of cooking terms, and much more.

But what makes this book truly special is its ability to fit your unique life-style. No matter what the occasion or time of day, whether you live alone or with a family of four, we've included great ideas for one delicious dish after another, with the variety and flexibility you may have only dreamed of before today. Going out? Staying in? Need a fast idea for company? Feel like having something on the hearty side? How about a rich-tasting guilt-free dessert to treat yourself?

There's something for everyone: recipes for desserts, snacks, soups, and light meals, a chapter filled with great ideas for meatless dishes.

Every recipe includes a per-serving analysis of calories, protein, fat, carbohydrate, calcium, sodium, cholesterol, and dietary fiber, based on the most current nutritional research, and you'll find recipes that are cholesterol-, fat-, and/or sodium-reduced.

Naturally, each recipe provides the Selection™ Information, to tell you exactly how it fits into the Weight Watchers food plan. You'll also find that many of our recipes are accompanied by a menu suggestion to help you in your meal planning; our handy index will help you find that special recipe quickly and easily.

Since 1962, Weight Watchers has grown from a handful of people to millions of enrollments. Today, Weight Watchers is a recognized leader in the weight-control field. Members of all ages, from children to senior citizens, attend weekly meetings virtually around the globe. Growing numbers of people enjoy our popular expanding line of convenience foods, best-selling cookbooks, engagement calendars, and exercise audio cassettes.

Recipes that fit your needs, plus the satisfaction of knowing they're brought to you by weight-control and nutrition experts . . . no wonder we called it *Simply Light Cooking*!

READING THE RECIPES

To help you keep track of your choices on the Food Plan, we've provided the Selection Information for each recipe. You'll see, for example, that one serving of a recipe provides 1 Milk, 2 Proteins, and 15 Optional Calories. (Be sure to recalculate the Selection Information if you make any changes to a recipe.)

Each recipe also includes a per-serving nutritional analysis of calories, protein, fat, carbohydrate, calcium, sodium, cholesterol, and dietary fiber. These figures are for the recipe *exactly as shown*. For example, the nutritional analyses for recipes containing cooked items such as rice, pasta, or vegetables assume that no extra salt or fat will be added during cooking. If you decide to add salt or fat, you alter the nutritional information shown for the recipe—whether or not the changes affect the Selection Information.

Many recipes are reduced in sodium or cholesterol, or have 30 percent or less calories from fat. Oftentimes we've used egg substitutes, reduced-fat cheeses, and low-sodium broths in recipes with excellent results:

- "Reduced cholesterol" means that a dish containing 2 or more Proteins has 50 milligrams or less of cholesterol per serving. All other recipes so noted contain 25 milligrams or less of cholesterol per serving.

- "Reduced fat" indicates that 30 percent or less of the calories come from fat.

- "Reduced sodium" means that a dish containing 2 or more Proteins has 400 milligrams or less of sodium per serving. All other recipes so noted contain 200 milligrams or less of sodium per serving.

TIPS, TACTICS, AND TECHNIQUES

Try these helpful and time-saving hints for working smart in the kitchen:

Become Familiar with the Recipe

When trying a recipe for the first time, take a few minutes to read through the ingredients and directions. That way, you'll know everything you'll need and exactly what you'll have to do to prepare the dish successfully. It will save you from working halfway through a recipe, only to realize that you need to marinate something overnight or that you're missing an important spice.

Once you understand the recipe and are certain you have everything you'll need, make sure you have everything within easy reach: the ingredients, the recipe, and the utensils.

Be Certain You Have the Right Tools

Use nonstick cookware whenever possible. This wonderful invention is a real boon to those looking to control their fat intake because it lets you cook without adding fat. You can quickly make your own nonstick pan by spraying an ordinary pan with nonstick cooking spray (which adds few, if any, calories to food).

Use Cooked Meats to Save Cooking Time

Many of the recipes in this book call for cooked meats or poultry to help you work more efficiently and save cooking time. There are a few sources of cooked meats you can turn to, including leftovers and deli meats, such as barbecued chicken, roast beef, or ham from your supermarket's take-out department.

Thaw Overnight or in the Microwave Oven

Thaw frozen ingredients overnight in the refrigerator rather than on the counter where they can become contaminated by bacteria while thawing. Of course, if you have a microwave oven, you can thaw any ingredient in a matter of minutes.

For Best Results, Start with Preparation Amounts

Be aware that the weights of fresh fruits and vegetables shown in our recipes mean the weights *before* any peeling or cutting. If a recipe calls for 1 pound of apples, cored, pared, and diced, begin with a full pound of apples; then prepare them according to the recipe.

Measure Food Carefully

It is very important when preparing a recipe to weigh and measure ingredients carefully. This is essential both for your success with the recipe and for the accuracy of the Selection Information and nutrition analysis. Never gauge amounts by guesswork. Here are a few guidelines to keep in mind:

Foods should be weighed on a food scale. Liquids should be measured in a standard glass or clear plastic measuring cup. For amounts of less than ¼ cup, use standard measuring spoons.

Dry ingredients should be measured in metal or plastic measuring cups that come in ¼-, ⅓-, ½-, and 1-cup sizes. Be sure to level the amount with a knife or spatula. To measure less than ¼ cup, use standard measuring spoons and level the contents the same way.

Dash means approximately 1/16 of a teaspoon (½ of a ⅛-teaspoon measure or ¼ of a ¼-teaspoon measure).

Weights in recipes are given in pounds and fractions of a pound. Here are the ounce equivalents:

1 pound = 16 ounces
¾ pound = 12 ounces
½ pound = 8 ounces
¼ pound = 4 ounces

MAXIMUM TASTE AND NUTRITION WITH FEW INGREDIENTS

We did our best to create flavorful recipes that require as few ingredients as possible. Some recipes use a few more ingredients than others, but all are simple, easy to follow, and delicious. And all of them will keep you in the kitchen for less time than you may have thought possible!

Mix Those Ingredients Well!
When you are preparing a recipe for more than one serving, mix the ingredients well and be sure to divide servings evenly. This will help ensure that each portion will contain equal amounts of all ingredients.

Tips on Multiplying or Dividing Recipes
For best results, use caution when multiplying (doubling, tripling, etc.) or dividing (halving, etc.) recipes:

• Seasonings should not automatically be multiplied or divided. Begin by using less of each seasoning than the multiplied or divided recipe would call for. Then increase these amounts gradually to taste.

- Adjust cooking times and base your judgment on how the dish looks visually, rather than solely on cooking time.

Marinating Cues

Many marinades contain acidic ingredients that can react unfavorably to aluminum. Therefore, it's best to marinate foods in glass or stainless-steel containers. Even a securely fastened leakproof plastic bag makes a great marinating container—and one that doesn't require cleaning!

Some Notes on Refrigerating and Freezing

Always allow foods to cool slightly before chilling or freezing them since placing hot food in the refrigerator or freezer may affect the efficiency of the appliance. Divide large quantities of food into smaller portions before refrigerating or freezing so they will cool faster, reducing the chance of spoilage. Cover any food to be refrigerated or frozen in moisture- and vapor-resistant wrap.

Oven Techniques

Always check as directed to determine whether a dish is done rather than relying exclusively on the cooking time indicated in a recipe.

Keep tabs on the accuracy of your oven thermostat by checking it from time to time. Any discrepancy may affect the quality of your cooking. To determine whether the thermostat is registering correctly, place an oven thermometer on a rack centered in the oven. Set the oven temperature, wait 10 to 15 minutes, then check the thermometer. If the actual oven temperature doesn't match the temperature setting, adjust the setting higher or lower as needed to compensate for the difference.

Prevent heat loss and rapid changes in oven temperature by closing the oven door promptly after putting food in and avoiding opening the door unnecessarily.

Place baking pans in the middle of the center rack to permit air to circulate freely, helping food to bake evenly. Use one oven rack at a time. If you must use more than one rack at the same time, position the racks so that they divide the oven into thirds. Stagger the pans so that they're not directly above each other. Again, this helps air circulate well and keeps baking even.

Here's another helpful baking tip: When you're using only some of the cups in a muffin pan, prevent the pan from warping or burning by partially filling the empty cups with water. When you're ready to remove the muffins, carefully drain off the boiling hot water.

When broiling, unless a recipe indicates otherwise, use the standard distance of 4 inches from the heat source.

Successful Microwaving

Perhaps no other culinary innovation has had the tremendous impact on food preparation that the microwave oven has. Cooking and defrosting has never been faster or easier. And since the microwave oven cooks without heating up the kitchen, it's an especially appealing cooking tool in warm weather. A microwave oven at the office allows you to enjoy soup or leftovers that need a quick heating.

The recipes in *Simply Light Cooking* make generous use of the microwave oven. They were tested in 650–700-watt microwave ovens with variable power levels. These levels control the percentage of power introduced into the oven cavity and automatically cycle power on and off. Lower power levels cook more slowly; higher levels cook faster. The power levels may also vary depending on the brand of oven. Our recipes use these power levels:

High (100%)
Medium-High (60–70%)
Medium (50%)
Low (10–20%)

Adjust the recipes if the levels in your microwave oven are different from these. In a lower-wattage oven, increase the cooking time. For a higher-wattage oven, decrease the cooking time slightly.

When cooking in your microwave oven, be sure to use cookware that is specifically recommended for use in the microwave oven, such as microwavable casseroles with matching covers. When food is arranged on a microwavable plate or in custard cups, try using an inverted microwavable pie plate or saucer as a cover.

SOME SPECIAL NOTES ABOUT OUR INGREDIENTS

Bacon. Some recipes include bacon because of its special taste and savory aroma. Whenever possible, we've provided a recipe variation that does not use bacon.

Broth. Canned ready-to-serve low-sodium broth is used in many of the recipes to add flavor to a dish while keeping the sodium level under control.

Butter. Although most of our recipes use lower-saturated-fat alternatives (such as nonstick cooking spray, margarine, vegetable oil, or olive oil), at times a small amount of butter is used in a recipe because of its flavor-enhancing capabilities. When the recipe calls for butter or whipped butter, you may use the lightly salted kind unless sweet butter is specified. Of course, if you prefer not to cook with butter, you can always prepare the variation of the recipe that does not use butter.

Cheese. The cheese used in our recipes is very often the reduced-fat variety, since other types add a substantial amount of fat to a dish. Reduced-fat cheeses have another advantage for health-conscious cooks—they're also often lower in sodium as well.

Eggs. Because of the danger of salmonella, certain precautions should be taken with eggs:

- Never use cracked or dirty eggs.

- Buy eggs stored in a refrigerator case only.

- Refrigerate eggs as soon as you get home from the supermarket. Store eggs in their carton to prevent their absorbing odors from the refrigerator. Don't wash them before storing or using.

- Do not eat raw eggs or foods made with raw eggs.

- Cook eggs until both the whites and the yolks are firm (not runny or loose). Over well is safer than sunny side up.

- Don't leave eggs, either raw or cooked, out of the refrigerator for more than two hours.

- Use fresh eggs within five weeks of purchase and cooked ones within one week.

- Refrigerate leftover uncooked egg whites and yolks immediately and discard any you don't use after four days.

- Wash any areas of the kitchen that come in contact with raw eggs with hot soapy water.

- Serve eggs and egg-rich foods promptly after cooking.

- Egg substitutes are made mostly of egg white (the high-protein portion of the egg). They are cholesterol free (some brands are also fat free) and are usually available in the supermarket freezer section.

- Keep frozen egg substitutes in the freezer until needed. Thaw the container in the refrigerator. Put the container under cold running water to hasten thawing when you're in a hurry.

Fruits. Fruits and fruit juices (canned and frozen) used in these recipes should not contain added sugar, although sugar substitutes are permitted. Canned fruit may be packed in its own juice or in another fruit juice, blend of juices, or water.

Gelatin. Since gelatin burns very easily, when dissolving unflavored gelatin over direct heat, keep the heat low and stir constantly.

Liqueurs. If you don't have the liqueur specified in a recipe, you may substitute one of your favorites.

Oils. Vegetable oils have specific properties that make them work well in certain recipes and they are sometimes interchangeable. When no particular type is specified in a recipe, you may use safflower, sunflower, soybean, corn, cottonseed, or any combination of these. However, because olive, walnut, and peanut oils add their distinctive flavors to a recipe, be sure to use these when specified.

Chinese sesame oil is available in light and dark varieties. When this oil is required in a recipe, use the dark kind. The light variety is bland, whereas the dark variety, which is made from toasted sesame seeds, has a rich amber color and characteristic sesame flavor. Feel free to use the light variety as a substitute for any other vegetable oil called for in a recipe.

Be sure to store nut and seed oils (such as walnut, hazelnut, peanut, almond, and sesame oils) in the refrigerator, rather than the cupboard, after they have been opened. This will prevent their spoiling or developing odors.

Shellfish. Always buy clams and mussels live and make sure they have tightly closed shells. If you spot a slightly open shell, give it a hard tap. It should snap shut. Do not use any that won't snap tightly shut.

It is important that fresh clams be given a thorough cleaning before cooking. To remove sand thoroughly from clams, place them in a large bowl covered with cornmeal and some water. Refrigerate overnight. Before preparing them, discard the cornmeal mixture, thoroughly scrub the clams with a brush or scrubbing pad, and rinse them under cold running water.

Ground Beef. Select lean ground beef to keep your intake of fat and cholesterol as low as possible.

Vegetables. Vegetables should be fresh, unless otherwise indicated. If you choose to substitute the canned or frozen varieties, adjust cooking times accordingly. Be aware that using canned or thawed frozen vegetables may also increase the sodium content of the recipe.

Peppers. Chili peppers contain volatile oils that can make your skin and eyes burn. When working with these hot peppers, you may want to wear rubber gloves. Be careful not to touch your face or eyes while handling hot peppers. After handling these peppers, thoroughly wash your hands and the knife and cutting board to remove all traces of the peppers.

Lemon or Orange Zest. The zest of a fruit is the peel without any of the pith (white membrane). To remove zest from the fruit, use a zester or vegetable peeler; wrap fruit in plastic wrap and refrigerate for use at another time.

Lettuce. When lettuce is called for in the recipes, it is assumed that either iceberg or romaine will be used. Four lettuce leaves provide one Vegetable Selection. If you use any other type of lettuce, such as Boston or Bibb, eight lettuce leaves provide one Vegetable Selection.

Whipped Topping. This lower-calorie alternative to whipped cream is used in a few dessert recipes.

Seasonings. We recommend using fresh herbs in many of our recipes. When appropriate, the amount of dried herb that may be substituted is also included. If the recipe does not have a dried alternative, use fresh only. When substituting fresh spices for ground spices, use approximately 8 times the amount (for example, 1 teaspoon minced pared gingerroot instead of ⅛ teaspoon ground ginger).

One Final Note
We sometimes use unusual ingredients in our recipes, such as sun-dried tomatoes, shiitake mushrooms, and balsamic and raspberry vinegars. When possible, however, we've given you the choice of using more common ingredients as alternatives.

SIMPLY LIGHT COOKING

BREAKFAST

OFTEN TOUTED AS THE MOST IMPORTANT MEAL, BREAKFAST sets the pace for the day. While some of us revel in a leisurely breakfast to let the reality of morning sink in, others would rather grab little more than coffee and a grapefruit. Regardless, knowing that you've had this meal invariably helps most of us stay happy and sated until noon. To honor the sanctity of individual breakfast preferences, most of these recipes serve one. If breakfast must be on the go, take-along meals like Scramble-in-a-Pocket or Blueberry Cottage Cheese are easy to pack and neat to eat. Worried that the whole family won't eat a good breakfast? Break out Apple and Cheddar Corn Muffins or Zucchini-Lemon Muffins. One of these with a glass of skim milk is the perfect fast-food breakfast. Cheese and Salmon Bagel is easy to assemble and suits those with a taste for the savory. If it takes a hot breakfast to get you moving, Apple Nut Oatmeal wakes up the old standard while Hot Couscous Breakfast, served with fruit and skim milk, is altogether new. Refreshing and dessertlike, Peach and Strawberry Breakfast Parfait seems like a summer natural, but you can enjoy this year round with canned fruit. Make this the night before so all you need to do is spoon right in! For some, nothing is faster than a breakfast drink. Creamy Peanut Butter and Banana Shake does the trick—protein, milk, and fruit in one frosty glass. With the promise of these meals ahead of you, we know you won't miss a chance to have breakfast!

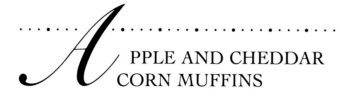

APPLE AND CHEDDAR CORN MUFFINS

For a complete breakfast, remember to include 1 serving of Milk or Protein.

Apple and Cheddar Corn Muffins

with Reduced-Calorie Apricot Spread

Coffee or Tea

MAKES 12 SERVINGS, 1 MUFFIN EACH
(SHOWN WITH SAVORY ZUCCHINI MUFFINS; SEE PAGE 228)

1⅔ cups plus 1 teaspoon all-purpose flour
1½ ounces uncooked yellow cornmeal
1 tablespoon double-acting baking powder
¾ pound apples, cored, pared, and finely chopped
½ cup thawed frozen whole-kernel corn

2¼ ounces reduced-fat Cheddar cheese, shredded
⅓ cup granulated sugar
Dash ground cinnamon
Dash ground nutmeg
⅓ cup plus 2 teaspoons corn oil
3 eggs, lightly beaten

1 Preheat oven to 400°F. Line twelve 2½-inch-diameter muffin-pan cups with paper baking cups; set aside.

2 In large mixing bowl combine flour, cornmeal, and baking powder. Add apples, corn, cheese, sugar, cinnamon, and nutmeg, stirring to combine. In small mixing bowl beat together oil and eggs; stir into flour mixture (*do not beat or overmix*).

3 Fill each baking cup with an equal amount of batter (each will be about ⅔ full). Bake in middle of center oven rack for 15 minutes (until muffins are golden and a toothpick inserted in center comes out dry). Set pan on wire rack and let cool.

EACH SERVING PROVIDES: 1½ FATS; ½ PROTEIN; 1 BREAD; ¼ FRUIT; 25 OPTIONAL CALORIES
PER SERVING: 214 CALORIES; 5 G PROTEIN; 9 G FAT; 27 G CARBOHYDRATE; 110 MG CALCIUM; 160 MG SODIUM; 57 MG CHOLESTEROL; 1 G DIETARY FIBER
REDUCED SODIUM

ZUCCHINI-LEMON MUFFINS

Pair a tasty muffin with reduced-calorie hot cocoa for a fuss-free breakfast.

MAKES 12 SERVINGS, 1 MUFFIN EACH

2¼ cups all-purpose flour
½ cup granulated sugar
2 teaspoons double-acting
　　baking powder
1 teaspoon baking soda
1½ cups shredded zucchini

¾ cup thawed frozen egg
　　substitute
¼ cup vegetable oil
2 tablespoons lemon juice
1 teaspoon grated lemon peel

1　Preheat oven to 350°F. Line twelve 2½-inch muffin-pan cups with paper baking cups; set aside.

2　In large mixing bowl combine flour, sugar, baking powder, and baking soda; set aside. In medium mixing bowl combine remaining ingredients, stirring to combine; add to flour mixture and stir until moistened (*do not beat or overmix*).

3　Fill each baking cup with an equal amount of batter (each will be about ⅔ full). Bake in middle of center oven rack for 20 minutes (until muffins are golden and a toothpick inserted in center comes out dry). Remove muffins from pan to wire rack and let cool.

EACH SERVING PROVIDES: 1 FAT; ¼ PROTEIN; ¼ VEGETABLE; 1 BREAD; 40 OPTIONAL CALORIES
PER SERVING: 167 CALORIES; 4 G PROTEIN; 5 G FAT; 27 G CARBOHYDRATE; 47 MG CALCIUM; 161 MG SODIUM; 0 MG CHOLESTEROL; 1 G DIETARY FIBER
REDUCED CHOLESTEROL, FAT AND SODIUM

POTATO OMELET

MAKES 6 SERVINGS

1 package (six ½-cup servings)
   au gratin potatoes and sauce
   mix
¼ cup sliced scallions (green
   onions)

1 tablespoon margarine
9 eggs, lightly beaten, divided

1 Preheat oven to 375°F. Prepare potatoes and sauce mix according to package directions (*do not bake*); stir in scallions and set aside.

2 Spray 10-inch nonstick skillet that has an oven-safe or removable handle with nonstick cooking spray; melt margarine in skillet. Pour half of the eggs into skillet and cook over medium-high heat until bottom is set, about 1 minute.

3 Spread potato-scallion mixture over center of eggs; pour remaining eggs over potato mixture.

4 Transfer skillet to oven and bake until eggs are set, about 15 minutes. Invert omelet onto serving platter.

EACH SERVING PROVIDES: ½ FAT; 1½ PROTEINS; 1 BREAD; 40 OPTIONAL CALORIES
PER SERVING: 261 CALORIES; 13 G PROTEIN; 15 G FAT; 21 G CARBOHYDRATE; 120 MG CALCIUM; 577 MG SODIUM; 319 MG CHOLESTEROL; 0.1 G DIETARY FIBER (THIS FIGURE DOES NOT INCLUDE AU GRATIN POTATOES; NUTRITION ANALYSIS NOT AVAILABLE)

Potato Omelet

Canadian-Style Bacon

*Toasted English
Muffin with Reduced-
Calorie Strawberry
Spread*

Coffee or Tea

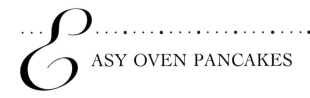

EASY OVEN PANCAKES

To make this fancy breakfast a complete meal, combine these scrumptious pancakes with grilled Canadian-style bacon.

MAKES 2 SERVINGS, 3 PANCAKES EACH

⅓ cup plus 2 teaspoons
   buttermilk baking mix
¼ cup plain low-fat yogurt
2 tablespoons plus 2 teaspoons
   apricot *or* peach nectar

1½ teaspoons grated orange peel
½ teaspoon poppy seed

1   Preheat oven to 400°F. In small mixing bowl combine all ingredients, stirring until smooth.

2   Spray nonstick baking sheet with nonstick cooking spray. Using a heaping tablespoon of batter for each pancake, drop batter onto baking sheet, making 6 pancakes and leaving a space of about 1 inch between each. Bake for 10 minutes, or until pancakes are browned on bottom; using pancake turner, turn pancakes over and cook until other sides are browned, about 2 minutes.

EACH SERVING PROVIDES: 1 BREAD; ¼ FRUIT; 40 OPTIONAL CALORIES
PER SERVING: 121 CALORIES; 3 G PROTEIN; 3 G FAT; 19 G CARBOHYDRATE; 96 MG CALCIUM; 283 MG SODIUM; 2 MG CHOLESTEROL; 14 G DIETARY FIBER
REDUCED CHOLESTEROL AND FAT

CHEESE TOAST

MAKES 1 SERVING

3 tablespoons part-skim ricotta
   cheese
1 tablespoon thawed frozen egg
   substitute
1 tablespoon light cream cheese

½ teaspoon granulated sugar
½ teaspoon cornstarch
½ teaspoon vanilla extract
2 slices raisin bread, lightly
   toasted

1   Preheat toaster oven to 350°F. In small bowl combine all ingredients except bread.

2   Set bread on toaster-oven tray; spread half of the cheese mixture on each slice of bread. Bake until cheese mixture is puffed, about 5 minutes.

EACH SERVING PROVIDES: 1 PROTEIN; 2 BREADS; 50 OPTIONAL CALORIES

PER SERVING: 251 CALORIES; 11 G PROTEIN; 8 G FAT; 34 G CARBOHYDRATE; 186 MG CALCIUM; 340 MG SODIUM; 23 MG CHOLESTEROL; DIETARY FIBER DATA NOT AVAILABLE

REDUCED CHOLESTEROL AND FAT

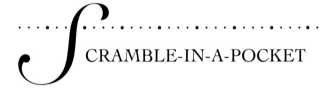CRAMBLE-IN-A-POCKET

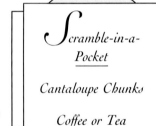

Scramble-in-a-Pocket

Cantaloupe Chunks

Coffee or Tea

MAKES 1 SERVING

½ teaspoon olive *or* vegetable oil
½ cup sliced mushrooms
¼ cup diced red onion
¼ cup diced red *or* green bell pepper

¼ cup thawed frozen egg substitute
1 tablespoon light cream cheese, softened
1 small pita (1 ounce)

1   In small nonstick skillet heat oil; add mushrooms, onion, and pepper and cook over medium-high heat, stirring frequently, until pepper is tender-crisp, about 1 minute.

2   Add egg substitute and cream cheese and cook, stirring constantly, until egg substitute is set, about 2 minutes.

3   Using a sharp knife, cut ¼ of the way around edge of pita; open to form pocket. Fill pocket with egg substitute mixture.

EACH SERVING PROVIDES: ½ FAT; 1 PROTEIN; 2 VEGETABLES; 1 BREAD; 35 OPTIONAL CALORIES

PER SERVING: 190 CALORIES; 11 G PROTEIN; 5 G FAT; 26 G CARBOHYDRATE; 58 MG CALCIUM; 344 MG SODIUM; 7 MG CHOLESTEROL; 2 G DIETARY FIBER

REDUCED CHOLESTEROL AND FAT

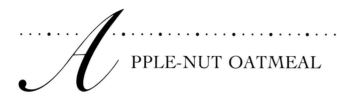

APPLE-NUT OATMEAL

Cereal and milk go hand-in-hand. So don't forget the milk!

MAKES 1 SERVING

¾ ounce uncooked quick-cooking
    oats
¾ ounce dried apple slices, diced
½ ounce shelled walnuts, toasted
    and chopped

1 tablespoon half-and-half (blend
    of milk and cream)

1 In small saucepan bring *⅔ cup water* to a boil; stir in oats and apple. Reduce heat to medium and cook, stirring frequently, until liquid is absorbed, 2 to 3 minutes.

2 Transfer to serving bowl; top with walnuts and half-and-half.

EACH SERVING PROVIDES: 1 FAT; ½ PROTEIN; 1 BREAD; 1 FRUIT; 25 OPTIONAL CALORIES
PER SERVING: 244 CALORIES; 6 G PROTEIN; 12 G FAT; 31 G CARBOHYDRATE; 43 MG CALCIUM; 27 MG SODIUM; 6 MG CHOLESTEROL; 2 G DIETARY FIBER (THIS FIGURE DOES NOT INCLUDE APPLE SLICES; NUTRITION ANALYSIS NOT AVAILABLE)
REDUCED CHOLESTEROL AND SODIUM

RICE-CAKE PORRIDGE

MAKES 1 SERVING

½ cup skim *or* nonfat milk
½ small apple (about 2 ounces),
    cored, pared, and chopped
1 tablespoon dark raisins *or* dried
    currants

1 teaspoon honey
2 plain rice cakes, broken into
    pieces

1 In 1-quart saucepan combine all ingredients except rice cakes; cook over high heat until mixture comes to a boil.

2 Remove from heat; stir in rice cake pieces. Cover and let stand until rice cakes soften, about 5 minutes.

EACH SERVING PROVIDES: ½ MILK; 1 BREAD; 1 FRUIT; 20 OPTIONAL CALORIES

PER SERVING: 189 CALORIES; 7 G PROTEIN; 4 G FAT; 42 G CARBOHYDRATE; 157 MG CALCIUM; 85 MG SODIUM; 2 MG CHOLESTEROL; 1 G DIETARY FIBER (THIS FIGURE DOES NOT INCLUDE RICE CAKES; NUTRITION ANALYSIS NOT AVAILABLE)

REDUCED CHOLESTEROL, FAT AND SODIUM

$\mathscr{H}$OT COUSCOUS BREAKFAST

This unusual breakfast is sure to satisfy. Combine it with fresh fruit and skim milk for your next morning meal.

MAKES 1 SERVING

¼ teaspoon grated orange peel
1 ounce uncooked couscous (dry precooked semolina)

½ ounce toasted almonds, sliced
1 tablespoon half-and-half (blend of milk and cream)

1 In small saucepan combine *¼ cup water* and the orange peel and bring to a boil; remove from heat and stir in couscous. Cover and let stand for 5 minutes.

2 Transfer couscous to serving bowl; top with almonds and half-and-half.

EACH SERVING PROVIDES: 1 FAT; ½ PROTEIN; 1 BREAD; 25 OPTIONAL CALORIES

PER SERVING: 210 CALORIES; 7 G PROTEIN; 9 G FAT; 26 G CARBOHYDRATE; 61 MG CALCIUM; 11 MG SODIUM; 6 MG CHOLESTEROL; 1 G DIETARY FIBER (THIS FIGURE DOES NOT INCLUDE COUSCOUS; NUTRITION ANALYSIS NOT AVAILABLE)

REDUCED CHOLESTEROL AND SODIUM

GRANOLA

Yogurt makes a great accompaniment.

MAKES 2 SERVINGS, ABOUT ⅓ CUP EACH

¾ ounce uncooked quick-cooking oats	1 teaspoon vegetable oil
½ ounce sliced almonds	1 teaspoon maple syrup
2 teaspoons shredded coconut	¼ teaspoon vanilla extract
1 teaspoon wheat germ	2 tablespoons golden raisins *or*
¼ teaspoon ground cinnamon	¾ ounce mixed dried fruit

Granola

Plain Low-Fat Yogurt

Mixed Berries

Coffee or Tea

Sparkling Orange Juice (orange juice and club soda with mint sprig)

1 Preheat oven to 375°F. In medium mixing bowl combine first 5 ingredients.

2 In small bowl combine oil, syrup, and vanilla; add to oat mixture and toss to combine.

3 On nonstick baking sheet spread oat mixture. Bake, stirring frequently, until lightly browned, 8 to 10 minutes. Transfer baking sheet to wire rack and let cool.

4 Transfer oat mixture to medium mixing bowl; add dried fruit and toss to combine. Store in airtight container for up to 1 week.

EACH SERVING PROVIDES: 1 FAT; ¼ PROTEIN; ½ BREAD; ½ FRUIT; 25 OPTIONAL CALORIES

PER SERVING: 151 CALORIES; 4 G PROTEIN; 7 G FAT; 19 G CARBOHYDRATE; 36 MG CALCIUM; 7 MG SODIUM; 0 MG CHOLESTEROL; 2 G DIETARY FIBER

Serving Suggestion —Spread ¾ cup plain low-fat yogurt in shallow bowl. Sprinkle with 1 serving Granola and top with ½ cup whole strawberries, halved, and 3 tablespoons each blueberries and raspberries. Garnish with mint sprigs. Add 1 Milk and 1 Fruit to Serving Information.

PER SERVING: 308 CALORIES; 14 G PROTEIN; 10 G FAT; 43 G CARBOHYDRATE; 365 MG CALCIUM; 129 MG SODIUM; 10 MG CHOLESTEROL; 5 G DIETARY FIBER
REDUCED CHOLESTEROL AND SODIUM

CHEESE AND SALMON BAGEL

MAKES 1 SERVING

1 tablespoon light cream cheese
1 mini bagel (1 ounce), cut in half horizontally and toasted
1 teaspoon rinsed drained capers

1 ounce thinly sliced smoked salmon (lox)
2 thin tomato slices
2 medium red onion slices

Cheese and Salmon Bagel

Orange and Grapefruit Sections

Coffee or Tea

Spread cream cheese over one cut side of toasted bagel; top with capers, salmon, tomato, and onion. Top with remaining half of toasted bagel.

EACH SERVING PROVIDES: 1 PROTEIN; 1 VEGETABLE; 1 BREAD; 35 OPTIONAL CALORIES

PER SERVING: 152 CALORIES; 10 G PROTEIN; 4 G FAT; 19 G CARBOHYDRATE; 42 MG CALCIUM; 553 MG SODIUM; 14 MG CHOLESTEROL; 1 G DIETARY FIBER (THIS FIGURE DOES NOT INCLUDE CAPERS; NUTRITION ANALYSIS NOT AVAILABLE)

REDUCED CHOLESTEROL AND FAT

PEANUT BUTTER AND BANANA SHAKE

Start off your day on the nutty side with this luscious shake.

MAKES 1 SERVING

1 packet reduced-calorie vanilla *or* chocolate-flavored milk beverage
½ medium ripe banana, peeled and sliced

1½ teaspoons creamy peanut butter
4 ice cubes

1 In blender combine milk beverage and *¾ cup cold water* and process on high speed until thoroughly combined, about 30 seconds.

2 Add banana and peanut butter and process on low speed until smooth, scraping down sides of container as necessary.

3 Remove center of blender cover and, with blender running, add ice cubes, one at a time; process on high speed after each addition, until ice cubes are dissolved (mixture will be thick).

EACH SERVING PROVIDES: 1 MILK; ½ FAT; ½ PROTEIN; 1 FRUIT
PER SERVING: 170 CALORIES; 9 G PROTEIN; 4 G FAT; 26 G CARBOHYDRATE; 156 MG CALCIUM; 38 MG SODIUM; 0 MG CHOLESTEROL; 1 G DIETARY FIBER
REDUCED CHOLESTEROL, FAT AND SODIUM

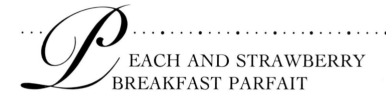

*P*EACH AND STRAWBERRY BREAKFAST PARFAIT

MAKES 1 SERVING

¾ cup plain nonfat yogurt
½ cup strawberries, cut into
    halves (reserve 1 whole
    strawberry for garnish)
1 teaspoon pourable all-fruit
    strawberry syrup

¼ cup chopped peach
½ teaspoon granulated sugar
½ teaspoon wheat germ

1 In small mixing bowl combine first 3 ingredients.

2 In separate small mixing bowl combine peach and sugar, stirring to coat.

3 Into 10-ounce parfait glass spoon half of the strawberry mixture; top with peach mixture and remaining strawberry mixture.

4 Garnish with reserved strawberry and sprinkle with wheat germ.

EACH SERVING PROVIDES: 1 MILK; 1 FRUIT; 35 OPTIONAL CALORIES
PER SERVING: 161 CALORIES; 11 G PROTEIN; 1 G FAT; 29 G CARBOHYDRATE; 352 MG CALCIUM; 134 MG SODIUM; 3 MG CHOLESTEROL; 3 G DIETARY FIBER
REDUCED CHOLESTEROL, FAT AND SODIUM

BLUEBERRY COTTAGE CHEESE

MAKES 1 SERVING

¾ cup fresh *or* thawed frozen
    blueberries (no sugar added),
    divided
⅓ cup low-fat cottage cheese
    (1% milk fat)

2 tablespoons apricot nectar
1 teaspoon shredded coconut
½ cup shredded lettuce leaves

Blueberry
Cottage
Cheese

Cinnamon Graham
Crackers

Coffee or Tea

1 In small mixing bowl combine ¼ cup blueberries and the cottage cheese;
stir well.

2 In blender combine remaining blueberries and the nectar and process on
high speed until pureed, about 1 minute.

3 Put cottage-cheese mixture in resealable plastic container and pour
blueberry-nectar mixture over. Sprinkle with coconut. Cover and refrigerate until ready to pack. Serve with shredded lettuce.

EACH SERVING PROVIDES: 1 PROTEIN; 1 VEGETABLE; 1 FRUIT; 35 OPTIONAL
CALORIES
PER SERVING: 145 CALORIES; 10 G PROTEIN; 2 G FAT; 24 G CARBOHYDRATE; 73 MG
CALCIUM; 317 MG SODIUM; 3 MG CHOLESTEROL; 3 G DIETARY FIBER
REDUCED CHOLESTEROL AND FAT

APPETIZERS

FEW WORDS CONJURE UP MORE CULINARY ANTICIPATION THAN *appetizer*. It promises both the expected and the unexpected. A first course, a snack, finger food, dip, or spread, an appetizer is anything that delights an appetite or stimulates one. It's no wonder restaurants have taken to calling these starters "appeteasers." With that in mind, the following collection of recipes reflects the spirit of the word. Warm Asparagus with Mushroom Vinaigrette or Roasted Peppers with Capers will satisfy traditionalists who favor appetizers served prior to a main course. For group gatherings or intimate tête-à-têtes, pair a crudite platter, crackers, or cocktail breads with Pesto-Spinach Dip, Citrus–Honey Mustard Dip, or the classic party dip—Onion. Exotic finger foods with an ethnic flavor, like Mini Calzones, Steamed Seafood Dumplings, and Spanakopitas (a mouthful that means spinach pies in Greek), will become conversation pieces as your guests hunt you down for "just one more." Garlic Knots, made easy with refrigerated pizza dough, are tasty rolls reminiscent of Italian garlic bread. They'll win rave reviews passed as hors d'oeuvre, or as part of a meal. Adapt the popular concept of grazing and plan a dinner around a balanced variety of these satisfying starters. Your family and friends won't forget all the delicious "apps" they sampled at your soiree. Be creative and indulge your appetite!

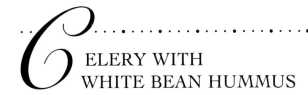

CELERY WITH WHITE BEAN HUMMUS

MAKES 2 SERVINGS

¼ pound rinsed drained canned white kidney (cannellini) beans

1 tablespoon tahini (sesame paste)

2 teaspoons chopped shallot

2 teaspoons freshly squeezed lemon juice

¼ teaspoon garlic powder
Dash pepper

1 tablespoon finely chopped fresh dill *or* ½ teaspoon dillweed

2 medium celery ribs, cut into ten 2-inch pieces

1 In food processor combine all ingredients except dill and celery and process until mixture resembles a smooth paste. Stir in dill.

2 Spread an equal amount of bean mixture onto each piece of celery.

EACH SERVING PROVIDES: ½ FAT; 1½ PROTEINS; ½ VEGETABLE

PER SERVING: 123 CALORIES; 7 G PROTEIN; 5 G FAT; 15 G CARBOHYDRATE; 74 MG CALCIUM; 162 MG SODIUM; 0 MG CHOLESTEROL; 5 G DIETARY FIBER

REDUCED CHOLESTEROL AND SODIUM

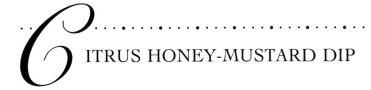

CITRUS HONEY-MUSTARD DIP

This tangy dip can be stored in the refrigerator for up to 4 days. Serve it with assorted fresh vegetables at your next gathering.

MAKES 4 SERVINGS, ABOUT 3 TABLESPOONS EACH

2 ounces firm-style tofu

2 tablespoons thawed frozen concentrated orange juice (no sugar added)

1 tablespoon plus 1 teaspoon reduced-calorie mayonnaise

2 teaspoons country Dijon-style mustard

2 teaspoons honey

In blender combine all ingredients until smooth.

EACH SERVING PROVIDES: ½ FAT; ¼ PROTEIN; ¼ FRUIT; 10 OPTIONAL CALORIES

PER SERVING: 62 CALORIES; 2 G PROTEIN; 3 G FAT; 8 G CARBOHYDRATE; 32 MG CALCIUM; 104 MG SODIUM; 2 MG CHOLESTEROL; 0.8 G DIETARY FIBER (THIS FIGURE DOES NOT INCLUDE TOFU; NUTRITION ANALYSIS NOT AVAILABLE)

REDUCED CHOLESTEROL AND SODIUM

ANTIPASTO DIP

Serve with assorted vegetables, melba rounds, or flat breads.

MAKES 4 SERVINGS, ABOUT ¼ CUP EACH

¼ cup plain low-fat yogurt
¼ cup light sour cream
6 large pitted black olives, finely chopped
2 tablespoons reduced-calorie mayonnaise
2 tablespoons finely chopped pimiento

2 tablespoons chopped radish
1 tablespoon seeded and finely chopped pepperoncini
½ teaspoon finely chopped rinsed drained capers

In small mixing bowl place all ingredients, stirring to combine thoroughly. Cover and refrigerate until flavors blend, at least 15 minutes.

EACH SERVING PROVIDES: 1 FAT; ⅛ VEGETABLE; 35 OPTIONAL CALORIES

PER SERVING: 64 CALORIES; 2 G PROTEIN; 5 G FAT; 3 G CARBOHYDRATE; 33 MG CALCIUM; 120 MG SODIUM; 8 MG CHOLESTEROL; 0.3 G DIETARY FIBER (THIS FIGURE DOES NOT INCLUDE PIMIENTO, PEPPERONCINI, AND CAPERS; NUTRITION ANALYSIS NOT AVAILABLE)

REDUCED CHOLESTEROL AND SODIUM

LIGHT GUACAMOLE

Tofu packs this dip with added nutrition. Serve it with assorted fresh vegetables or taco chips.

MAKES 4 SERVINGS, ABOUT ⅓ CUP EACH

(SHOWN WITH MEXICAN BURGER; SEE PAGE 187)

¼ pound firm-style tofu
¼ medium avocado (about 2 ounces), pared
½ medium tomato, chopped
¼ cup diced green bell pepper
¼ cup diced onion
1 garlic clove, minced

1 tablespoon diced fresh *or* drained canned green chili pepper
1 tablespoon freshly squeezed lime *or* lemon juice
Dash ground red pepper

1 In blender combine tofu and avocado and process until smooth, scraping down sides of container as necessary.

2 Transfer tofu-avocado mixture to small mixing bowl; add remaining ingredients and stir to combine.

EACH SERVING PROVIDES: ½ FAT; ½ PROTEIN; ½ VEGETABLE

PER SERVING: 69 CALORIES; 5 G PROTEIN; 4 G FAT; 5 G CARBOHYDRATE; 66 MG CALCIUM; 7 MG SODIUM; 0 MG CHOLESTEROL; 1 G DIETARY FIBER (THIS FIGURE DOES NOT INCLUDE TOFU; NUTRITION ANALYSIS NOT AVAILABLE)

REDUCED CHOLESTEROL AND SODIUM

PESTO-SPINACH DIP

MAKES 4 SERVINGS, ABOUT ⅓ CUP EACH

½ cup plain low-fat yogurt
⅓ cup light sour cream
¼ cup Pesto (see below)
   Dash ground nutmeg

½ cup well-drained cooked frozen
   chopped spinach
3 ounces sesame breadsticks

In medium mixing bowl, using a wire whisk, beat together yogurt, sour cream, Pesto, and nutmeg. Stir in spinach. Cover and refrigerate until ready to serve. Serve with breadsticks.

EACH SERVING (INCLUDING PESTO) PROVIDES: 1½ FATS; ¼ PROTEIN; ¼ VEGETABLE; 1 BREAD; 60 OPTIONAL CALORIES

PER SERVING: 244 CALORIES; 10 G PROTEIN; 13 G FAT; 23 G CARBOHYDRATE; 228 MG CALCIUM; 289 MG SODIUM; 13 MG CHOLESTEROL; 1 G DIETARY FIBER (THIS FIGURE DOES NOT INCLUDE BREADSTICKS; NUTRITION ANALYSIS NOT AVAILABLE)

REDUCED CHOLESTEROL

PESTO

For a super side dish combine 1 tablespoon pesto with ¾ cup hot cooked spaghetti and 2 teaspoons hot water.

YIELD: ¾ CUP

1½ cups firmly packed fresh basil
   leaves
⅓ cup less 1 teaspoon olive oil
6 garlic cloves, minced
2¼ ounces Parmesan cheese,
   grated

1½ ounces pignolias (pine nuts),
   toasted and finely chopped
Dash pepper

1 In food processor combine first 3 ingredients and process until basil is finely chopped, about 2 minutes, scraping down sides of work bowl as necessary.

2 Add remaining ingredients and, using on-off motion, process until combined.

3 Transfer Pesto to resealable plastic container and refrigerate for up to 2 weeks.

EACH 1-TABLESPOON SERVING PROVIDES: 1½ FATS; ¼ PROTEIN; 10 OPTIONAL CALORIES

PER SERVING: 101 CALORIES; 4 G PROTEIN; 9 G FAT; 3 G CARBOHYDRATE; 133 MG CALCIUM; 100 MG SODIUM; 4 MG CHOLESTEROL; DIETARY FIBER DATA NOT AVAILABLE

REDUCED CHOLESTEROL AND SODIUM

$\mathcal{C}$UCUMBER-SHRIMP SPREAD

Serve on cocktail bread, crispbreads, or rice cakes.

MAKES 2 SERVINGS

½ medium cucumber, pared and shredded
⅛ teaspoon salt
3 ounces frozen cooked tiny shrimp, thawed

2 tablespoons light sour cream
1½ teaspoons chopped fresh dill *or* ¼ teaspoon dillweed

1 In small mixing bowl combine cucumber and salt; let stand for 10 minutes. Place cucumber in center of clean kitchen towel. Gather together each corner of towel to enclose cucumber in pouch. Squeeze pouch to release excess liquid from cucumber, discarding liquid. Transfer cucumber to medium mixing bowl.

2 Add remaining ingredients and stir to combine.

EACH SERVING PROVIDES: ¾ PROTEIN; ½ VEGETABLE; 25 OPTIONAL CALORIES
PER SERVING: 73 CALORIES; 10 G PROTEIN; 2 G FAT; 2 G CARBOHYDRATE; 27 MG CALCIUM; 236 MG SODIUM; 88 MG CHOLESTEROL; 0.2 G DIETARY FIBER

$\mathcal{C}$ucumber-Shrimp Spread

with Lettuce and Tomato Slices on Reduced-Calorie Wheat Bread

Red Bell Pepper Rings and Whole Mushrooms

Orange and Grapefruit Sections

Iced Tea with Lemon Slice

ONION DIP

MAKES 4 SERVINGS

½ cup Yogurt Cheese (see below)
¼ cup light sour cream

1 packet instant onion broth and seasoning mix

Using a wire whisk, in small mixing bowl combine all ingredients until blended.

EACH SERVING (INCLUDING YOGURT CHEESE) PROVIDES: 45 OPTIONAL CALORIES
PER SERVING: 52 CALORIES; 4 G PROTEIN; 3 G FAT; 3 G CARBOHYDRATE; 60 MG CALCIUM; 209 MG SODIUM; 6 MG CHOLESTEROL; 0 G DIETARY FIBER

REDUCED CHOLESTEROL

YOGURT CHEESE

Yogurt cheese requires a little advance planning because the yogurt will need to drain for 24 hours.

YIELD: 2¼ CUPS

4½ cups plain low-fat yogurt*

1 Line a large sieve with a double thickness of cheesecloth. Set sieve in medium mixing bowl and spoon in yogurt. Cover and refrigerate for 24 hours. Discard liquid in bowl.

2 Transfer yogurt cheese to resealable plastic container and refrigerate for up to 1 week. Pour off any accumulated liquid before using.

EACH ¾-CUP SERVING PROVIDES: 1 MILK; 10 OPTIONAL CALORIES
PER SERVING: 150 CALORIES; 16 G PROTEIN; 4 G FAT; 7 G CARBOHYDRATE; 359 MG CALCIUM; 108 MG SODIUM; 8 MG CHOLESTEROL; 0 G DIETARY FIBER

* Use yogurt that does not contain gelatin.
REDUCED CHOLESTEROL, FAT AND SODIUM

MINI CALZONES

An Italian specialty that uses refrigerated buttermilk flaky biscuits, making preparation a cinch.

MAKES 10 SERVINGS, 1 CALZONE EACH

2½ teaspoons olive *or* vegetable oil
½ cup finely chopped red onion
½ cup finely chopped red bell pepper
1 garlic clove, minced
4 large plum tomatoes, blanched, peeled, seeded, and chopped
1 tablespoon finely chopped fresh basil
1 tablespoon finely chopped Italian (flat-leaf) parsley
½ cup plus 2 tablespoons part-skim ricotta cheese
⅛ teaspoon oregano leaves
10 ready-to-bake refrigerated buttermilk flaky biscuits (1 ounce each)

1 Preheat oven to 400°F. In 9-inch nonstick skillet heat oil; add onion, pepper, and garlic and cook over medium-high heat, stirring frequently, until onion is softened, about 3 minutes. Add tomatoes, basil, and parsley and cook, stirring constantly, until moisture has evaporated, about 2 minutes. Set aside and let cool slightly. Stir in cheese and oregano.

2 Between 2 sheets of wax paper roll each biscuit into a 5-inch circle. Spoon an equal amount of vegetable-cheese mixture onto center of each biscuit; fold each biscuit in half to enclose filling. Press edge of each biscuit with tines of fork to seal filling.

3 Arrange calzones on nonstick baking sheet and bake until golden, about 10 minutes. Serve immediately.

EACH SERVING PROVIDES: ¼ FAT; ¼ PROTEIN; ½ VEGETABLE; 1 BREAD

PER SERVING: 125 CALORIES; 4 G PROTEIN; 6 G FAT; 15 G CARBOHYDRATE; 49 MG CALCIUM; 317 MG SODIUM; 5 MG CHOLESTEROL; 0.5 DIETARY FIBER (THIS FIGURE DOES NOT INCLUDE BISCUITS; NUTRITION ANALYSIS NOT AVAILABLE)

REDUCED CHOLESTEROL

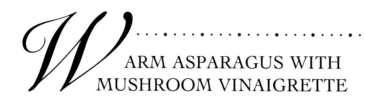

WARM ASPARAGUS WITH MUSHROOM VINAIGRETTE

This elegant appetizer can also be served as a side dish.

MAKES 2 SERVINGS

12 thin asparagus spears
2 teaspoons olive oil
1½ teaspoons country Dijon-style mustard

1½ teaspoons balsamic *or* red wine vinegar
Dash pepper
½ cup sliced mushrooms

1 In 1-quart microwavable casserole arrange asparagus; add *½ cup water.* Cover and microwave on High (100%) for 2 minutes.

2 Rearrange asparagus in casserole, moving those that have been in the center to the edge. Rotate dish ¼ turn and microwave on High for 2 minutes. Let stand for 1 minute, until asparagus are tender.

3 While asparagus are standing, prepare mushroom mixture. Using a wire whisk, in small microwavable mixing bowl beat together *2 tablespoons water,* the oil, mustard, vinegar, and pepper. Add mushrooms and stir to coat. Cover and microwave on High for 2 minutes.

4 To serve, on each of 2 serving plates arrange 6 asparagus spears, discarding cooking liquid; top each portion with half of the mushroom vinaigrette.

EACH SERVING PROVIDES: 1 FAT; 1½ VEGETABLES
PER SERVING: 63 CALORIES; 2 G PROTEIN; 5 G FAT; 4 G CARBOHYDRATE; 14 MG CALCIUM; 114 MG SODIUM; 0 MG CHOLESTEROL; 1 G DIETARY FIBER
REDUCED CHOLESTEROL AND SODIUM

ROASTED PEPPERS WITH CAPERS

MAKES 2 SERVINGS

1 medium red bell pepper	1 tablespoon rinsed drained capers
1 medium green bell pepper	2 teaspoons olive oil, divided
1 medium yellow bell pepper	Dash ground pepper
1 tablespoon chopped fresh basil	1 garlic clove, sliced

1   Preheat broiler. On baking sheet lined with heavy-duty foil, broil peppers 3 inches from heat source, turning frequently, until charred on all sides. Let stand until cool enough to handle, about 15 minutes.

2   Fit strainer into small mixing bowl; peel peppers over strainer, removing and discarding stem ends and seeds and allowing juice from peppers to drip into bowl. Cut peppers into ½-inch-wide strips and add to bowl with juice. Add basil, capers, 1 teaspoon oil, and the ground pepper and stir to combine.

3   In small nonstick skillet heat remaining oil; add garlic and cook over medium heat, stirring frequently, until thoroughly heated, about 1 minute. Add to pepper mixture and stir to combine. Serve immediately.

EACH SERVING PROVIDES: 1 FAT; 3 VEGETABLES

PER SERVING: 71 CALORIES; 1 G PROTEIN; 5 G FAT; 7 G CARBOHYDRATE; 22 MG CALCIUM; 114 MG SODIUM; 0 MG CHOLESTEROL; 2 G DIETARY FIBER (THIS FIGURE DOES NOT INCLUDE CAPERS; NUTRITION ANALYSIS NOT AVAILABLE)

REDUCED CHOLESTEROL AND SODIUM

 NTIPASTO PLATTER

Serve with Italian bread and iced tea for that perfect summer meal.

Antipasto Platter

Italian Bread with Reduced-Calorie Margarine

Raspberries sprinkled with Confectioners' Sugar

Light White Wine

MAKES 2 SERVINGS

1 tablespoon plus 1 teaspoon red wine vinegar
2 teaspoons olive oil
¼ teaspoon oregano leaves
  Dash pepper
½ cup drained canned artichoke hearts
¼ cup thinly sliced yellow squash

1½ cups torn mixed lettuce leaves
2 ounces rinsed drained canned chick-peas
10 small black olives, pitted and cut into halves
¼ cup julienne-cut red bell pepper
1½ ounces part-skim mozzarella cheese, shredded

1 Using a wire whisk, in medium glass or stainless-steel mixing bowl combine *2 tablespoons water*, the vinegar, oil, oregano, and pepper. Add artichoke hearts and squash and stir to coat. Cover and let stand at room temperature for at least 10 minutes or up to 2 hours.

2 On serving platter arrange lettuce. Drain artichoke-squash mixture, reserving marinade. Arrange artichoke-squash mixture, chick-peas, olives, and bell pepper on lettuce; top with cheese and reserved marinade.

EACH SERVING PROVIDES: 1½ FATS; 1½ PROTEINS; 2½ VEGETABLES
PER SERVING: 179 CALORIES; 9 G PROTEIN; 11 G FAT; 13 G CARBOHYDRATE; 205 MG CALCIUM; 319 MG SODIUM; 12 MG CHOLESTEROL; 4 G DIETARY FIBER
REDUCED CHOLESTEROL

STEAMED SEAFOOD DUMPLINGS

MAKES 2 SERVINGS, 5 DUMPLINGS EACH

1½ ounces sea scallops
1½ ounces shelled and deveined
    shrimp
1 egg white
1 teaspoon reduced-sodium soy
    sauce, divided
1 garlic clove, chopped
½ teaspoon grated pared
    gingerroot

½ cup water chestnuts, chopped
10 wonton skins (wrappers),
    3 × 3-inch squares
3 tablespoons duck sauce
1 tablespoon hot Chinese *or*
    Dijon-style mustard

1   In food processor combine scallops, shrimp, egg white, ½ teaspoon soy sauce, the garlic, and gingerroot and process until finely chopped, about 1 minute. Transfer to medium mixing bowl; add water chestnuts and stir to combine.

2   Set vegetable steamer in 4-quart saucepan; add water to saucepan, being sure water does not touch bottom of steamer. Remove steamer, cover saucepan, and bring water to a boil.

3   On clean work surface arrange wonton skins; top each wonton skin with an equal amount of seafood mixture. Lightly moisten edges of 1 wonton skin with cold water, fold corners of wonton skin over filling, and press to seal. Repeat procedure with remaining wonton skins.

4   Spray vegetable steamer with nonstick cooking spray and set in saucepan. Arrange dumplings in steamer, cover saucepan, and steam for 10 minutes.

5   In small serving bowl combine remaining soy sauce, the duck sauce, and mustard. Serve with dumplings for dipping.

EACH SERVING PROVIDES: ¾ PROTEIN; 1 BREAD; 50 OPTIONAL CALORIES

PER SERVING: 216 CALORIES; 14 G PROTEIN; 2 G FAT; 35 G CARBOHYDRATE; 25 MG CALCIUM; 439 MG SODIUM; 39 MG CHOLESTEROL; DIETARY FIBER DATA NOT AVAILABLE

REDUCED FAT

GARLIC KNOTS

Serve these scrumptious rolls hot out of the oven. They're as delicious as any you will find in an Italian restaurant.

MAKES 10 SERVINGS, 2 KNOTS EACH
(SHOWN WITH ONION AND FENNEL SOUP
AU GRATIN; SEE PAGE 38)

1 package refrigerated ready-to-bake pizza crust dough (10 ounces)
1 tablespoon plus 2 teaspoons olive oil

1 tablespoon whipped butter
2 garlic cloves, minced
    Dash oregano leaves

1   Preheat oven to 425°F. Unroll dough and cut in half crosswise, then cut each half into ten 1-inch-wide strips, making 20 strips.

2   Tie each strip of dough into a loose knot and arrange on nonstick baking sheet, leaving a space of about 1 inch between each knot. Set aside.

3   In small saucepan combine remaining ingredients and cook over medium heat until butter is melted, about 1 minute.

4   Using a pastry brush, lightly brush half of the garlic-oil mixture evenly over each knot. Bake in middle of center oven rack until lightly browned, 10 to 12 minutes. Lightly brush knots evenly with the remaining garlic-oil mixture and transfer to serving plate. Serve immediately.

EACH SERVING PROVIDES: ½ FAT; 1 BREAD; 5 OPTIONAL CALORIES
PER SERVING: 100 CALORIES; 2 G PROTEIN; 4 G FAT; 13 G CARBOHYDRATE; 1 MG CALCIUM; 144 MG SODIUM; 2 MG CHOLESTEROL; DIETARY FIBER DATA NOT AVAILABLE
REDUCED CHOLESTEROL AND SODIUM

PHYLLO-CHEESE BUNDLES

MAKES 4 SERVINGS

¼ cup shredded yellow squash
¼ cup shredded zucchini
¼ cup finely chopped red bell
    pepper
¼ cup finely chopped onion
1 garlic clove, minced
6 sheets frozen phyllo dough
    (12 × 17 inches each),
    thawed* and cut crosswise
    into halves

⅔ cup low-fat cottage cheese
    (1% milk fat)
4 scallions (green onions), each 6
    inches long, green portion
    only, blanched

1 Preheat oven to 375°F. Spray nonstick skillet with nonstick cooking spray and heat; add squash, zucchini, pepper, onion, and garlic and cook over medium heat, stirring frequently, until moisture has evaporated, 3 to 4 minutes. Set aside and let cool.

2 Spray clean work surface with nonstick cooking spray. Arrange 4 phyllo dough halves side by side on prepared work surface; top each with 2 phyllo dough halves, making 4 stacks, each consisting of 3 halves. Spray surface of each stack with nonstick cooking spray.

3 Add cottage cheese to vegetable mixture and stir to combine. Spoon ¼ of the cottage cheese–vegetable mixture onto center of 1 stack of phyllo dough. Bring corners of stack together and gently twist, forming a bundle. Repeat procedure, using remaining cottage cheese–vegetable mixture and phyllo dough stacks, making 3 more bundles. Tie a scallion around the twisted portion of each bundle to secure.

4 Arrange bundles on nonstick baking sheet and bake until golden brown, about 15 minutes. Serve immediately.

EACH SERVING PROVIDES: ½ PROTEIN; ½ VEGETABLE; 1 BREAD

PER SERVING: 134 CALORIES; 8 G PROTEIN; 1 G FAT; 24 G CARBOHYDRATE; 39 MG CALCIUM; 281 MG SODIUM; 2 MG CHOLESTEROL; 1 G DIETARY FIBER (THIS FIGURE DOES NOT INCLUDE PHYLLO DOUGH; NUTRITION ANALYSIS NOT AVAILABLE)

REDUCED CHOLESTEROL AND FAT

* Phyllo dough must be thawed in the refrigerator for at least 8 hours, or overnight.

SPANAKOPITAS

MAKES 4 SERVINGS, 2 SPANAKOPITAS EACH

½ cup thawed and well-drained frozen chopped spinach
½ cup finely chopped scallions (green onions), white portion and some green
1 garlic clove, minced
3 sheets frozen phyllo dough (12 × 17 inches each), thawed*

1½ ounces feta cheese, crumbled
1 tablespoon finely chopped fresh Italian (flat-leaf) parsley
1 tablespoon finely chopped fresh dill
Dash pepper
Dash grated lemon peel

1 Preheat oven to 375°F. Spray 9-inch nonstick skillet with nonstick cooking spray and heat; add spinach, scallions, and garlic and cook over medium-high heat, stirring frequently, until all moisture has evaporated, about 3 minutes. Transfer to small mixing bowl; set aside and let cool.

2 Spray clean work surface with nonstick cooking spray. Arrange 2 phyllo dough sheets side by side on prepared work surface. Cut remaining phyllo dough sheet in half crosswise and set one half on each whole phyllo dough sheet, making 2 stacks. Starting from narrow end, cut each stack into 4 equal strips. Spray surface of strips with nonstick cooking spray and set aside.

3 Add remaining ingredients to spinach mixture and stir to combine. Spoon ⅛ of spinach-cheese mixture onto narrow end of 1 strip. Fold 1 corner of strip diagonally over filling so the narrow end meets the wide side, making a triangle. Continue folding, alternating from left to right until entire strip is folded. Repeat procedure, using remaining spinach-cheese mixture and phyllo dough strips, making 7 more spanakopitas.

4 Arrange spanakopitas on nonstick baking sheet and bake until golden, about 15 minutes. Serve immediately.

EACH SERVING PROVIDES: ½ PROTEIN; ½ VEGETABLE; ½ BREAD

PER SERVING: 87 CALORIES; 4 G PROTEIN; 2 G FAT; 13 G CARBOHYDRATE; 96 MG CALCIUM; 203 MG SODIUM; 9 MG CHOLESTEROL; 1 G DIETARY FIBER (THIS FIGURE DOES NOT INCLUDE PHYLLO DOUGH; NUTRITION ANALYSIS NOT AVAILABLE)

REDUCED CHOLESTEROL AND FAT

* Phyllo dough must be thawed in the refrigerator for at least 8 hours, or overnight.

SOUPS

ITS AROMA A SILENT DINNER BELL, A BIG POT OF HOMEMADE SOUP brewing gathers the whole family. A cup, mug, or steaming bowl has always been food for body and soul. These recipes will not only live up to your expectations, they'll become new favorites because of their versatility and convenient preparation. Our version of Creamy Tomato Soup is sure to please even the most discriminating soup critic, while tasty twists on it, like Creamy Tomato-Corn Soup or Tomato Soup with Chicken Meatballs, sate more adventurous appetites. Potato and Leek Soup and Onion and Fennel Soup Au Gratin prepared with a hunk of French bread and just-broiled cheese are gourmet-style soups you can enjoy at home. Warm days are the perfect times for Cold Melon or Cold Cucumber Soup. Tote lunch soups in an insulated container to keep cool, or serve them as a refreshing first course. Vegetable soups get style and substance when tortellini is added, and are souped up with a wide variety of veggies. Sweet Potato and Turkey Soup cures post-Thanksgiving blues. Remember, a hearty soup with bread and a simple salad are the basis for a wonderful meal. So simmer it, chill it, but above all, enjoy it. Soup's on!

COLD MELON SOUP

MAKES 2 SERVINGS, ABOUT 1½ CUPS EACH

2 cups cantaloupe chunks
1 tablespoon thawed frozen
   concentrated orange juice (no
   sugar added)

1 teaspoon lemon-lime flavored
   sugar-free drink mix (4
   calories per 8-fluid-ounce
   serving of prepared drink mix)

In blender combine cantaloupe, *1 cup water,* the orange juice concentrate, and drink mix and process on high speed until drink mix is dissolved. Transfer to serving bowl; cover and refrigerate until chilled.

EACH SERVING PROVIDES: 1¼ FRUITS; 8 OPTIONAL CALORIES
PER SERVING: 72 CALORIES; 2 G PROTEIN; 0.5 G FAT; 17 G CARBOHYDRATE; 20 MG CALCIUM; 15 MG SODIUM; 0 MG CHOLESTEROL; 1 G DIETARY FIBER
REDUCED CHOLESTEROL, FAT AND SODIUM

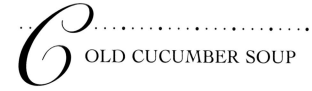

COLD CUCUMBER SOUP

MAKES 2 SERVINGS, ABOUT ¾ CUP EACH

1 medium cucumber, pared,
   seeded, shredded, and
   divided
½ cup plain low-fat yogurt
3 tablespoons light sour cream
1 tablespoon plus 1 teaspoon
   reduced-calorie mayonnaise

1 packet instant chicken broth
   and seasoning mix
1 teaspoon minced shallot *or*
   onion
   Dash white pepper
1 tablespoon chopped fresh dill

1   In blender combine all ingredients except 2 tablespoons of the cucumber and the dill; add *¾ cup cold water* and process on high speed, scraping down sides of container as necessary, until pureed, about 2 minutes.

2 Stir in reserved cucumber and dill. Cover and refrigerate until flavors blend, at least 30 minutes.

EACH SERVING PROVIDES: ¼ MILK; 1 FAT; 1 VEGETABLE; 55 OPTIONAL CALORIES
PER SERVING: 118 CALORIES; 6 G PROTEIN; 7 G FAT; 10 G CARBOHYDRATE; 125 MG CALCIUM; 594 MG SODIUM; 14 MG CHOLESTEROL; 0.4 G DIETARY FIBER
REDUCED CHOLESTEROL

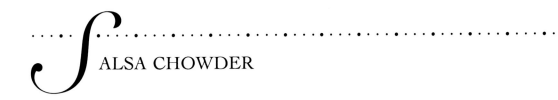

$\int$ ALSA CHOWDER

A mere six ingredients are combined into a hearty chowder.

MAKES 2 SERVINGS, ABOUT 1 CUP EACH

½ cup chopped onion
½ cup chopped red bell pepper
2 teaspoons margarine
1 cup frozen whole-kernel corn

1 cup canned ready-to-serve low-sodium chicken broth
½ cup mild chunky salsa

In 1-quart microwavable casserole combine onion, pepper, and margarine; cover and microwave on High (100%) until onion is translucent, about 2 minutes. Add remaining ingredients and stir to combine; microwave on Medium (50%) for 4 minutes, stirring every 2 minutes, until mixture is thoroughly heated.

EACH SERVING PROVIDES: 1 FAT; 1½ VEGETABLES; 1 BREAD; 20 OPTIONAL CALORIES
PER SERVING: 157 CALORIES; 4 G PROTEIN; 5 G FAT; 26 G CARBOHYDRATE; 16 MG CALCIUM; 435 MG SODIUM; 0 MG CHOLESTEROL; 3 G DIETARY FIBER (THIS FIGURE DOES NOT INCLUDE SALSA; NUTRITION ANALYSIS NOT AVAILABLE)
REDUCED CHOLESTEROL AND FAT

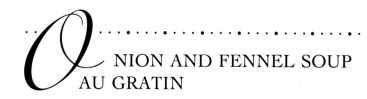

ONION AND FENNEL SOUP AU GRATIN

MAKES 2 SERVINGS, ABOUT 1½ CUPS EACH
(SHOWN WITH GARLIC KNOTS; SEE PAGE 31)

2 teaspoons margarine
1½ cups chopped onions
½ cup chopped fennel
1 packet instant onion broth
and seasoning mix,
dissolved in ¾ cup warm
water

Dash white pepper
2 slices French bread (1 ounce
each), toasted
1½ ounces reduced-fat Swiss
cheese, shredded

1 In 1-quart nonstick saucepan melt margarine; add onions and fennel and cook over medium-high heat, stirring frequently, until onions are translucent, about 2 minutes.

2 Add *½ cup water,* the dissolved broth mix, and pepper and bring mixture to a boil. Reduce heat to low and let simmer until flavors blend, about 15 minutes.

3 Preheat broiler. Set 2 flameproof bowls on baking sheet. Ladle half of the soup into each bowl; top each portion with 1 slice of bread and then half of the cheese. Broil until cheese is melted, about 2 minutes.

EACH SERVING PROVIDES: 1 FAT; 1 PROTEIN; 2 VEGETABLES; 1 BREAD; 5 OPTIONAL CALORIES
PER SERVING: 234 CALORIES; 12 G PROTEIN; 9 G FAT; 27 G CARBOHYDRATE; 319 MG CALCIUM; 655 MG SODIUM; 16 MG CHOLESTEROL; 3 G DIETARY FIBER
REDUCED CHOLESTEROL

CREAMY TOMATO-CORN SOUP

MAKES 2 SERVINGS, ABOUT 1½ CUPS EACH

2 cups canned stewed tomatoes, slightly pureed
½ cup evaporated skimmed milk
½ cup frozen whole-kernel corn

2 tablespoons half-and-half (blend of milk and cream)
1 tablespoon whipped butter
Dash white pepper

In 1-quart microwavable casserole combine tomatoes, milk, and corn and microwave on Medium (50%) for 5 minutes, until corn is heated. Add remaining ingredients and stir to combine; microwave on Medium for 2 minutes. Let stand for 3 minutes, until flavors blend.

EACH SERVING PROVIDES: ½ MILK; 2 VEGETABLES; ½ BREAD; 50 OPTIONAL CALORIES
PER SERVING: 206 CALORIES; 9 G PROTEIN; 6 G FAT; 33 G CARBOHYDRATE; 288 MG CALCIUM; 768 MG SODIUM; 19 MG CHOLESTEROL; 1 G DIETARY FIBER (THIS FIGURE DOES NOT INCLUDE STEWED TOMATOES; NUTRITION ANALYSIS NOT AVAILABLE)
REDUCED CHOLESTEROL AND FAT

NOODLE SOUP

Homemade noodle soup with all the flavor you expect and none of the effort.

MAKES 2 SERVINGS, ABOUT 1 CUP EACH

½ cup shredded carrot
¼ cup chopped onion
¼ cup diagonally sliced celery
2 teaspoons margarine

1 cup canned ready-to-serve low-sodium chicken broth
1½ ounces uncooked medium *or* thin egg noodles

In 1-quart microwavable casserole combine carrot, onion, celery, and margarine; cover and microwave on High (100%) for 1 minute. Add broth and *¹/₂ cup water* and stir to combine. Cover and microwave on High for 5 minutes. Stir in noodles; cover and microwave on Medium (50%) for 3 minutes, stirring every minute. Let stand for 2 minutes, until noodles are softened.

EACH SERVING PROVIDES: 1 FAT; 1 VEGETABLE; 1 BREAD; 20 OPTIONAL CALORIES
PER SERVING: 151 CALORIES; 5 G PROTEIN; 6 G FAT; 21 G CARBOHYDRATE; 26 MG CALCIUM; 99 MG SODIUM; 20 MG CHOLESTEROL; 2 G DIETARY FIBER
REDUCED CHOLESTEROL AND SODIUM

ITALIAN CABBAGE AND BEAN SOUP

MAKES 2 SERVINGS, ABOUT 1½ CUPS EACH

1 teaspoon olive oil
½ cup chopped onion
½ cup chopped celery
½ cup sliced carrot
1 garlic clove, minced
1½ cups shredded green cabbage
1 cup canned Italian tomatoes (reserve liquid), seeded and chopped

¼ pound rinsed drained canned white kidney (cannellini) beans
2 packets instant onion broth and seasoning mix
½ teaspoon chopped fresh parsley
¼ teaspoon pepper

1 In 2-quart nonstick saucepan heat oil; add onion, celery, carrot, and garlic and cook over medium-high heat, stirring occasionally, until celery is softened, 2 to 3 minutes. Add cabbage and cook, stirring frequently, until cabbage begins to wilt, 1 to 2 minutes.

2 Add tomatoes with reserved liquid, the beans, broth mix, parsley, and pepper; stir to combine. Reduce heat to low and let simmer, stirring occasionally, until carrot is tender, 15 to 20 minutes.

EACH SERVING PROVIDES: ½ FAT; 1 PROTEIN; 4 VEGETABLES; 10 OPTIONAL CALORIES
PER SERVING: 166 CALORIES; 9 G PROTEIN; 3 G FAT; 28 G CARBOHYDRATE; 109 MG CALCIUM; 1,125 MG SODIUM; 0 MG CHOLESTEROL; 8 G DIETARY FIBER
REDUCED CHOLESTEROL AND FAT

P OTATO AND LEEK SOUP

Tote heated leftover soup to the office in a wide-mouth insulated vacuum container.

MAKES 4 SERVINGS, ABOUT 1¼ CUPS EACH

3 cups chopped thoroughly washed leeks (white portion only)
1 tablespoon plus 1 teaspoon reduced-calorie margarine (tub)

4 cups skim *or* nonfat milk
2 packets instant chicken broth and seasoning mix
1½ ounces uncooked instant potato flakes

1 In 3-quart microwavable casserole combine leeks and margarine; cover and microwave on High (100%) for 5 minutes, stirring once after 3 minutes, until leeks are translucent.

2 Stir in milk and broth mix; microwave, uncovered, on Medium (50%) for 4 minutes.

3 Stir in potato flakes and microwave on Medium for 5 minutes, stirring once after 2 minutes, until soup thickens slightly.

EACH SERVING PROVIDES: 1 MILK; ½ FAT; 1½ VEGETABLES; ½ BREAD; 5 OPTIONAL CALORIES

PER SERVING: 192 CALORIES; 11 G PROTEIN, 3 G FAT; 32 G CARBOHYDRATE; 351 MG CALCIUM; 689 MG SODIUM; 5 MG CHOLESTEROL; 1 G DIETARY FIBER (THIS FIGURE DOES NOT INCLUDE POTATO FLAKES; NUTRITION ANALYSIS NOT AVAILABLE)

REDUCED CHOLESTEROL AND FAT

P otato and Leek Soup

Special Turkey Sandwich (sliced roast turkey with sliced reduced-fat Swiss cheese, shredded lettuce, tomato slices, and reduced-calorie Thousand Island dressing on reduced-calorie wheat bread)

Cherries

Coffee, Tea, or Mineral Water

CREAMY TOMATO SOUP

MAKES 4 SERVINGS, ABOUT 1¼ CUPS EACH

2 teaspoons olive *or* vegetable oil
½ cup chopped onion
2 garlic cloves, minced
2 tablespoons all-purpose flour
2 cups Italian tomatoes (reserve liquid), seeded and pureed
2 tablespoons chopped fresh basil *or* 1 teaspoon basil leaves

2 packets instant vegetable broth and seasoning mix
1 cup cooked ditalini *or* small shell macaroni
¼ cup half-and-half (blend of milk and cream)

1 In 3-quart nonstick saucepan heat oil; add onion and garlic and cook over medium-high heat, stirring occasionally, until onion is softened, 1 to 2 minutes.

2 Sprinkle mixture with flour and stir quickly to combine. Continuing to stir, add *3 cups water,* the tomatoes with reserved liquid, the basil, and broth mix. Reduce heat to low and let simmer, stirring occasionally, until flavors blend, 20 to 25 minutes.

3 Stir in ditalini and half-and-half and cook until heated through, 3 to 5 minutes (*do not boil*).

EACH SERVING PROVIDES: ½ FAT; 1¼ VEGETABLES; ½ BREAD; 45 OPTIONAL CALORIES
PER SERVING: 133 CALORIES; 4 G PROTEIN; 5 G FAT; 20 G CARBOHYDRATE; 6 MG CALCIUM; 585 MG SODIUM; 6 MG CHOLESTEROL; 2 G DIETARY FIBER

REDUCED CHOLESTEROL AND FAT

Creamy Tomato Soup

Chicken Salad Pita (diced cooked chicken with chopped celery, reduced-calorie mayonnaise, green bell pepper rings, and tomato slices in whole wheat pita)

Red Grapes

Coffee, Tea, or Mineral Water

HEARTY TORTELLINI-VEGETABLE SOUP

MAKES 4 SERVINGS, ABOUT 3 CUPS EACH

3 cups quartered small
    mushrooms
1 cup chopped onions
1 cup chopped carrots
1 cup chopped zucchini
1 tablespoon plus 1 teaspoon
    olive *or* vegetable oil
2 small garlic cloves, minced
4 cups thoroughly washed and
    drained spinach leaves*

3 cups canned stewed tomatoes
2 cups canned ready-to-serve
    low-sodium chicken broth
2 tablespoons chopped fresh
    Italian (flat-leaf) parsley
2 tablespoons chopped fresh dill
    or basil
56 frozen tortellini (stuffed with
    ricotta cheese)†

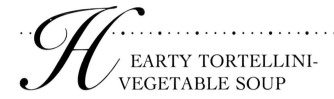

Hearty Tortellini-Vegetable Soup

Tossed Salad with Reduced-Calorie Italian Dressing

Club Soda

1 In 4-quart microwavable casserole combine mushrooms, onions, carrots, zucchini, oil, and garlic and stir to coat. Cover and microwave on High (100%) for 6 minutes, stirring once halfway through cooking.

2 Add remaining ingredients except tortellini and stir to combine. Cover and microwave on High for 6 minutes, stirring once halfway through cooking.

3 Add tortellini and stir to combine; cover and microwave on Medium (50%) for 5 minutes. Let stand for 5 minutes, stirring after 3 minutes, until tortellini are soft.

EACH SERVING PROVIDES: 1 FAT; 1 PROTEIN; 5 VEGETABLES; 1 BREAD; 40 OPTIONAL CALORIES
PER SERVING: 288 CALORIES; 14 G PROTEIN; 8 G FAT; 45 G CARBOHYDRATE; 248 MG CALCIUM; 760 MG SODIUM; 23 MG CHOLESTEROL; 4 G DIETARY FIBER (THIS FIGURE DOES NOT INCLUDE STEWED TOMATOES AND TORTELLINI; NUTRITION ANALYSIS NOT AVAILABLE)
REDUCED CHOLESTEROL AND FAT

* 4 cups fresh spinach will yield about 1 cup cooked spinach.

† 56 frozen tortellini will yield about 2 cups cooked tortellini.

ZUCCHINI SOUP

MAKES 2 SERVINGS, ABOUT 1¼ CUPS EACH

½ cup diced onion
1 teaspoon vegetable oil
1 cup shredded zucchini, divided
1 cup low-fat milk (1% milk fat)
¼ pound rinsed drained canned
    white kidney (cannellini)
    beans

1 packet instant chicken broth
    and seasoning mix
Dash white pepper

1 In 1-quart microwavable bowl combine onion and oil and stir to coat. Cover and microwave on High (100%) for 2 minutes, stirring once halfway through cooking, until onion is translucent.

2 Add ¾ cup zucchini, the milk, beans, *½ cup water,* and the broth mix. Cover and microwave on High for 6 minutes, stirring every 2 minutes. Microwave on Medium-High (70%) for 3 minutes.

3 Remove cover and let soup cool slightly. Pour into work bowl of food processor and process until pureed, 1 to 2 minutes. Transfer soup to serving bowl; stir in remaining zucchini and pepper.

EACH SERVING PROVIDES: ½ MILK; ½ FAT; 1 PROTEIN; 1½ VEGETABLES; 5 OPTIONAL CALORIES
PER SERVING: 165 CALORIES; 11 G PROTEIN; 4 G FAT; 22 G CARBOHYDRATE; 191 MG CALCIUM; 676 MG SODIUM; 5 MG CHOLESTEROL; 5 G DIETARY FIBER
REDUCED CHOLESTEROL AND FAT

TOMATO SOUP WITH CHICKEN MEATBALLS

MAKES 1 SERVING, ABOUT 1½ CUPS

3 ounces ground chicken
¼ cup finely chopped onion, divided
2 teaspoons chopped fresh Italian (flat-leaf) parsley, divided
¼ cup finely chopped celery
½ teaspoon vegetable oil

1 cup tomato juice
½ cup canned ready-to-serve low-sodium chicken broth
¼ teaspoon paprika
¼ cup cooked elbow macaroni
Dash pepper

1 In small mixing bowl combine chicken, 1 tablespoon onion, and 1 teaspoon parsley. Shape into 6 equal meatballs; set aside.

2 In 1-quart microwavable casserole combine remaining onion, the celery, and oil, stirring to coat. Cover and microwave on High (100%) for 2 minutes, stirring once halfway through cooking, until onion is translucent.

3 Add tomato juice, broth, and paprika and stir to combine; microwave on High for 2 minutes. Add meatballs; cover and microwave on High for 2 minutes.

4 Add macaroni, remaining parsley, and the pepper and stir to combine. Microwave on High for 30 seconds, until meatballs are no longer pink.

EACH SERVING PROVIDES: ½ FAT; 2 PROTEINS; 2 VEGETABLES; ½ BREAD; 20 OPTIONAL CALORIES

PER SERVING: 278 CALORIES; 20 G PROTEIN; 11 G FAT; 26 G CARBOHYDRATE; 73 MG CALCIUM; 1,005 MG SODIUM; 71 MG CHOLESTEROL; 2 G DIETARY FIBER

Tomato Soup with Chicken Meatballs

Garlic Bread (Italian bread with reduced-calorie margarine and garlic powder, broiled)

Tossed Salad with Reduced-Calorie Thousand Island Dressing

Unsweetened Orange-Flavored Seltzer

 SWEET POTATO– TURKEY SOUP

MAKES 4 SERVINGS, ABOUT 1 CUP EACH

2 teaspoons margarine
1 cup sliced carrots
1 cup sliced celery
1 cup diced onions
1 garlic clove, minced
3 cups canned stewed tomatoes, pureed

6 ounces diced pared sweet potato *or* yam
¼ teaspoon thyme leaves
¼ pound cooked, skinned, and boned turkey, cut into cubes

1 In 2-quart nonstick saucepan melt margarine; add carrots, celery, onions, and garlic and cook over medium-high heat, stirring frequently, until celery is tender, about 5 minutes.

2 Add tomatoes, sweet potato, and thyme and stir to combine. Cook, stirring occasionally, until mixture comes to a boil. Reduce heat to low and let simmer until sweet potato is tender, about 15 minutes.

3 Add turkey to soup and stir to combine. Cook until turkey is thoroughly heated, 1 to 2 minutes.

EACH SERVING PROVIDES: ½ FAT; 1 PROTEIN; 3 VEGETABLES; ¼ BREAD; 10 OPTIONAL CALORIES
PER SERVING: 191 CALORIES; 12 G PROTEIN; 4 G FAT; 30 G CARBOHYDRATE; 111 MG CALCIUM; 572 MG SODIUM; 22 MG CHOLESTEROL; 3 G DIETARY FIBER (THIS FIGURE DOES NOT INCLUDE STEWED TOMATOES; NUTRITION ANALYSIS NOT AVAILABLE)

REDUCED CHOLESTEROL AND FAT

Sweet Potato-Turkey Soup

Carrot, Celery, Tomato, and Romaine Lettuce Salad with Italian Dressing

Cinnamon-Spiced Applesauce

Coffee, Tea, or Mineral Water

SALADS

THE DAYS WHEN A SALAD WAS A HUNK OF ICEBERG AND SLICE of tomato are gone! Salads have come into their own, and the more exotic, flavorful, or filled with crunchy goodness, the better. It's not surprising that salads have gained such popularity—nothing is easier than tossing together a quick one, especially when you're looking for a light meal. An inspiring variety of cold, warm, sweet, and savory salads fill this chapter. Some, like our Classic Tomato Salad, feature ingredients you can't get enough of. Others court the exotic, featuring almonds, bananas, berries, coconut, and honey paired irreverently but tastefully with cucumbers, carrots, tomatoes, and walnuts. Some favorites are revamped. California Potato Salad, a far cry from the mayonnaise and potato standard, is jazzed up with avocado and cilantro. Honey-Mustard Cole Slaw is sweeter than its deli cousin. The mainstay of many salads—lettuce—moves over to make room for pasta and rice, the perfect foil for scallops, citrus, or vegetables. Seafood salads, beef, chicken, and, yes, even the ubiquitous tuna salad are revisited. For a splash, apple cider and raspberry vinegars, sesame and peanut oils and citrus juices give an added punch of flavor. Most of these recipes are quick to prepare, but many benefit from chilling time to let flavors meld. So grab your cutting board and make quick work of these special salads.

CLASSIC TOMATO SALAD

MAKES 2 SERVINGS

2 medium tomatoes, thinly sliced

½ cup thinly sliced red onion (separated into rings)

¼ medium avocado (about 2 ounces), pared and thinly sliced

1½ teaspoons freshly squeezed lime *or* lemon juice

½ teaspoon olive oil

¼ teaspoon granulated sugar
Dash pepper

1 On serving platter decoratively arrange tomatoes and onion.

2 In shallow mixing bowl combine avocado and lime juice and turn to coat. Decoratively arrange avocado on platter with tomatoes and onion. Drizzle oil evenly over tomatoes. Sprinkle sugar and pepper over tomatoes.

3 Cover platter and refrigerate until chilled, about 1 hour.

EACH SERVING PROVIDES: 1¼ FATS; 2½ VEGETABLES; 3 OPTIONAL CALORIES
PER SERVING: 86 CALORIES; 2 G PROTEIN; 5 G FAT; 11 G CARBOHYDRATE; 22 MG CALCIUM; 14 MG SODIUM; 0 MG CHOLESTEROL; 3 G DIETARY FIBER
REDUCED CHOLESTEROL AND SODIUM

TOMATO SALAD WITH PESTO DRESSING

MAKES 2 SERVINGS

2 cups torn lettuce leaves

1 medium tomato, sliced

2 tablespoons thinly sliced red onion

2 tablespoons Pesto (see page 22)

1 tablespoon plus 1½ teaspoons canned ready-to-serve low-sodium chicken broth

1 teaspoon red wine vinegar

1   On serving platter arrange lettuce; decoratively arrange tomato and onion over lettuce.

2   Using a wire whisk, in small mixing bowl beat together remaining ingredients; spoon over salad. Serve immediately.

EACH SERVING (INCLUDING PESTO) PROVIDES: 1½ FATS; ¼ PROTEIN; 3⅛ VEGETABLES; 10 OPTIONAL CALORIES

PER SERVING: 129 CALORIES; 5 G PROTEIN; 9 G FAT; 9 G CARBOHYDRATE; 178 MG CALCIUM; 113 MG SODIUM; 4 MG CHOLESTEROL; 2 G DIETARY FIBER

REDUCED CHOLESTEROL AND SODIUM

MINTED TOMATO-ORANGE SALAD

MAKES 2 SERVINGS

1 small navel orange (about 6 ounces)
1 large tomato, sliced
2 teaspoons chopped fresh mint

2 teaspoons chopped chives
1 teaspoon vegetable oil
1 teaspoon white wine vinegar

1   Over small bowl (to catch juice) peel and section orange, reserving juice.

2   On serving platter decoratively arrange orange sections and tomato slices; sprinkle with mint and chives.

3   Add oil and vinegar to reserved orange juice and, using a wire whisk, beat until combined. Pour over tomato slices and orange sections.

EACH SERVING PROVIDES: ½ FAT; 1½ VEGETABLES; ½ FRUIT

PER SERVING: 64 CALORIES; 1 G PROTEIN; 2 G FAT; 11 G CARBOHYDRATE; 31 MG CALCIUM; 7 MG SODIUM; 0 MG CHOLESTEROL; 3 G DIETARY FIBER

REDUCED CHOLESTEROL AND SODIUM

HONEY-MUSTARD COLESLAW

For ease of preparation, use your food processor to shred the cabbage and carrots for this tangy slaw.

MAKES 4 SERVINGS

6 cups shredded green cabbage
1 cup shredded carrots
¼ cup finely chopped scallions (green onions), white portion and some green
¼ cup finely chopped green bell pepper

1 tablespoon plus 1 teaspoon vegetable oil
1 tablespoon Dijon-style mustard
1 tablespoon seasoned rice vinegar
1 tablespoon honey

1 In large mixing bowl combine cabbage, carrots, scallions, and pepper.

2 In small bowl combine remaining ingredients, stirring until blended. Pour over cabbage mixture and toss to coat thoroughly.

EACH SERVING PROVIDES: 1 FAT; 3¾ VEGETABLES; 15 OPTIONAL CALORIES
PER SERVING: 106 CALORIES; 2 G PROTEIN; 5 G FAT; 15 G CARBOHYDRATE; 61 MG CALCIUM; 164 MG SODIUM; 0 MG CHOLESTEROL; 4 G DIETARY FIBER
REDUCED CHOLESTEROL AND SODIUM

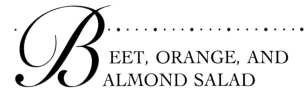

BEET, ORANGE, AND ALMOND SALAD

MAKES 2 SERVINGS

1 small navel orange (about 6 ounces)
1½ cups drained canned whole beets, cut into quarters
2 tablespoons sliced scallion (green onion)

1 teaspoon seasoned rice vinegar
½ teaspoon Chinese sesame oil
½ teaspoon olive oil
½ ounce slivered almonds, toasted

1 Over small bowl (to catch juice) peel and section orange, reserving juice. In medium mixing bowl place orange sections, beets, and scallion, tossing to combine.

2 Add vinegar and oils to reserved orange juice and, using a wire whisk, beat to combine. Add to beet mixture and toss to coat.

3 To serve, transfer salad to serving bowl and sprinkle with almonds.

EACH SERVING PROVIDES: 1 FAT; ¼ PROTEIN; 1½ VEGETABLES; ½ FRUIT
PER SERVING: 133 CALORIES; 3 G PROTEIN; 6 G FAT; 19 G CARBOHYDRATE; 70 MG CALCIUM; 318 MG SODIUM; 0 MG CHOLESTEROL; 4 G DIETARY FIBER
REDUCED CHOLESTEROL

CALIFORNIA POTATO SALAD

MAKES 2 SERVINGS

½ pound cooked red potatoes, pared and diced
½ cup sliced celery
¼ cup sliced scallions (green onions)
¼ cup diced red bell pepper
¼ medium avocado (about 2 ounces), pared and diced

1 tablespoon freshly squeezed lime juice
1 teaspoon chopped fresh cilantro (Chinese parsley) *or* Italian (flat-leaf) parsley
1 teaspoon granulated sugar
Dash pepper

Using a rubber scraper, in medium mixing bowl combine all ingredients, stirring to coat.

EACH SERVING PROVIDES: 1 FAT; 1 VEGETABLE; 1 BREAD; 10 OPTIONAL CALORIES
PER SERVING: 147 CALORIES; 3 G PROTEIN; 4 G FAT; 27 G CARBOHYDRATE; 22 MG CALCIUM; 38 MG SODIUM; 0 MG CHOLESTEROL; 3 G DIETARY FIBER
REDUCED CHOLESTEROL, FAT AND SODIUM

WALNUT-FRUIT SALAD

MAKES 2 SERVINGS

2 teaspoons olive oil
1 teaspoon champagne vinegar *or* white wine vinegar
½ teaspoon freshly squeezed lemon juice
½ teaspoon Dijon-style mustard
3 cups torn lettuce leaves

1 medium Belgian endive (about ¼ pound), separated into leaves
2 small plum tomatoes, diced
1 medium kiwi fruit (about ¼ pound), pared and sliced
½ ounce walnuts, chopped

1   Using a wire whisk, in large mixing bowl combine oil, vinegar, lemon juice, and mustard. Add lettuce, endive, and tomatoes and toss to coat.

2   Transfer salad to serving bowl; top with kiwi fruit and walnuts. Serve immediately.

EACH SERVING PROVIDES: 1½ FATS; ¼ PROTEIN; 4 VEGETABLES; ½ FRUIT
PER SERVING: 148 CALORIES; 3 G PROTEIN; 10 G FAT; 15 G CARBOHYDRATE; 79 MG CALCIUM; 55 MG SODIUM; 0 MG CHOLESTEROL; 5 G DIETARY FIBER
REDUCED CHOLESTEROL AND SODIUM

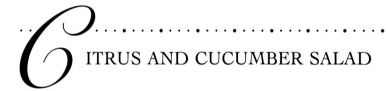

CITRUS AND CUCUMBER SALAD

MAKES 2 SERVINGS

1 medium grapefruit (about 1 pound)
1 small navel orange (about 6 ounces)
8 lettuce leaves

½ cup sliced pared cucumber
2 teaspoons olive oil
1 teaspoon chopped fresh mint
1 teaspoon seasoned rice vinegar

1   Over small mixing bowl (to catch juices) peel and section grapefruit and orange, reserving juices.

2   Line serving platter with lettuce. Decoratively arrange grapefruit sections, orange sections, and cucumber slices on lettuce.

3   Using a wire whisk, add oil, mint, and vinegar to reserved grapefruit and orange juices. Spoon over salad.

EACH SERVING PROVIDES: 1 FAT; 1½ VEGETABLES; 1½ FRUITS
PER SERVING: 117 CALORIES; 2 G PROTEIN; 5 G FAT; 19 G CARBOHYDRATE; 65 MG CALCIUM; 21 MG SODIUM; 0 MG CHOLESTEROL; 3 G DIETARY FIBER
REDUCED CHOLESTEROL AND SODIUM

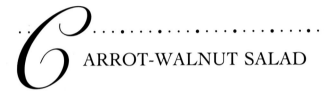

CARROT-WALNUT SALAD

For an attractive presentation, serve this colorful salad on a platter lined with lettuce or cabbage leaves.

MAKES 2 SERVINGS

¼ cup dark raisins
2 cups shredded carrots
½ ounce walnuts, coarsely chopped
2 tablespoons chopped scallion (green onion)

2 tablespoons chopped celery
2 tablespoons chopped green bell pepper
1½ teaspoons apple cider vinegar
1 teaspoon vegetable oil

1   In small bowl combine raisins and *¼ cup warm water;* set aside.

2   In medium mixing bowl place remaining ingredients; toss to combine. Drain raisins, reserving 1 tablespoon water. Add raisins and reserved water to carrot mixture and toss to combine.

3   Cover and refrigerate until ready to serve.

EACH SERVING PROVIDES: 1 FAT; ¼ PROTEIN; 2¼ VEGETABLES; 1 FRUIT
PER SERVING: 172 CALORIES; 3 G PROTEIN; 7 G FAT; 28 G CARBOHYDRATE; 52 MG CALCIUM; 48 MG SODIUM; 0 MG CHOLESTEROL; 5 G DIETARY FIBER
REDUCED CHOLESTEROL AND SODIUM

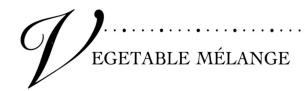

VEGETABLE MÉLANGE

MAKES 2 SERVINGS

1 cup thawed Spaghetti Squash
   (see page 208)
½ cup broccoli florets, blanched
1 cup cauliflower florets,
   blanched
½ cup sliced carrot, blanched
¼ cup sliced zucchini
¼ cup sliced yellow squash

1 tablespoon sliced scallion
   (green onion)
2 teaspoons reduced-calorie
   margarine
2 teaspoons lemon juice
   Dash pepper
1 teaspoon grated lemon peel

In 4-quart microwavable casserole combine all ingredients except lemon peel. Cover and microwave on Medium (50%) for 5 minutes, stirring once every 2 minutes. Add lemon peel and stir to combine. Let stand 1 minute before serving or serve at room temperature.

EACH SERVING (INCLUDING SPAGHETTI SQUASH) PROVIDES: ½ FAT; 3 VEGETABLES
PER SERVING: 82 CALORIES; 3 G PROTEIN; 3 G FAT; 14 G CARBOHYDRATE; 57 MG CALCIUM; 76 MG SODIUM; 0 MG CHOLESTEROL; 1 G DIETARY FIBER (THIS FIGURE DOES NOT INCLUDE BROCCOLI FLORETS; NUTRITION ANALYSIS NOT AVAILABLE)
REDUCED CHOLESTEROL, FAT AND SODIUM

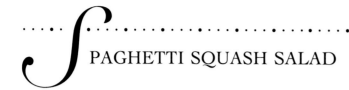

SPAGHETTI SQUASH SALAD

For an attractive presentation, serve this salad in the shell of the spaghetti squash.

MAKES 2 SERVINGS

2 cups thawed Spaghetti Squash (see page 208)
½ cup sliced radishes
½ cup sliced scallions (green onions)
½ cup diced tomato
1 tablespoon teriyaki sauce
1 tablespoon seasoned rice vinegar

1½ teaspoons peanut *or* vegetable oil
1 teaspoon minced pared gingerroot
1 garlic clove, minced
½ teaspoon Chinese sesame oil
½ teaspoon honey

In large salad bowl place all ingredients and toss to combine.

EACH SERVING (INCLUDING SPAGHETTI SQUASH) PROVIDES: 1 FAT; 3½ VEGETABLES; 5 OPTIONAL CALORIES
PER SERVING: 138 CALORIES; 3 G PROTEIN; 6 G FAT; 21 G CARBOHYDRATE; 66 MG CALCIUM; 429 MG SODIUM; 0 MG CHOLESTEROL; 2 G DIETARY FIBER
REDUCED CHOLESTEROL

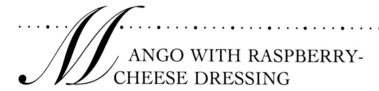

MANGO WITH RASPBERRY-CHEESE DRESSING

MAKES 2 SERVINGS

¼ cup raspberries
¼ cup Yogurt Cheese (see page 24)
1 teaspoon honey
4 lettuce leaves

1 small mango (about ½ pound), pared, pitted, and thinly sliced
2 teaspoons shredded coconut, toasted

1 In blender process raspberries until pureed. Press raspberries through sieve into small mixing bowl, discarding seeds. Add Yogurt Cheese and honey and stir to combine.

2 On serving platter arrange lettuce; top with mango and coconut. Drizzle Yogurt Cheese mixture over mango and coconut.

EACH SERVING (INCLUDING YOGURT CHEESE) PROVIDES: ½ VEGETABLE; 1 FRUIT; 45 OPTIONAL CALORIES

PER SERVING: 105 CALORIES; 4 G PROTEIN; 2 G FAT; 21 G CARBOHYDRATE; 82 MG CALCIUM; 25 MG SODIUM; 1 MG CHOLESTEROL; 2 G DIETARY FIBER

REDUCED CHOLESTEROL, FAT AND SODIUM

BANANA-BERRY CHEESE PLATTER

MAKES 2 SERVINGS

1 medium banana (about 6 ounces), peeled and sliced
¾ cup sliced strawberries
1 tablespoon half-and-half (blend of milk and cream)
1 cup low-fat cottage cheese (2% milk fat)

½ ounce chopped dry roasted almonds (no salt added); reserve 1 teaspoon for garnish
2 teaspoons pourable all-fruit strawberry syrup

Banana-Berry Cheese Platter

Crispbreads with Margarine

Sparkling Mineral Water

1 In medium mixing bowl combine banana, strawberries, and half-and-half and toss to coat.

2 In separate medium mixing bowl combine cottage cheese and all but reserved almonds.

3 To serve, arrange cottage cheese mixture in center of serving platter; spoon fruit mixture around cottage cheese mixture. Drizzle with syrup and sprinkle with reserved almonds.

EACH SERVING PROVIDES: ½ FAT; 1¾ PROTEINS; 1½ FRUITS; 35 OPTIONAL CALORIES

PER SERVING: 235 CALORIES; 18 G PROTEIN; 7 G FAT; 26 G CARBOHYDRATE; 115 MG CALCIUM; 468 MG SODIUM; 12 MG CHOLESTEROL; 3 G DIETARY FIBER

REDUCED CHOLESTEROL AND FAT

PIMIENTO-CHEESE SALAD

MAKES 1 SERVING

½ cup rinsed drained pimientos, sliced
¼ cup diced zucchini
¾ ounce part-skim mozzarella cheese, diced

¼ ounce (2 teaspoons) pignolias (pine nuts)
1 teaspoon red wine vinegar
½ teaspoon olive oil
1 cup shredded lettuce leaves

1 In medium mixing bowl combine all ingredients except lettuce.

2 Pack resealable plastic container with pimiento-cheese mixture. Serve with lettuce.

EACH SERVING PROVIDES: 1 FAT; 1¼ PROTEINS; 3½ VEGETABLES

PER SERVING: 150 CALORIES; 9 G PROTEIN; 10 G FAT; 10 G CARBOHYDRATE; 189 MG CALCIUM; 128 MG SODIUM; 12 MG CHOLESTEROL; 1 G DIETARY FIBER (THIS FIGURE DOES NOT INCLUDE PIMIENTOS AND PIGNOLIAS; NUTRITION ANALYSIS NOT AVAILABLE)

REDUCED CHOLESTEROL AND SODIUM

*Pimiento-Cheese
Salad*

Sesame Breadsticks

Tangerine

*Coffee, Tea, or
Mineral Water*

KENTUCKY SALAD WITH BACON

MAKES 2 SERVINGS

2 cups torn lettuce
2 cups thoroughly washed and drained spinach leaves
½ cup sliced pimiento (thin strips)
¼ cup drained canned whole-kernel corn, chilled
2 tablespoons sliced scallion (green onion)

½ ounce (about 1 tablespoon) bacon bits (made from real bacon)
1 tablespoon light sour cream
2 teaspoons olive oil
1 teaspoon Dijon-style mustard
1 tablespoon apple cider vinegar

1 Line serving platter with lettuce and spinach; top with pimiento, corn, scallion, and bacon bits.

2 Using a wire whisk, in small mixing bowl combine remaining ingredients and *1 tablespoon water,* mixing well. Pour over salad.

EACH SERVING PROVIDES: 1 FAT; 4½ VEGETABLES; ¼ BREAD; 55 OPTIONAL CALORIES

PER SERVING: 150 CALORIES; 6 G PROTEIN; 10 G FAT; 12 G CARBOHYDRATE; 101 MG CALCIUM; 249 MG SODIUM; 9 MG CHOLESTEROL; 2 G DIETARY FIBER (THIS FIGURE DOES NOT INCLUDE PIMIENTO; NUTRITION ANALYSIS NOT AVAILABLE)

Variation: Kentucky Salad—Omit bacon bits. In Serving Information, decrease Optional Calories to 15.

PER SERVING: 109 CALORIES; 4 G PROTEIN; 6 G FAT; 12 G CARBOHYDRATE; 101 MG CALCIUM; 136 MG SODIUM; 3 MG CHOLESTEROL; 2 G DIETARY FIBER (THIS FIGURE DOES NOT INCLUDE PIMIENTO; NUTRITION ANALYSIS NOT AVAILABLE)

REDUCED CHOLESTEROL

ITALIAN SALAD WITH YOGURT CHEESE

MAKES 2 SERVINGS

2 cups torn lettuce leaves
2 large plum tomatoes, sliced
½ cup sliced red onion
¾ cup Yogurt Cheese (see page 24)

¼ cup fresh basil, divided
1 teaspoon olive oil
Dash pepper

Italian Salad with Yogurt Cheese

Watermelon Balls

Iced Coffee

1 Line serving platter with lettuce; top with tomatoes and onion. Divide Yogurt Cheese into 4 equal portions and arrange on platter.

2 Thinly slice half of the basil and arrange on Yogurt Cheese. Decoratively arrange remaining basil on platter. Drizzle an equal amount of oil over each portion of Yogurt Cheese and then sprinkle with pepper.

EACH SERVING (INCLUDING YOGURT CHEESE) PROVIDES: ½ MILK; ½ FAT; 3½ VEGETABLES; 5 OPTIONAL CALORIES

PER SERVING: 134 CALORIES; 10 G PROTEIN; 5 G FAT; 12 G CARBOHYDRATE; 279 MG CALCIUM; 65 MG SODIUM; 4 MG CHOLESTEROL; 2 G DIETARY FIBER

REDUCED CHOLESTEROL AND SODIUM

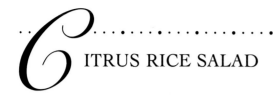

CITRUS RICE SALAD

For a touch of luxury, substitute wild rice for the brown rice in this recipe. Keep in mind, however, that wild rice takes about one hour to cook.

MAKES 2 SERVINGS

½ cup orange sections (no sugar added)
½ cup cooked long-grain rice, chilled
½ cup cooked fast-cooking whole grain brown rice, chilled
½ ounce sliced almonds, toasted, divided
2 tablespoons sliced scallion (green onion)
2 tablespoons diced red bell pepper

2 tablespoons dried currants *or* dark raisins
2 tablespoons orange juice (no sugar added)
1 tablespoon raspberry *or* apple cider vinegar
1½ teaspoons freshly squeezed lime juice
1 teaspoon olive oil
⅛ teaspoon grated orange peel
Dash white pepper

1 In medium mixing bowl combine orange sections, rice, ¼ ounce almonds, the scallion, bell pepper, and currants; set aside.

2 In small mixing bowl combine orange juice, vinegar, lime juice, oil, orange peel, and white pepper, mixing well. Pour over rice mixture and toss to coat. Cover and refrigerate until chilled, about 30 minutes.

3 To serve, arrange rice mixture in serving bowl; sprinkle with remaining almonds.

EACH SERVING PROVIDES: 1 FAT; ¼ PROTEIN; ¼ VEGETABLE; 1 BREAD; 1 FRUIT; 10 OPTIONAL CALORIES

PER SERVING: 232 CALORIES; 5 G PROTEIN; 7 G FAT; 41 G CARBOHYDRATE; 57 MG CALCIUM; 9 MG SODIUM; 0 MG CHOLESTEROL; 3 G DIETARY FIBER

REDUCED CHOLESTEROL, FAT AND SODIUM

WHITE BEAN SALAD

This flavorful salad is a great lunch to take to the office. Prepare it the night before and pack it in a resealable plastic container. Be sure to pack the lettuce separately to keep it crisp. It's ready to go when you are!

White Bean Salad

Spicy Peach Yogurt (plain low-fat yogurt mixed with peach slices and ground cinnamon)

Unsweetened Orange-Flavored Seltzer

MAKES 2 SERVINGS

1 cup thawed frozen whole-kernel corn

4 ounces rinsed drained canned white kidney (cannellini) beans

6 cherry tomatoes, cut into quarters

¼ cup diced red bell pepper

¼ cup sliced scallions (green onions)

¼ cup chopped radishes

2 tablespoons seeded and minced green chili pepper

1 tablespoon plus 1 teaspoon red wine vinegar

2 teaspoons olive oil

2 teaspoons freshly squeezed lime juice

1 garlic clove, minced
   Dash taco seasoning

2 cups torn lettuce leaves

1 In medium mixing bowl place all ingredients except lettuce and toss to combine thoroughly. Cover and refrigerate until flavors blend, at least 30 minutes.

2 To serve, line serving platter with lettuce. Toss bean mixture and arrange on lettuce.

EACH SERVING PROVIDES: 1 FAT; 1 PROTEIN; 3¼ VEGETABLES; 1 BREAD

PER SERVING: 212 CALORIES; 9 G PROTEIN; 6 G FAT; 35 G CARBOHYDRATE; 80 MG CALCIUM; 137 MG SODIUM; 0 MG CHOLESTEROL; 7 G DIETARY FIBER

REDUCED CHOLESTEROL, FAT AND SODIUM

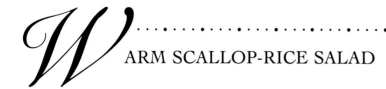

WARM SCALLOP-RICE SALAD

Serve on a bed of colorful salad greens for added visual appeal.

MAKES 2 SERVINGS

¼ cup sliced thoroughly washed leek (white portion only)
¼ cup diced red bell pepper
1 garlic clove, sliced
2 ounces uncooked fast-cooking whole grain brown rice
5 ounces bay *or* sea scallops (cut into quarters)

1 tablespoon lemon juice
2 teaspoons olive *or* vegetable oil
1½ teaspoons red wine vinegar
1½ teaspoons prepared horseradish
2 drops hot sauce
Mixed salad greens (optional)

1 In 1-quart microwavable casserole combine leek, pepper, and garlic; cover and microwave on High (100%) for 2 minutes, until leek is tender.

2 Add rice and *¾ cup water* and stir to combine; microwave (uncovered) on High for 5 minutes, stirring once halfway through cooking. Cover and microwave on Medium (50%) for 3 minutes.

3 Add scallops, cover, and microwave on Medium for 3 minutes. Let stand for 1 minute, until scallops are opaque.

4 Add remaining ingredients and stir to combine. Serve over greens if desired.

EACH SERVING PROVIDES: 1 FAT; 1 PROTEIN; ½ VEGETABLE; 1 BREAD
PER SERVING: 215 CALORIES; 14 G PROTEIN; 6 G FAT; 28 G CARBOHYDRATE; 31 MG CALCIUM; 137 MG SODIUM; 23 MG CHOLESTEROL; 1 G DIETARY FIBER
REDUCED CHOLESTEROL, FAT AND SODIUM

ORIENTAL BEEF SALAD

Use leftover rice in this unusual salad.

MAKES 1 SERVING

1 teaspoon reduced-sodium soy
   sauce
1 teaspoon rice vinegar
½ teaspoon Chinese sesame oil
½ teaspoon peanut oil
1 ounce cooked roast beef, cut
   into strips
½ cup cooked long-grain rice,
   chilled

¼ cup canned mandarin orange
   sections with 1 tablespoon
   juice (no sugar added)
2 tablespoons finely diced red *or*
   yellow bell pepper
1 tablespoon sliced scallion
   (green onion)
1 teaspoon sesame seed, toasted

*Oriental Beef
Salad*

*Fresh Fruit Salad
sprinkled with Toasted
Shredded Coconut*

*Tea with Lemon
Wedge*

1 In medium mixing bowl combine soy sauce, vinegar, and oils; add beef
  and turn to coat. Cover and refrigerate for 30 minutes.

2 Add remaining ingredients to beef mixture and toss to combine.

EACH SERVING PROVIDES: 1 FAT; 1 PROTEIN; ¼ VEGETABLE; 1 BREAD; ½ FRUIT; 20
OPTIONAL CALORIES

PER SERVING: 273 CALORIES; 12 G PROTEIN; 8 G FAT; 37 G CARBOHYDRATE; 54 MG
CALCIUM; 226 MG SODIUM; 23 MG CHOLESTEROL; 1 G DIETARY FIBER (THIS FIGURE
DOES NOT INCLUDE SESAME SEED; NUTRITION ANALYSIS NOT AVAILABLE)
REDUCED CHOLESTEROL AND FAT

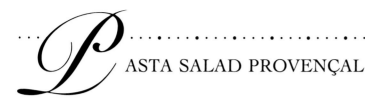

PASTA SALAD PROVENÇAL

MAKES 2 SERVINGS

2½ teaspoons olive oil
1½ teaspoons red wine vinegar
    Dash pepper
  1 cup cooked shell macaroni,
    chilled
  ½ cup sugar snap peas, blanched
  2 ounces drained canned tuna
    (packed in water)
  2 small plum tomatoes, cut
    lengthwise into wedges

  2 tablespoons thinly sliced red
    onion
  3 large black olives, pitted and
    sliced
  1 tablespoon chopped fresh
    basil
  1 tablespoon rinsed drained
    capers

*Pasta Salad
Provençal*

*Mozzarella Melt
(shredded mozzarella
cheese sprinkled on
Italian bread, broiled)*

Honeydew Melon Balls

Light White Wine

Using a wire whisk, in medium mixing bowl beat together *1 tablespoon water,* the oil, vinegar, and pepper. Add remaining ingredients and toss to coat. Cover and refrigerate until ready to serve.

EACH SERVING PROVIDES: 1½ FATS; ½ PROTEIN; 1⅛ VEGETABLES; 1 BREAD

PER SERVING: 162 CALORIES; 11 G PROTEIN; 7 G FAT; 14 G CARBOHYDRATE; 44 MG CALCIUM; 273 MG SODIUM; 12 MG CHOLESTEROL; 2 G DIETARY FIBER (THIS FIGURE DOES NOT INCLUDE CAPERS; NUTRITION ANALYSIS NOT AVAILABLE)

REDUCED CHOLESTEROL

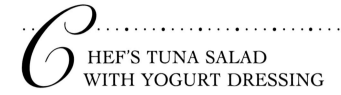

CHEF'S TUNA SALAD WITH YOGURT DRESSING

MAKES 1 SERVING

2 tablespoons plain low-fat
    yogurt
2 teaspoons ketchup
2 teaspoons reduced-calorie
    mayonnaise
1 teaspoon pickle relish
    Dash pepper
½ cup torn lettuce leaves

¼ cup shredded carrot
1 medium tomato, cut into 8
    equal wedges
1 hard-cooked egg, quartered
1 ounce drained canned tuna
    (packed in water)
3 large black olives, pitted and
    sliced

*Chef's Tuna Salad
with Yogurt Dressing*

Seeded Roll

Strawberries

*Coffee, Tea, or
Mineral Water*

1 Using a wire whisk, in small mixing bowl beat together yogurt, ketchup,
  mayonnaise, relish, and pepper. Transfer to small resealable plastic container; cover and refrigerate until ready to pack.

2 Line separate resealable plastic container with lettuce; top with carrot,
  tomato, egg, tuna, and olives. Cover and refrigerate until ready to pack.

3 To serve, pour yogurt dressing over salad.

EACH SERVING PROVIDES: 1½ FATS; 1½ PROTEINS; 3½ VEGETABLES; 35 OPTIONAL
CALORIES
PER SERVING: 237 CALORIES; 18 G PROTEIN; 10 G FAT; 18 G CARBOHYDRATE; 134 MG
CALCIUM; 532 MG SODIUM; 229 MG CHOLESTEROL; 3 G DIETARY FIBER

CHICKEN AND MELON SALAD

MAKES 2 SERVINGS

2 ounces julienne-cut cooked, skinned, and boned chicken
2 tablespoons dry sherry
2 tablespoons seasoned rice vinegar
1 tablespoon teriyaki sauce
2 cups shredded lettuce
1 cup cantaloupe chunks
½ cup julienne-cut red bell pepper

½ cup julienne-cut carrot
½ cup diagonally sliced celery
¼ cup diagonally sliced scallions (green onions), white portion and some green
¼ cup alfalfa sprouts
½ ounce shelled roasted unsalted peanuts, coarsely chopped

Chicken and Melon Salad

French Bread with Reduced-Calorie Margarine

Reduced-Calorie Chocolate Pudding with Whipped Topping

Iced Tea with Lemon Slice

1 In small glass or stainless-steel mixing bowl combine chicken, sherry, vinegar, and teriyaki sauce; set aside.

2 Line serving platter with lettuce; decoratively arrange cantaloupe, pepper, carrot, celery, scallions, and sprouts on lettuce. Using a slotted spoon, arrange chicken on salad. Drizzle sherry mixture over salad and sprinkle with peanuts.

EACH SERVING PROVIDES: ½ FAT; 1¼ PROTEINS; 4 VEGETABLES; ½ FRUIT; 15 OPTIONAL CALORIES

PER SERVING: 212 CALORIES; 13 G PROTEIN; 6 G FAT; 24 G CARBOHYDRATE; 83 MG CALCIUM; 510 MG SODIUM; 25 MG CHOLESTEROL; 4 G DIETARY FIBER

REDUCED CHOLESTEROL AND FAT

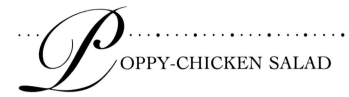

$\mathcal{P}$OPPY-CHICKEN SALAD

MAKES 1 SERVING

1 tablespoon light sour cream
2 teaspoons reduced-calorie
    mayonnaise
1 teaspoon freshly squeezed
    lemon juice
½ teaspoon poppy seed
2 ounces cooked chicken, diced
    and chilled
½ small apple (about 2 ounces),
    cored, pared, and cubed

2 tablespoons chopped celery
1 tablespoon chopped scallion
    (green onion)
  Dash pepper
½ cup torn romaine lettuce leaves
½ cup torn spinach leaves,
    trimmed, thoroughly
    washed, and drained

*$\mathcal{P}$oppy-Chicken
Salad*

Crispbreads

*Fruity Yogurt (plain
low-fat yogurt with
fruit cocktail)*

*Coffee, Tea, or
Mineral Water*

1 Using a wire whisk, in medium mixing bowl beat together the sour
   cream, mayonnaise, lemon juice, and poppy seed.

2 Add remaining ingredients except lettuce and spinach to sour cream
   mixture and toss to coat.

3 Line serving plate with lettuce and spinach; top with chicken mixture.
   Cover and refrigerate until ready to serve.

EACH SERVING PROVIDES: 1 FAT; 2 PROTEINS; 2¼ VEGETABLES; ½ FRUIT; 35 OP-
TIONAL CALORIES

PER SERVING: 211 CALORIES; 19 G PROTEIN; 10 G FAT; 12 G CARBOHYDRATE; 79 MG
CALCIUM; 141 MG SODIUM; 59 MG CHOLESTEROL; 3 G DIETARY FIBER

REDUCED SODIUM

 ARM CHICKEN AND POTATO SALAD

A satisfying dinner for those nights when you're on your own.

MAKES 1 SERVING

3 ounces chicken cutlet, cut into
 cubes
1 teaspoon cornstarch
1 teaspoon vegetable oil
¼ cup diced onion
¼ cup green bell pepper strips
½ cup canned ready-to-serve low-
 sodium chicken broth

¼ pound cooked small red
 potatoes, cut into quarters
1 tablespoon apple cider vinegar
½ teaspoon granulated sugar
 Dash pepper

*Warm Chicken
and Potato Salad*

Cooked Broccoli Spears

Cantaloupe Balls

*Iced Tea with Lemon
Wedge*

1 On sheet of wax paper dredge chicken in cornstarch; set aside.

2 In 9-inch nonstick skillet heat oil; add chicken and cook over medium-
 high heat, stirring frequently, until lightly browned on all sides, about
 3 minutes.

3 Add onion and bell pepper and cook, stirring frequently, until tender-
 crisp, about 2 minutes. Add broth and bring mixture to a boil. Add
 remaining ingredients and stir to combine. Reduce heat to low and let
 simmer until potatoes are heated through, about 5 minutes.

EACH SERVING PROVIDES: 1 FAT; 2 PROTEINS; 1 VEGETABLE; 1 BREAD; 40 OPTIONAL
CALORIES
PER SERVING: 281 CALORIES; 24 G PROTEIN; 7 G FAT; 31 G CARBOHYDRATE; 22 MG
CALCIUM; 93 MG SODIUM; 49 MG CHOLESTEROL; 3 G DIETARY FIBER

REDUCED CHOLESTEROL, FAT AND SODIUM

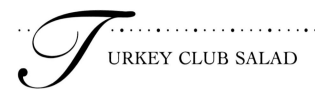# TURKEY CLUB SALAD

If you have leftover cooked chicken on hand, substitute it for the turkey in this salad version of the popular sandwich.

MAKES 2 SERVINGS

4 cups shredded lettuce
¼ pound sliced roast turkey, cut into strips
12 cherry tomatoes, cut into quarters
1 ounce seasoned croutons
¼ cup sliced red onion (separated into rings)

¼ cup plain low-fat yogurt
1 tablespoon plus 1 teaspoon reduced-calorie mayonnaise
½ ounce (about 1 tablespoon) bacon bits (made from real bacon)
2 teaspoons ketchup

Turkey Club Salad

Cantaloupe Chunks

Mixed Vegetable Juice with Celery Stick Stirrer

Onion Bouillon

1 Arrange half of the lettuce, turkey, tomatoes, croutons, and onion in each of two bowls.

2 In small mixing bowl combine remaining ingredients, mixing well. Top each salad with half of the yogurt mixture.

EACH SERVING PROVIDES: 1 FAT; 2 PROTEINS; 5¼ VEGETABLES; 1 BREAD; 65 OP-TIONAL CALORIES

PER SERVING: 295 CALORIES; 25 G PROTEIN; 13 G FAT; 21 G CARBOHYDRATE; 175 MG CALCIUM; 504 MG SODIUM; 55 MG CHOLESTEROL; 2 G DIETARY FIBER (THIS FIGURE DOES NOT INCLUDE CROUTONS; NUTRITION ANALYSIS NOT AVAILABLE)

REDUCED CHOLESTEROL

MEATLESS MAIN DISHES

I N THE PAST, MEATLESS CUISINE WAS ABOUT AS AMERICAN AS BEAN sprouts and tofu. More recently the benefits of a vegetarian diet have become apparent, not only as a means of combating high cholesterol and as a source of vitamins and fiber but as an important part of any well-balanced diet. And vegetarianism is easy on the environment. But if you still think people who eat meatless are missing out, think again. Recipes for Fettuccine Alfredo, Quesadillas with Three Cheeses, Broccoli and Cheddar Pizza, and Southwestern Bean Burgers will satisfy and delight every palate. Besides being a healthful way of eating, vegetarian cooking helps keep food bills down and adds excitement to meal planning. Experiment with different beans to create colorful, fiber-rich side dishes or main meals. Try substituting chick-peas or lentils for ground beef in meatloaf. Some great take-along lunches like Peanut–Apple Butter Sandwich will easily become part of your brown-bag repertoire. For a quick dinner, Vegetable Pita Pizza for one couldn't be simpler or more satisfying. Bulgur Chili and Miniature Falafel with Yogurt Sauce are great for the novice vegetarian. And while eating vegetarian doesn't mean just tofu and bean sprouts, we've included recipes with those popular ingredients as well.

HITE PIZZA

MAKES 8 SERVINGS

1 tablespoon plus 2 teaspoons olive oil

1 garlic clove, minced

1 package refrigerated ready-to-bake pizza-crust dough (10 ounces)

5¼ ounces part-skim mozzarella cheese, shredded

2 teaspoons grated Parmesan cheese

1 teaspoon chopped fresh parsley

⅛ teaspoon oregano leaves

¾ cup part-skim ricotta cheese

White Pizza

Tossed Salad with Italian Dressing

Fresh Fruit Salad

Light Beer

1 Preheat oven to 400°F. In small saucepan heat oil; add garlic and cook over medium heat, stirring frequently, until golden, about 1 minute; set aside.

2 Spray 12-inch round pizza pan with nonstick cooking spray; fit pizza crust dough into pan. Using a pastry brush, brush garlic-oil mixture evenly over dough, leaving ½ inch of outer edge of dough uncovered.

3 Sprinkle oiled surface of dough with mozzarella cheese. Bake for 10 minutes.

4 In small bowl combine Parmesan cheese, parsley, and oregano. Remove pizza from oven and drop ricotta cheese by 8 rounded tablespoonsful in a circular pattern onto pizza. Sprinkle pizza with Parmesan cheese mixture. Return to oven and bake until cheese is melted, 10 to 15 minutes. Cut into 8 equal slices.

EACH SERVING PROVIDES: ½ FAT; 1¼ PROTEINS; 1¼ BREADS; 10 OPTIONAL CALORIES

PER SERVING: 197 CALORIES; 10 G PROTEIN; 9 G FAT; 18 G CARBOHYDRATE; 190 MG CALCIUM; 293 MG SODIUM; 18 MG CHOLESTEROL; DIETARY FIBER DATA NOT AVAILABLE

REDUCED CHOLESTEROL

BROCCOLI AND CHEDDAR PIZZA

MAKES 8 SERVINGS

1 tablespoon plus 2 teaspoons olive oil

3 garlic cloves, minced

2 cups thawed frozen chopped broccoli

½ cup part-skim ricotta cheese

1 package refrigerated ready-to-bake pizza-crust dough (10 ounces)

1 teaspoon sesame seed

3 ounces reduced-fat Cheddar cheese, shredded

3 ounces part-skim mozzarella cheese, shredded

2 teaspoons grated Parmesan cheese

Dash pepper

Broccoli and Cheddar Pizza

Spinach, Mushroom, and Red Onion Salad with Olive Oil, Red Wine Vinegar, and Herbs

Honeydew Melon Wedge

White Wine Spritzer (dry white wine and club soda)

1 Preheat oven to 425°F. In 10-inch nonstick skillet heat oil; add garlic and cook over medium heat, stirring frequently, until golden, about 1 minute. Add broccoli and cook, stirring occasionally, until broccoli is thoroughly heated, 3 to 4 minutes. Remove from heat; stir in ricotta cheese and set aside.

2 Spray 12-inch round pizza pan with nonstick cooking spray; fit pizza-crust dough into pan. Spread broccoli mixture evenly over dough, leaving ½ inch of outer edge of dough uncovered. Sprinkle sesame seed over outer edge of dough. Sprinkle Cheddar and mozzarella cheeses over broccoli mixture, then sprinkle with Parmesan cheese and pepper.

3 Bake until pizza crust is lightly browned, 15 to 20 minutes.

EACH SERVING PROVIDES: ½ FAT; 1¼ PROTEINS; ½ VEGETABLE; 1¼ BREADS; 10 OPTIONAL CALORIES

PER SERVING: 208 CALORIES; 11 G PROTEIN; 9 G FAT; 19 G CARBOHYDRATE; 228 MG CALCIUM; 327 MG SODIUM; 19 MG CHOLESTEROL; 0.4 G DIETARY FIBER (THIS FIGURE DOES NOT INCLUDE PIZZA CRUST DOUGH; NUTRITION ANALYSIS NOT AVAILABLE)

REDUCED CHOLESTEROL

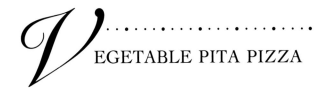

VEGETABLE PITA PIZZA

The perfect pizza for singles—no tempting leftovers lying around!

MAKES 1 SERVING

1 teaspoon olive oil
½ cup sliced pared baby *or* Japanese eggplant
¼ cup diced green bell pepper
¼ cup diced onion
1 garlic clove, minced
1 small pita (1 ounce), split in half horizontally and toasted

1 small plum tomato, sliced
1½ ounces part-skim mozzarella cheese, shredded
1 tablespoon grated Parmesan cheese
¼ teaspoon Italian seasoning

1 Preheat broiler. In small nonstick skillet heat oil; add eggplant, pepper, onion, and garlic and cook over medium heat, stirring frequently, until eggplant is lightly browned, about 3 minutes.

2 Arrange pita halves, cut-side up, on baking sheet. Top each pita half with half of the vegetable mixture, the tomato slices, cheeses, and Italian seasoning.

3 Broil 6 inches from heat source until cheeses are melted, about 1 minute.

EACH SERVING PROVIDES: 1 FAT; 2 PROTEINS; 2½ VEGETABLES; 1 BREAD; 30 OPTIONAL CALORIES
PER SERVING: 301 CALORIES; 17 G PROTEIN; 13 G FAT; 29 G CARBOHYDRATE; 383 MG CALCIUM; 483 MG SODIUM; 29 MG CHOLESTEROL; 3 G DIETARY FIBER
REDUCED CHOLESTEROL

Vegetable Pita Pizza

Cherry Tomatoes, Shredded Red Cabbage, and Sliced Celery on Romaine Lettuce Leaves with Reduced-Calorie Italian Dressing

Reduced-Calorie Strawberry-Flavored Gelatin with Shredded Coconut

Sparkling Mineral Water with Lemon Slice

TOFU "RAVIOLI"

Wonton skins, gingerroot, and Chinese sesame oil give this "ravioli" an Oriental flair.

MAKES 2 SERVINGS, 5 "RAVIOLI" EACH

½ pound firm-style tofu
2 tablespoons teriyaki sauce
2 tablespoons seasoned rice vinegar
¼ cup thinly sliced scallions (green onions)
20 wonton skins (wrappers), 3 × 3-inch squares
1½ teaspoons vegetable oil
1 cup finely chopped onions
2 garlic cloves, minced
1 teaspoon minced pared gingerroot
1 packet instant vegetable broth and seasoning mix, dissolved in 1½ cups hot water
¼ cup dry sherry
1 teaspoon cornstarch
1 teaspoon Chinese sesame oil

1   Using a fork, in medium glass or stainless-steel mixing bowl mash tofu. Add teriyaki sauce, vinegar, and scallions and stir to combine; let stand for 15 minutes.

2   Drain tofu mixture, reserving marinade. On clean work surface arrange wonton skins side by side. Using a pastry brush, brush 10 wonton skins with water and then top each with an equal amount of tofu mixture. Arrange remaining wonton skins over each portion of tofu mixture. Using tines of a fork, press edges of wontons together to seal; set aside.

3   In 12-inch nonstick skillet heat vegetable oil; add onions, garlic, and gingerroot and cook over medium-high heat until onions are translucent, about 1 minute.

4   In medium mixing bowl combine dissolved broth mix, the reserved marinade mixture, the sherry, cornstarch, and sesame oil, stirring to dissolve cornstarch. Stir into onion mixture and cook, stirring constantly, until mixture comes to a boil.

5   Reduce heat to low; add wontons 1 at a time to onion mixture. Cover
    and let simmer for 5 minutes.

EACH SERVING PROVIDES: 1¼ FATS; 2 PROTEINS; 1¼ VEGETABLES; 2 BREADS; 35
OPTIONAL CALORIES

PER SERVING: 516 CALORIES; 29 G PROTEIN; 16 G FAT; 61 G CARBOHYDRATE; 273 MG
CALCIUM; 1,201 MG SODIUM; 0 MG CHOLESTEROL; 2 G DIETARY FIBER (THIS FIGURE
DOES NOT INCLUDE WONTON SKINS; NUTRITION ANALYSIS NOT AVAILABLE)

REDUCED CHOLESTEROL AND FAT

TOFU-STUFFED TOMATO

MAKES 1 SERVING

1 large tomato, cut in half
  horizontally
½ cup drained canned whole-
  kernel corn
2 ounces firm-style tofu,
  mashed
2 tablespoons minced onion
2 tablespoons freshly squeezed
  lime juice

1½ teaspoons chopped fresh
  cilantro (Chinese parsley)
  or Italian (flat-leaf) parsley
1 teaspoon olive oil
  Dash hot sauce
  Dash pepper

*Tofu-Stuffed
Tomato*

Rice Cakes

Apricots

*Coffee, Tea, or
Mineral Water*

1   Scoop out pulp from each tomato half, reserving shells. Chop tomato
    pulp and transfer to medium mixing bowl.

2   Add remaining ingredients to tomato pulp and stir to combine. Cover
    and refrigerate until flavors blend, about 1 hour.

3   Spoon half of the tofu–tomato pulp mixture into each reserved tomato
    shell. Place tomato shells on serving platter; cover and refrigerate until
    ready to serve.

EACH SERVING PROVIDES: 1 FAT; 1 PROTEIN; 3¼ VEGETABLES; 1 BREAD

PER SERVING: 236 CALORIES; 13 G PROTEIN; 11 G FAT; 29 G CARBOHYDRATE; 137 MG
CALCIUM; 30 MG SODIUM; 0 MG CHOLESTEROL; 4 G DIETARY FIBER (THIS FIGURE
DOES NOT INCLUDE TOFU; NUTRITION ANALYSIS NOT AVAILABLE)

REDUCED CHOLESTEROL AND SODIUM

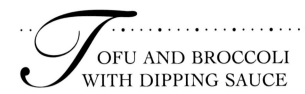

TOFU AND BROCCOLI WITH DIPPING SAUCE

MAKES 2 SERVINGS

1 packet instant vegetable broth and seasoning mix, dissolved in ¾ cup warm water
2 teaspoons reduced-sodium soy sauce
½ pound firm-style tofu, cut into 12 equal rectangular pieces
⅓ cup plus 2 teaspoons plain dried bread crumbs

½ teaspoon garlic powder
½ teaspoon Chinese five-spice powder
¼ cup thawed frozen egg substitute
1 cup broccoli florets, blanched
2 tablespoons sliced scallion (green onion)

1 In medium mixing bowl combine dissolved broth mix and the soy sauce; add tofu and turn to coat with marinade. Cover and refrigerate at least 20 minutes or up to 2 hours.

2 Drain tofu, reserving marinade. Preheat oven to 450°F. Spray nonstick baking sheet with nonstick cooking spray.

3 In small mixing bowl combine bread crumbs, garlic powder, and five-spice powder. Dip each piece of tofu in egg substitute, coating all sides. Dredge in bread crumb mixture and arrange on prepared baking sheet. Repeat procedure, using all remaining ingredients.

4 Arrange tofu and broccoli on baking sheet. Bake for 5 minutes; using pancake turner, turn tofu over and bake until golden brown, about 5 minutes.

5 In small saucepan cook reserved marinade over medium-high heat until mixture comes to a boil.

6 To serve, pour marinade into small serving bowl; stir in scallion. Serve as a dipping sauce for tofu and broccoli.

EACH SERVING PROVIDES: 2½ PROTEINS; 1⅛ VEGETABLES; 1 BREAD; 5 OPTIONAL CALORIES

PER SERVING: 282 CALORIES; 26 G PROTEIN; 11 G FAT; 25 G CARBOHYDRATE; 299 MG CALCIUM; 793 MG SODIUM; 1 MG CHOLESTEROL; 1 G DIETARY FIBER (THIS FIGURE DOES NOT INCLUDE TOFU AND BROCCOLI FLORETS; NUTRITION ANALYSIS NOT AVAILABLE)

REDUCED CHOLESTEROL

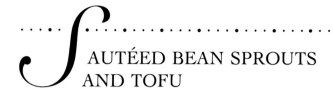

SAUTÉED BEAN SPROUTS AND TOFU

MAKES 2 SERVINGS

1 teaspoon vegetable oil
2 cups bean sprouts
1 cup broccoli florets, blanched
1 cup sliced carrots, blanched
1 tablespoon minced pared
   gingerroot
2 garlic cloves, minced
1 packet instant vegetable broth
   and seasoning mix, dissolved
   in ½ cup hot water

2 tablespoons reduced-sodium
   soy sauce
2 tablespoons seasoned rice
   vinegar
1 teaspoon cornstarch
1 teaspoon Chinese sesame oil
½ pound firm-style tofu, cubed
½ cup diagonally sliced celery
½ cup diagonally sliced scallions
   (green onions)

1 In 10-inch nonstick skillet heat vegetable oil; add bean sprouts and cook over high heat, stirring frequently, until tender-crisp, about 1 minute. Add broccoli, carrots, gingerroot, and garlic and stir to combine. Cover and let cook for 1 minute.

2 In 1-cup liquid measure combine dissolved broth mix, the soy sauce, vinegar, cornstarch, and sesame oil, stirring to dissolve cornstarch. Stir into vegetable mixture and cook, stirring constantly, until mixture comes to a boil. Continue to cook, stirring constantly, until mixture thickens, about 1 minute.

3 Remove skillet from heat; add remaining ingredients and stir to combine.

EACH SERVING PROVIDES: 1 FAT; 2 PROTEINS; 5 VEGETABLES; 10 OPTIONAL CALORIES
PER SERVING: 337 CALORIES; 26 G PROTEIN; 15 G FAT; 33 G CARBOHYDRATE; 324 MG CALCIUM; 1,158 MG SODIUM; 0 MG CHOLESTEROL; 4 G DIETARY FIBER (THIS FIGURE DOES NOT INCLUDE BROCCOLI FLORETS; NUTRITION ANALYSIS NOT AVAILABLE)
REDUCED CHOLESTEROL

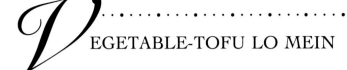

VEGETABLE-TOFU LO MEIN

An assortment of vegetables adds interest to this dish while helping you to feel satisfied.

MAKES 2 SERVINGS

½ cup bean sprouts
½ cup julienne-cut carrot
½ cup sliced scallions (green onions); reserve 1 tablespoon for garnish
1 packet instant vegetable broth and seasoning mix, dissolved in ½ cup warm water

2 tablespoons creamy peanut butter
1 tablespoon reduced-sodium soy sauce
½ teaspoon cornstarch
Dash pepper
¼ pound firm-style tofu, cubed
1½ cups cooked spaghetti (hot)

Vegetable-Tofu Lo Mein

Mixed Green Salad with Red Wine Vinegar and Herbs

Lime Sherbet

Tea with Lemon and Honey

1 Spray 10-inch nonstick skillet with nonstick cooking spray and heat; add bean sprouts and carrot and cook over medium-high heat, stirring frequently, until sprouts soften, about 2 minutes. Add scallions (except garnish) and stir to combine; cook until carrot is tender-crisp, about 1 minute.

2 Using a wire whisk, in small mixing bowl beat together dissolved broth mix, peanut butter, soy sauce, cornstarch, and pepper; stir into vegetable mixture. Add tofu and stir to combine.

3 Reduce heat to medium and cook until mixture thickens, about 5 minutes. Add spaghetti and toss to coat.

4. To serve, transfer vegetable-spaghetti mixture to serving bowl and sprinkle with reserved scallion.

EACH SERVING PROVIDES: 1 FAT; 2 PROTEINS; 1½ VEGETABLES; 1½ BREADS; 10 OPTIONAL CALORIES
PER SERVING: 364 CALORIES; 21 G PROTEIN; 14 G FAT; 43 G CARBOHYDRATE; 157 MG CALCIUM; 780 MG SODIUM; 0 MG CHOLESTEROL; 4 G DIETARY FIBER (THIS FIGURE DOES NOT INCLUDE TOFU; NUTRITION ANALYSIS NOT AVAILABLE)
REDUCED CHOLESTEROL

VEGETABLE FRIED RICE

MAKES 4 SERVINGS

1 tablespoon plus 1 teaspoon peanut oil
1 cup chopped onions
1 tablespoon minced pared gingerroot
2 garlic cloves, minced
2 cups coarsely chopped Chinese cabbage
½ cup julienne-cut carrot
½ cup julienne-cut red bell pepper
1½ cups cooked long-grain rice
1 packet instant vegetable broth and seasoning mix, dissolved in ¼ cup hot water

2 tablespoons reduced-sodium soy sauce
2 tablespoons dry sherry
¼ pound firm-style tofu, cubed
½ cup frozen peas
½ cup thawed frozen egg substitute
2 tablespoons sliced scallion (green onion)

1 In 10-inch nonstick skillet or wok heat oil; add onions, gingerroot, and garlic and cook over high heat, stirring quickly and frequently, until onions are translucent, about 1 minute.

2 Add cabbage, carrot, and bell pepper and cook, stirring quickly and frequently, until cabbage softens, about 5 minutes.

3 Add rice, dissolved broth mix, the soy sauce, and sherry and stir to combine; bring mixture to a boil. Add tofu and peas and cook until thoroughly heated, about 2 minutes.

4 Drizzle egg substitute over vegetable-rice mixture, stirring well to combine. Cook until egg substitute is set. Sprinkle with scallion.

EACH SERVING PROVIDES: 1 FAT; 1 PROTEIN; 2 VEGETABLES; 1 BREAD; 10 OPTIONAL CALORIES
PER SERVING: 258 CALORIES; 12 G PROTEIN; 7 G FAT; 35 G CARBOHYDRATE; 131 MG CALCIUM; 568 MG SODIUM; 0 MG CHOLESTEROL; 3 G DIETARY FIBER (THIS FIGURE DOES NOT INCLUDE TOFU; NUTRITION ANALYSIS NOT AVAILABLE)
REDUCED CHOLESTEROL AND FAT

CHICK-PEA STEW

MAKES 2 SERVINGS

1 cup chopped onions
2 garlic cloves, minced
2 teaspoons olive *or* vegetable oil
⅛ teaspoon oregano leaves
⅛ teaspoon crushed red pepper
  flakes
1 bay leaf

½ pound rinsed drained canned
  chick-peas, divided
½ cup tomato sauce
½ cup canned stewed tomatoes
  (reserve liquid), chopped
1 teaspoon chopped fresh basil
  or ⅛ teaspoon basil leaves

1 In 1-quart microwavable casserole combine onions, garlic, oil, oregano, pepper, and bay leaf. Cover and microwave on High (100%) for 3 minutes, stirring halfway through cooking time, until onions are translucent. Set aside.

2 In blender combine 2 ounces chick-peas and the tomato sauce and process on high speed until chick-peas are pureed, about 1 minute.

3 Add pureed chick-peas, the remaining chick-peas, tomatoes with reserved liquid, basil, and *1 tablespoon water* to onion mixture and stir to combine. Cover and microwave on High for 3 minutes, stirring every minute, until mixture is thoroughly heated. Remove and discard bay leaf.

EACH SERVING PROVIDES: 1 FAT; 2 PROTEINS; 2 VEGETABLES

PER SERVING: 246 CALORIES; 10 G PROTEIN; 8 G FAT; 36 G CARBOHYDRATE; 103 MG CALCIUM; 757 MG SODIUM; 0 MG CHOLESTEROL; 8 G DIETARY FIBER (THIS FIGURE DOES NOT INCLUDE STEWED TOMATOES; NUTRITION ANALYSIS NOT AVAILABLE)

REDUCED CHOLESTEROL AND FAT

Chick-Pea Stew

*Cooked Noodles
sprinkled with Poppy
Seed*

*Cooked Sliced Zucchini
and Pearl Onions*

*Spinach and
Mushroom Salad with
Imitation Bacon Bits
and Reduced-Calorie
French Dressing*

*Pear Wedges sprinkled
with Cinnamon*

*Club Soda with Lime
Wedge*

RICE AND BEAN CASSEROLE

Rice and beans—a classic vegetarian combination.

MAKES 2 SERVINGS, ABOUT 1 CUP EACH

2 teaspoons margarine
¼ cup diced onion
¼ cup diced red *or* green bell
　pepper
1 garlic clove, minced
½ pound rinsed drained canned
　black-eyed peas

1 cup skim *or* nonfat milk
1 bay leaf
2 ounces fast-cooking whole
　grain brown rice
⅛ teaspoon thyme leaves
⅛ teaspoon rubbed sage
　Dash pepper

1 In 1-quart microwavable casserole microwave margarine on High (100%) for 30 seconds, until melted.

2 Add onion, bell pepper, and garlic and stir to combine; cover and microwave on High for 2 minutes, stirring once halfway through cooking, until onion is translucent.

3 Add black-eyed peas, milk, *1 tablespoon water,* and the bay leaf; microwave on High for 2 minutes, until mixture is boiling. Stir in rice; cover and microwave on High for 4 minutes.

4 Microwave on Medium (50%) for 2½ minutes. Stir in seasonings; cover and microwave on Medium for 2½ minutes. Let stand for 2 minutes until liquid is absorbed. Remove and discard bay leaf.

EACH SERVING PROVIDES: ½ MILK; 1 FAT; 2 PROTEINS; ½ VEGETABLE; 1 BREAD
PER SERVING: 315 CALORIES; 16 G PROTEIN; 6 G FAT; 54 G CARBOHYDRATE; 209 MG CALCIUM; 507 MG SODIUM (ESTIMATED); 2 MG CHOLESTEROL; 12 G DIETARY FIBER
REDUCED CHOLESTEROL AND FAT

Rice and Bean Casserole

*Cooked Broccoli Spears
with Reduced-Calorie
Margarine*

*Tossed Salad with
Reduced-Calorie
Buttermilk Dressing*

Strawberry Ice Milk

*Coffee, Tea, or
Mineral Water*

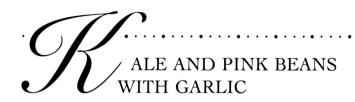

KALE AND PINK BEANS WITH GARLIC

Trying to increase the amount of fiber in your diet? This recipe may be of interest to you.

MAKES 2 SERVINGS

2 teaspoons olive oil
2 garlic cloves, minced
4 cups thoroughly washed and drained kale,* chopped

½ packet instant vegetable broth and seasoning mix
¼ pound rinsed drained canned pink beans

1 In 1-quart microwavable casserole combine oil and garlic; cover and microwave on High (100%) for 1 minute.

2 Add kale, *1 tablespoon water,* and the broth mix to garlic and stir to combine. Cover and microwave on High for 2½ minutes. Add beans and stir to combine; microwave on High for 2½ minutes. Let stand for 1 minute, until kale is wilted and beans are heated through.

EACH SERVING PROVIDES: 1 FAT; 1 PROTEIN; 1 VEGETABLE; 3 OPTIONAL CALORIES
PER SERVING: 172 CALORIES; 9 G PROTEIN; 6 G FAT; 24 G CARBOHYDRATE; 209 MG CALCIUM; 417 MG SODIUM; 0 MG CHOLESTEROL; 12 G DIETARY FIBER
REDUCED CHOLESTEROL AND FAT

* 4 cups fresh kale yield about 1 cup cooked kale.

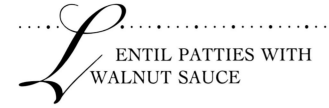

LENTIL PATTIES WITH WALNUT SAUCE

MAKES 2 SERVINGS, 2 LENTIL PATTIES EACH

6 ounces rinsed drained canned lentils
¼ cup seasoned dried bread crumbs
1 egg white
1 garlic clove, minced
1 teaspoon margarine

¼ cup finely chopped onion
1½ teaspoons all-purpose flour
½ cup low-fat milk (1% milk fat)
¼ cup minced fresh parsley
1 ounce finely chopped walnuts
Dash ground nutmeg

1   Using a fork, in medium mixing bowl mash lentils slightly; add bread crumbs, egg white, and garlic and mix well. Shape into 4 equal patties.

2   Spray 9-inch nonstick skillet with nonstick cooking spray; add patties and cook over medium-high heat until browned, about 4 minutes on each side. Transfer patties to serving platter; set aside and keep warm.

3   In same skillet melt margarine; add onion and cook over high heat, stirring frequently, until softened, about 1 minute.

4   Reduce heat to medium. Sprinkle flour over onion and stir quickly to combine. Continue to cook, stirring constantly, for 1 minute. Gradually stir in milk. Add parsley, walnuts, and nutmeg and cook, stirring frequently, until mixture thickens, about 2 minutes.

5   Serve with walnut sauce.

EACH SERVING PROVIDES: ¼ MILK; 1½ FATS; 2 PROTEINS; ¼ VEGETABLE; ½ BREAD; 35 OPTIONAL CALORIES
PER SERVING: 313 CALORIES; 16 G PROTEIN; 12 G FAT; 37 G CARBOHYDRATE; 137 MG CALCIUM; 484 MG SODIUM; 3 MG CHOLESTEROL; 5 G DIETARY FIBER
REDUCED CHOLESTEROL

Lentil Patties with Walnut Sauce

Cooked Brown Rice with Sliced Mushrooms

Cooked French-Style Green Beans

Cantaloupe Wedge

Coffee, Tea, or Mineral Water

SOUTHWESTERN BEAN BURGERS

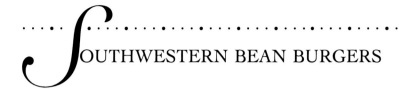

MAKES 2 SERVINGS, 2 BURGERS EACH

6 ounces rinsed drained canned
    white kidney (cannellini)
    beans, mashed
1 cup mild salsa, divided
½ cup plain dried bread crumbs
1 tablespoon minced fresh
    cilantro (Chinese parsley) *or*
    Italian (flat-leaf) parsley

Dash hot sauce
¾ ounce reduced-fat Cheddar
    cheese, shredded

Southwestern Bean Burgers

Tomato Slices, Red Onion Slices, and Shredded Lettuce

Whole Wheat Pita

Fruit Salad

Light Beer

1 In medium mixing bowl combine beans, ½ cup salsa, the bread crumbs, cilantro, and hot sauce. Shape into 4 equal patties. Wrap patties and refrigerate until firm, about 20 minutes.

2 Spray 12-inch nonstick skillet with nonstick cooking spray and heat; add patties and cook over medium heat until browned, about 5 minutes on each side.

3 To serve, top each burger with an equal amount of the remaining salsa and the cheese.

EACH SERVING PROVIDES: 2 PROTEINS; 1 VEGETABLE; 1 BREAD; 30 OPTIONAL CALORIES

PER SERVING: 264 CALORIES; 13 G PROTEIN; 4 G FAT; 43 G CARBOHYDRATE; 156 MG CALCIUM; 1,159 MG SODIUM; 9 MG CHOLESTEROL; 7 G DIETARY FIBER (THIS FIGURE DOES NOT INCLUDE SALSA; NUTRITION ANALYSIS NOT AVAILABLE)

REDUCED CHOLESTEROL AND FAT

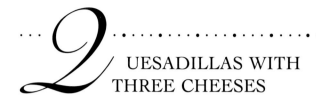

QUESADILLAS WITH THREE CHEESES

For that extra special touch, serve with a topping of light sour cream.

MAKES 2 SERVINGS, 2 QUESADILLAS EACH

1 teaspoon olive *or* vegetable
　oil, divided
¼ cup thinly sliced onion
¼ cup red *or* green bell pepper
　strips
1 garlic clove, minced
1½ ounces reduced-fat Cheddar
　cheese, shredded
1 tablespoon plus 1½ teaspoons
　whipped cream cheese

1 tablespoon grated Parmesan
　cheese
Dash ground cumin
Dash crushed red pepper
　flakes
2 flour tortillas (6-inch diameter
　each)
Cherry tomato, lime slice, and
　Italian parsley for garnish
　(optional)

1　In small nonstick skillet heat ¾ teaspoon oil; add onion, bell pepper, and garlic and cook until bell pepper is tender-crisp, 2 to 3 minutes. Set aside.

2　Using a fork, in small mixing bowl combine remaining ingredients, except tortillas, stirring to combine.

3　Preheat oven to 450°F. Onto bottom half of 1 tortilla spoon half of the vegetable mixture; top with half of the cheese mixture. Fold tortilla in half and gently press to close. Repeat procedure with remaining vegetable mixture, cheese mixture, and tortilla.

4　Arrange filled tortillas on nonstick baking sheet and brush each with half of the remaining oil. Bake until cheeses are melted, about 5 minutes. Cut each tortilla in half, making 4 quesadillas. Garnish with tomato, lime, and parsley as desired.

EACH SERVING PROVIDES: ½ FAT; 1 PROTEIN; ½ VEGETABLE; 1 BREAD; 40 OPTIONAL CALORIES

PER SERVING: 205 CALORIES; 10 G PROTEIN; 11 G FAT; 16 G CARBOHYDRATE; 276 MG CALCIUM; 364 MG SODIUM; 24 MG CHOLESTEROL; 1 G DIETARY FIBER

REDUCED CHOLESTEROL

BULGUR CHILI

Bulgur and beans are combined in this meatless chili.

MAKES 2 SERVINGS

¼ cup chopped onion
¼ cup chopped red *or* green bell
    pepper
1 small jalapeño pepper, seeded
    and chopped
2 garlic cloves, minced
¾ cup canned Italian tomatoes
    (reserve liquid), seeded and
    pureed
2 ounces uncooked bulgur
    (cracked wheat)

1 teaspoon chili powder
4 ounces rinsed drained canned
    black (turtle) beans
10 small pimiento-stuffed green
    olives, cut lengthwise into
    halves
    Dash pepper
1½ ounces reduced-fat Cheddar
    cheese, shredded

Bulgur Chili

*Warm Taco Shell
Pieces*

Cooked Green Beans

Honeydew Melon Balls

Light Beer

1 Spray 1-quart microwavable casserole with nonstick cooking spray; add onion, bell pepper, jalapeño pepper, garlic, and *1 tablespoon water.* Cover and microwave on High (100%) for 2 minutes, stirring once halfway through cooking, until onion is translucent.

2 Add *1¼ cups water,* the tomatoes with reserved liquid, bulgur, and chili powder; cover and microwave on Medium-High (70%) for 10 minutes, stirring once halfway through cooking, until liquid is absorbed.

3 Add beans, olives, and pepper to bulgur mixture and stir to combine; cover and microwave on High for 3 minutes, stirring every minute, until mixture is thoroughly heated. Let stand for 5 minutes, until liquid is absorbed.

4 To serve, sprinkle with cheese.

EACH SERVING PROVIDES: ½ FAT; 2 PROTEINS; 1¼ VEGETABLES; 1 BREAD
PER SERVING: 284 CALORIES; 15 G PROTEIN; 7 G FAT; 42 G CARBOHYDRATE; 269 MG CALCIUM; 855 MG SODIUM (ESTIMATED); 15 MG CHOLESTEROL; 10 G DIETARY FIBER
REDUCED CHOLESTEROL AND FAT

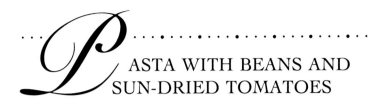

PASTA WITH BEANS AND SUN-DRIED TOMATOES

Cook the pasta while you prepare the bean mixture. For added appeal, sprinkle with freshly grated Parmesan cheese before serving.

MAKES 2 SERVINGS

2 teaspoons olive *or* vegetable oil
1 cup chopped onions
1 garlic clove, mashed
½ pound rinsed drained canned white kidney (cannellini) beans
2½ cups canned Italian tomatoes (reserve liquid), seeded and chopped

4 sun-dried tomato halves (not packed in oil), cut into strips
1 tablespoon dry white table wine
1½ cups cooked thin spaghetti (hot)
2 tablespoons chopped fresh Italian (flat-leaf) parsley

1   In 10-inch nonstick skillet heat oil; add onions and garlic and cook until onions are translucent, about 2 minutes. Add beans, Italian tomatoes with reserved liquid, the sun-dried tomatoes, and wine; stir to combine and bring to a boil.

2   Reduce heat to low and let simmer, stirring occasionally, until flavors blend, about 8 minutes.

3   To serve, arrange spaghetti on serving platter; top with bean-tomato mixture. Sprinkle with parsley.

EACH SERVING PROVIDES: 1 FAT; 2 PROTEINS; 4½ VEGETABLES; 1½ BREADS; 5 OPTIONAL CALORIES
PER SERVING: 433 CALORIES; 19 G PROTEIN; 7 G FAT; 74 G CARBOHYDRATE; 161 MG CALCIUM; 736 MG SODIUM; 0 MG CHOLESTEROL; 14 G DIETARY FIBER

Variation: Pasta with Beans—Omit sun-dried tomato halves from recipe. In Serving Information decrease Vegetables to 3½.

PER SERVING: 417 CALORIES; 19 G PROTEIN; 7 G FAT; 70 G CARBOHYDRATE; 155 MG CALCIUM; 729 MG SODIUM; 0 MG CHOLESTEROL; 13 G DIETARY FIBER
REDUCED CHOLESTEROL AND FAT

FETTUCCINE ALFREDO

MAKES 2 SERVINGS

1 cup White Sauce (see below)
½ cup part-skim ricotta cheese
1½ ounces Parmesan cheese,
    grated

Dash pepper
1¾ cups cooked fettuccine (hot)
1 tablespoon chopped fresh
    Italian (flat-leaf) parsley

1   In 1-quart nonstick saucepan cook White Sauce over low heat, stirring frequently, until heated, about 3 minutes. Stir in cheeses and pepper and cook until cheeses are melted, about 1 minute.

2   To serve, in serving bowl arrange fettuccine; top with sauce and sprinkle with parsley.

EACH SERVING (INCLUDING WHITE SAUCE) PROVIDES: ½ MILK; 1 FAT; 2 PROTEINS; 2 BREADS; 25 OPTIONAL CALORIES

PER SERVING: 510 CALORIES; 27 G PROTEIN; 22 G FAT; 49 G CARBOHYDRATE; 634 MG CALCIUM; 694 MG SODIUM; 97 MG CHOLESTEROL; 3 G DIETARY FIBER

WHITE SAUCE

YIELD: 1 CUP

1 tablespoon whipped butter
2 teaspoons margarine
1 tablespoon plus 1½ teaspoons
    all-purpose flour
1 cup low-fat milk (1% milk fat)

Dash salt
Dash white pepper
Dash ground nutmeg
Dash paprika

1   In 1-quart nonstick saucepan melt butter and margarine over low heat. Using a wire whisk, stir in flour and cook, stirring constantly, for 1 minute. Gradually stir in milk and seasonings. Continuing to stir, increase heat to medium-high and cook until mixture comes to a boil. Let cool slightly.

2 Transfer White Sauce to resealable plastic container and refrigerate for up to 1 week.

EACH ½-CUP SERVING PROVIDES: ½ MILK; 1 FAT; ¼ BREAD; 25 OPTIONAL CALORIES

PER SERVING: 141 CALORIES; 5 G PROTEIN; 9 G FAT; 10 G CARBOHYDRATE; 154 MG CALCIUM; 211 MG SODIUM; 15 MG CHOLESTEROL; 0.2 G DIETARY FIBER

REDUCED CHOLESTEROL

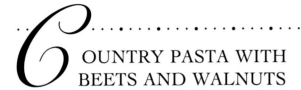

COUNTRY PASTA WITH BEETS AND WALNUTS

MAKES 4 SERVINGS

2 teaspoons olive oil
1 cup diced red onions
1 ounce walnuts, chopped
2 garlic cloves, minced
1 teaspoon all-purpose flour
1 cup low-fat milk (1% milk fat)
3 ounces Camembert cheese (rind and paper removed), cut into small pieces

2 cups fresh cooked *or* drained canned julienne-cut beets
2 cups cooked penne *or* ziti macaroni

1 In 10-inch nonstick skillet heat oil; add onions, walnuts, and garlic and cook over medium-high heat, stirring frequently, until onions are translucent, about 1 minute. Sprinkle flour over onion mixture and stir quickly to combine; cook, stirring constantly, for 1 minute.

2 Remove skillet from heat and stir in milk. Return skillet to medium heat; stir in cheese and cook, stirring frequently, until cheese melts and mixture thickens, about 5 minutes.

3 Add beets and pasta and toss to coat; cook until heated through, 1 to 2 minutes.

EACH SERVING PROVIDES: ¼ MILK; 1 FAT; 1¼ PROTEINS; 1½ VEGETABLES; 1 BREAD; 3 OPTIONAL CALORIES

PER SERVING: 298 CALORIES; 12 G PROTEIN; 13 G FAT; 34 G CARBOHYDRATE; 191 MG CALCIUM; 254 MG SODIUM; 18 MG CHOLESTEROL; 4 G DIETARY FIBER

REDUCED CHOLESTEROL

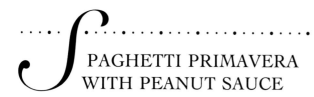

SPAGHETTI PRIMAVERA WITH PEANUT SAUCE

MAKES 2 SERVINGS (PICTURED ON JACKET)

¼ cup dark raisins
2 tablespoons creamy peanut butter
2 tablespoons chutney
½ cup sliced scallions (green onions)
½ cup red bell pepper strips
½ cut green bell pepper strips

½ cup peapods
¼ cup sliced zucchini
¼ cup summer squash
1 garlic clove, minced
2 cups cooked thin spaghetti (hot)
  Dash crushed red pepper flakes

1 In small cup combine raisins and *¼ cup warm water;* set aside.

2 In 1-quart microwavable casserole combine peanut butter and chutney. Cover and microwave on High (100%) for 1 minute. Add scallions, bell pepper, peapods, zucchini, squash, and garlic and stir to combine. Cover and microwave on Medium (50%) for 3 minutes, stirring once halfway through cooking.

3 Drain raisins, reserving liquid. Add raisins, spaghetti, and red pepper to peanut butter mixture and toss to coat. Cover and microwave on Medium for 1 minute. (If peanut butter mixture is very thick, add some of the reserved liquid from the raisins.)

EACH SERVING PROVIDES: 1 FAT; 1 PROTEIN; 2½ VEGETABLE; 2 BREADS; 1 FRUIT; 30 OPTIONAL CALORIES

PER SERVING: 408 CALORIES; 13 G PROTEIN; 9 G FAT; 71 G CARBOHYDRATE; 49 MG CALCIUM; 116 MG SODIUM; 0 MG CHOLESTEROL; 5 G DIETARY FIBER

REDUCED CHOLESTEROL, FAT AND SODIUM

MACARONI AND VEGETABLES WITH CHEESE SAUCE

We've used cooked broccoli and cauliflower in this recipe. It's a wonderful way to recycle leftover vegetables.

MAKES 1 SERVING

1 teaspoon margarine
1 garlic clove, minced
½ cup low-fat milk (1% milk fat)
2 teaspoons all-purpose flour
¼ teaspoon salt
2¼ ounces reduced-fat Cheddar cheese, shredded, divided

½ teaspoon Worcestershire sauce
¾ cup cooked elbow macaroni
½ cup cooked broccoli florets
½ cup cooked cauliflower florets

Macaroni and Vegetables with Cheese Sauce

Cooked Carrot Sticks with Reduced-Calorie Margarine

Tossed Salad with Reduced-Calorie Thousand Island Dressing

Cinnamon-Spiced Baked Apple

Coffee or Tea

1 In 1-quart microwavable casserole combine margarine and garlic; microwave on High (100%) for 30 seconds, until margarine is melted.

2 In 1-cup liquid measure combine milk, flour, and salt, stirring to dissolve flour. Using a wire whisk, stir into margarine-garlic mixture. Cover and microwave on High for 1 minute. Stir in 2 ounces cheese and the Worcestershire sauce. Microwave on High for 2 minutes, until mixture thickens.

3 Add macaroni, broccoli, and cauliflower to cheese sauce and stir to coat. Microwave on Medium-High (70%) for 2 minutes, until thoroughly heated. Top with remaining cheese. Microwave on High for 30 seconds, until cheese is melted.

EACH SERVING PROVIDES: ½ MILK; 1 FAT; 3 PROTEINS; 2 VEGETABLES; 1½ BREADS; 20 OPTIONAL CALORIES

PER SERVING: 496 CALORIES; 31 G PROTEIN; 17 G FAT; 50 G CARBOHYDRATE; 776 MG CALCIUM; 1,144 MG SODIUM; 50 MG CHOLESTEROL; 3 G DIETARY FIBER (THIS FIGURE DOES NOT INCLUDE BROCCOLI FLORETS; NUTRITION ANALYSIS NOT AVAILABLE)

REDUCED CHOLESTEROL

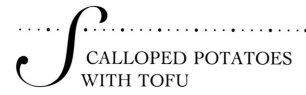

SCALLOPED POTATOES WITH TOFU

MAKES 6 SERVINGS

1 package (six ½-cup servings) cheesy scalloped potato mix
1½ pounds firm-style tofu, cubed

1 tablespoon chopped fresh Italian (flat-leaf) parsley

1   Preheat oven to 400°F. Prepare potato mix according to package directions. Add tofu to potato mixture and stir to combine.

2   Spray 2-quart casserole with nonstick cooking spray and arrange potato-tofu mixture in casserole. Bake until golden, 30 to 35 minutes. Sprinkle with parsley.

EACH SERVING PROVIDES: 2 PROTEINS; 1 BREAD; 40 OPTIONAL CALORIES

PER SERVING: 316 CALORIES; 21 G PROTEIN; 17 G FAT; 25 G CARBOHYDRATE; 287 MG CALCIUM; 559 MG SODIUM; 14 MG CHOLESTEROL; DIETARY FIBER DATA NOT AVAILABLE

REDUCED CHOLESTEROL

Scalloped Potatoes with Tofu

Cooked Brussels Sprouts and Pearl Onions

Tossed Salad with Croutons and French Dressing

Cinnamon-Spiced Warm Applesauce

Coffee, Tea, or Mineral Water

RÖSTI POTATOES WITH VEGETABLES

MAKES 2 SERVINGS

5-ounce baking potato, pared
2 tablespoons chopped chives
⅛ teaspoon pepper
2 teaspoons vegetable oil
½ cup julienne-cut red bell pepper
½ cup julienne-cut zucchini

½ cup julienne-cut yellow squash
¼ cup sliced mushrooms
1½ ounces reduced-fat Swiss cheese, shredded

1 Using largest holes on a hand grater, grate potato. Transfer potato to small mixing bowl; add chives and pepper and stir to combine.

2 In 12-inch nonstick skillet heat oil; spread potato mixture on bottom of skillet, making 2 circles. Cook over medium heat until potato circles are lightly browned on bottom, 3 to 4 minutes; using pancake turner, turn potato circles over and cook until the other sides are lightly browned, 2 to 3 minutes. Transfer to nonstick baking sheet.

3 Preheat broiler. Spray same skillet with nonstick cooking spray and heat; add bell pepper and cook over medium-high heat, stirring frequently, for 1 minute. Add zucchini, yellow squash, and mushrooms and cook, stirring frequently, until pepper is tender-crisp, 2 to 3 minutes. Spoon half of the vegetable mixture over each potato "pancake"; top each portion with half of the cheese.

4 Broil "pancakes" 5 to 6 inches from heat source until cheese melts, 1 to 2 minutes.

EACH SERVING PROVIDES: 1 FAT; 1 PROTEIN; 1¾ VEGETABLES; ½ BREAD
PER SERVING: 184 CALORIES; 10 G PROTEIN; 9 G FAT; 18 G CARBOHYDRATE; 284 MG CALCIUM; 41 MG SODIUM; 15 MG CHOLESTEROL; 2 G DIETARY FIBER
REDUCED CHOLESTEROL AND SODIUM

CHEESE FONDUE

Serve with French-bread cubes and assorted fresh vegetables for dipping.

MAKES 2 SERVINGS

1 cup White Sauce (see page 94)

1½ ounces reduced-fat Swiss cheese, shredded

1 tablespoon country Dijon-style mustard

1 teaspoon Worcestershire sauce

In 1-quart nonstick saucepan cook White Sauce over low heat, stirring frequently, until heated, about 3 minutes. Stir in remaining ingredients and cook, stirring constantly, until cheese is melted, about 1 minute. Serve immediately.

EACH SERVING (INCLUDING WHITE SAUCE) PROVIDES: ½ MILK; 1 FAT; 1 PROTEIN; ¼ BREAD; 25 OPTIONAL CALORIES

PER SERVING: 220 CALORIES; 12 G PROTEIN; 13 G FAT; 13 G CARBOHYDRATE; 417 MG CALCIUM; 497 MG SODIUM; 30 MG CHOLESTEROL; 0.2 G DIETARY FIBER

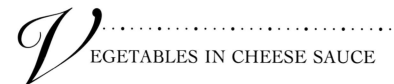

VEGETABLES IN CHEESE SAUCE

MAKES 2 SERVINGS

1 cup White Sauce (see page 94)

1½ ounces reduced-fat Cheddar cheese, shredded

½ teaspoon Italian seasoning

1 cup broccoli florets, blanched

½ cup cauliflower florets, blanched

½ cup sliced carrot, blanched

½ cup red bell pepper strips, blanched

½ cup sliced onion

In 2½-quart nonstick saucepan cook White Sauce over low heat, stirring frequently, until heated, about 3 minutes. Stir in cheese and Italian seasoning and cook, stirring constantly, until cheese is melted, about 1 minute. Add vegetables and stir to coat. Serve immediately.

EACH SERVING (INCLUDING WHITE SAUCE) PROVIDES: ½ MILK; 1 FAT; 1 PROTEIN; 4 VEGETABLES; ¼ BREAD; 25 OPTIONAL CALORIES

PER SERVING: 286 CALORIES; 15 G PROTEIN; 13 G FAT; 27 G CARBOHYDRATE; 411 MG CALCIUM; 409 MG SODIUM; 30 MG CHOLESTEROL; 4 G DIETARY FIBER (THIS FIGURE DOES NOT INCLUDE BROCCOLI FLORETS; NUTRITION ANALYSIS NOT AVAILABLE)

SQUASH FRITTATA

MAKES 2 SERVINGS

1 cup thawed Spaghetti Squash (see page 208)
1 cup thawed frozen egg substitute
2 tablespoons chopped fresh Italian (flat-leaf) parsley

1 tablespoon grated Parmesan cheese
Dash ground red pepper
Dash onion powder
Dash garlic powder

1 In large mixing bowl combine all ingredients, mixing well. Spray 7-inch microwavable pie plate with nonstick cooking spray and spread mixture over bottom of plate.

2 Microwave on High (100%) for 6 minutes. Stir outside of mixture toward center of pie plate.

3 Microwave on Medium (50%) for 6 minutes, stirring mixture once halfway through cooking. Let stand 1 minute before serving.

EACH SERVING (INCLUDING SPAGHETTI SQUASH) PROVIDES: 2 PROTEINS; 1 VEGETABLE; 15 OPTIONAL CALORIES

PER SERVING: 89 CALORIES; 12 G PROTEIN; 1 G FAT; 8 G CARBOHYDRATE; 94 MG CALCIUM; 221 MG SODIUM; 2 MG CHOLESTEROL; DIETARY FIBER DATA NOT AVAILABLE

REDUCED CHOLESTEROL, FAT AND SODIUM

Squash Frittata

Cooked Sliced Zucchini, Stewed Tomatoes, and Chopped Fresh Basil

Italian Bread with Reduced-Calorie Margarine

Lemon Sherbet with Blueberries

Coffee, Tea, or Mineral Water

CHEDDAR CORN CAKES

Serve these tangy cakes for brunch, a light lunch, or a midweek supper.

MAKES 2 SERVINGS, 5 CAKES EACH

1 teaspoon olive oil
½ cup chopped scallions (green onions)
½ cup diced red bell pepper
1½ ounces reduced-fat Cheddar cheese, shredded
½ cup thawed frozen whole-kernel corn

⅓ cup plus 2 teaspoons all-purpose flour
1 teaspoon double-acting baking powder
½ cup low-fat buttermilk (1% milk fat)
2 eggs, separated
2 egg whites

Cheddar Corn Cakes

Cooked Asparagus Spears with Grated Lemon Peel

Mixed Green Salad with Reduced-Calorie Italian Dressing

Cranberry Spritzer (cranberry juice cocktail and club soda)

1 In small nonstick skillet heat oil; add scallions and pepper and cook over medium-high heat, stirring occasionally, until scallions are tender, about 1 minute. Remove from heat and set aside.

2 Preheat oven to 400°F. In large mixing bowl combine cheese, corn, flour, and baking powder; set aside.

3 Using a wire whisk, in small mixing bowl beat together milk and egg yolks; set aside.

4 Using mixer on high speed, in medium mixing bowl beat the 4 egg whites until stiff but not dry.

5 Stir milk–egg yolk mixture into dry ingredients; fold in beaten egg whites.

6 Spray nonstick baking sheet with nonstick cooking spray. Drop batter by ½-cup measures onto baking sheet, making 10 cakes, and leaving a space between each. Bake until golden, about 6 minutes.

EACH SERVING PROVIDES: ¼ MILK; ½ FAT; 2 PROTEINS; 1 VEGETABLE; 1½ BREADS; 20 OPTIONAL CALORIES

PER SERVING: 338 CALORIES; 22 G PROTEIN; 12 G FAT; 34 G CARBOHYDRATE; 413 MG CALCIUM; 549 MG SODIUM; 230 MG CHOLESTEROL; 2 G DIETARY FIBER

MOZZARELLA AND PESTO TOASTS

MAKES 2 SERVINGS, 1 TOAST EACH

1½ ounces part-skim mozzarella cheese, shredded
2 tablespoons Pesto (see page 22)

2 slices reduced-calorie Italian bread, toasted

1 Preheat broiler. In small mixing bowl combine cheese and Pesto.

2 Spread half of cheese mixture on each slice of toast. Arrange toast slices on baking sheet and broil until cheese is melted, about 2 minutes.

EACH SERVING (INCLUDING PESTO) PROVIDES: 1½ FATS; 1¼ PROTEINS; ½ BREAD; 10 OPTIONAL CALORIES

PER SERVING: 195 CALORIES; 11 G PROTEIN; 13 G FAT; 12 G CARBOHYDRATE; 290 MG CALCIUM; 294 MG SODIUM; 17 MG CHOLESTEROL; 0.4 G DIETARY FIBER

REDUCED CHOLESTEROL

ITALIAN-STYLE SPAGHETTI SQUASH

MAKES 2 SERVINGS

2 cups thawed Spaghetti Squash (see page 208)
½ cup part-skim ricotta cheese
½ cup cauliflower florets, blanched, chopped
1 cup canned stewed tomatoes, finely chopped

1 tablespoon grated Parmesan cheese
1 tablespoon finely chopped Italian (flat-leaf) parsley
1 tablespoon finely chopped fresh basil

1 On microwavable plate arrange Spaghetti Squash. In small mixing bowl combine ricotta cheese and cauliflower. Spoon cheese-cauliflower mixture over Spaghetti Squash; top with tomatoes.

2 Microwave on Medium (50%) for 6 minutes, rotating plate ½ turn halfway through cooking, until thoroughly heated.

3 In small bowl combine remaining ingredients and sprinkle over tomatoes.

EACH SERVING (INCLUDING SPAGHETTI SQUASH) PROVIDES: 1 PROTEIN; 3½ VEG-ETABLES; 15 OPTIONAL CALORIES

PER SERVING: 190 CALORIES; 11 G PROTEIN; 7 G FAT; 24 G CARBOHYDRATE; 300 MG CALCIUM; 479 MG SODIUM; 21 MG CHOLESTEROL; 1 G DIETARY FIBER (THIS FIGURE DOES NOT INCLUDE STEWED TOMATOES; NUTRITION ANALYSIS NOT AVAILABLE)

REDUCED CHOLESTEROL

*P*OLENTA PARMESAN

MAKES 2 SERVINGS

2¼ ounces uncooked instant polenta (quick-cooking yellow cornmeal)
¾ ounce Parmesan cheese, grated
1 teaspoon margarine

⅛ teaspoon garlic powder
½ cup tomato sauce
1½ ounces part-skim mozzarella cheese, shredded

Polenta Parmesan

Cooked Broccoli Spears

Tomato, Zucchini, Black Olive, and Romaine Lettuce Salad with Reduced-Calorie Italian Dressing

Green Grapes

Amaretti Cookies

Coffee or Tea

1 In 1½-quart saucepan bring *1½ cups water* to a full boil. Stir in polenta, Parmesan cheese, margarine, and garlic powder. Reduce heat to medium and cook, stirring constantly, for 4 minutes.

2 Spray 8-inch flameproof pie pan with nonstick cooking spray; pour polenta mixture into pie pan. Preheat broiler.

3 Pour tomato sauce over polenta mixture; sprinkle with mozzarella cheese. Broil until cheese is golden, about 2 minutes.

EACH SERVING PROVIDES: ½ FAT; 1½ PROTEINS; ½ VEGETABLE; 1½ BREADS

PER SERVING: 255 CALORIES; 13 G PROTEIN; 9 G FAT; 30 G CARBOHYDRATE; 295 MG CALCIUM; 689 MG SODIUM; 21 MG CHOLESTEROL; 3 G DIETARY FIBER

REDUCED CHOLESTEROL

RICE CAKE MELTS

MAKES 2 SERVINGS, 2 RICE CAKES EACH

4 rice cakes, any type
1½ ounces reduced-fat Swiss *or* Cheddar cheese, shredded
6 cherry tomatoes, cut into halves

1 tablespoon plus 1 teaspoon pickle relish
1 tablespoon reduced-calorie buttermilk dressing (30 calories per tablespoon)

1 Preheat oven to 450°F. On nonstick baking sheet arrange rice cakes; top each with ¼ of the cheese and tomato halves.

2 Bake until cheese melts, about 2 minutes. Transfer rice cakes to serving platter; top each with an equal amount of pickle relish and buttermilk dressing.

EACH SERVING PROVIDES: 1 PROTEIN; ½ VEGETABLE; 1 BREAD; 35 OPTIONAL CALORIES

PER SERVING: 172 CALORIES; 10 G PROTEIN; 5 G FAT; 22 G CARBOHYDRATE; 267 MG CALCIUM; 191 MG SODIUM; 15 MG CHOLESTEROL; 0.4 G DIETARY FIBER (THIS FIGURE DOES NOT INCLUDE RICE CAKES; NUTRITION ANALYSIS NOT AVAILABLE)

REDUCED CHOLESTEROL, FAT AND SODIUM

Rice Cake Melts

Bean and Vegetable Toss (rinsed, drained, canned red kidney beans with torn Boston lettuce leaves, tomato wedges, cauliflower florets, and Thousand Island dressing)

Strawberries with Whipped Topping

Coffee, Tea, or Mineral Water

ITALIAN SOUFFLÉ SANDWICH

MAKES 1 SERVING

2 slices reduced-calorie wheat bread
¾ ounce provolone cheese, shredded
2 tablespoons tomato sauce
¼ cup thawed frozen egg substitute

¼ cup evaporated skimmed milk
1 egg white
⅛ teaspoon basil leaves
⅛ teaspoon oregano leaves
Dash pepper
2 teaspoons grated Parmesan cheese

1 Preheat oven to 375°F. Spray a ¾-cup casserole with nonstick cooking spray and arrange 1 bread slice in casserole. Sprinkle with provolone cheese, then top with tomato sauce and remaining bread slice.

2 Using a wire whisk, in small mixing bowl beat together egg substitute, milk, egg white, basil, oregano, and pepper. Pour egg substitute mixture over sandwich; sprinkle with Parmesan cheese.

3 Bake for 25 minutes until a knife inserted in center comes out dry. Serve immediately.

EACH SERVING PROVIDES: ½ MILK; 2 PROTEINS; ¼ VEGETABLE; 1 BREAD; 40 OPTIONAL CALORIES

PER SERVING: 272 CALORIES; 25 G PROTEIN; 8 G FAT; 30 G CARBOHYDRATE; 465 MG CALCIUM; 831 MG SODIUM; 20 MG CHOLESTEROL; 4 G DIETARY FIBER

REDUCED CHOLESTEROL AND FAT

PEANUT–APPLE BUTTER SANDWICH

MAKES 1 SERVING

1 tablespoon creamy peanut butter
1 tablespoon light cream cheese
1 tablespoon golden raisins, chopped

2 slices reduced-calorie wheat bread (40 calories per slice)
1½ teaspoons apple butter

1 In small mixing bowl combine peanut butter, cream cheese, and raisins.

2 Spread peanut butter mixture on 1 slice of bread; top with apple butter and remaining slice of bread. Cut sandwich in half.

EACH SERVING PROVIDES: 1 FAT; 1 PROTEIN; 1 BREAD; ½ FRUIT; 50 OPTIONAL CALORIES

PER SERVING: 249 CALORIES; 10 G PROTEIN; 12 G FAT; 33 G CARBOHYDRATE; 71 MG CALCIUM; 347 MG SODIUM; 7 MG CHOLESTEROL; 5 G DIETARY FIBER

REDUCED CHOLESTEROL

Peanut–Apple Butter Sandwich

Carrot Sticks and Cauliflower Florets

Raspberry Yogurt (plain low-fat yogurt with reduced-calorie raspberry spread)

Chocolate Chip Cookies

Coffee, Tea, or Mineral Water

VEGETABLE FRITTATA

MAKES 8 SERVINGS

2 tablespoons plus 2 teaspoons olive *or* vegetable oil, divided
1 cup chopped thoroughly washed leeks (white portion and some green)
1 cup diced red bell peppers
1 cup sliced mushrooms
1 garlic clove, minced
¾ pound cooked sliced pared all-purpose potatoes

3 ounces reduced-fat Swiss cheese, shredded
2 cups thawed frozen egg substitute
3 tablespoons grated Parmesan cheese
Arugula for garnish (optional)

Vegetable Frittata

Pumpernickel-Raisin Bread with Reduced-Calorie Margarine

Cooked Asparagus Spears

Orange Sections

White Wine

1   In 10-inch nonstick skillet that has an oven-safe or removable handle, heat 2 teaspoons oil; add leeks, peppers, mushrooms, and garlic and cook over medium-high heat, stirring frequently, until leeks are tender, about 3 minutes. Transfer to medium mixing bowl; set aside.

2   Preheat oven to 400°F. To same skillet add remaining oil; arrange potatoes in a single layer in skillet and sprinkle Swiss cheese over potatoes.

3   Add egg substitute to leek mixture and carefully pour over potatoes and cheese in skillet. Cook over medium-high heat until bottom is set, about 5 minutes.

4   Sprinkle frittata with Parmesan cheese. Transfer skillet to oven and bake until mixture is set, about 10 minutes. Garnish with arugula.

EACH SERVING PROVIDES: 1 FAT; 1½ PROTEINS; ¾ VEGETABLE; ¼ BREAD; 20 OPTIONAL CALORIES
PER SERVING: 157 CALORIES; 11 G PROTEIN; 7 G FAT; 13 G CARBOHYDRATE; 190 MG CALCIUM; 137 MG SODIUM; 9 MG CHOLESTEROL; 1 G DIETARY FIBER
REDUCED CHOLESTEROL AND SODIUM

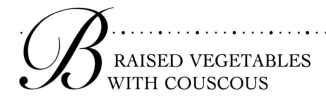

BRAISED VEGETABLES WITH COUSCOUS

MAKES 2 SERVINGS

2 teaspoons vegetable oil
1 cup sliced onions
½ cup sliced carrot
½ cup sliced celery
½ cup sliced zucchini
½ pound rinsed drained canned
    chick-peas
1 tablespoon dried currants

1 packet instant vegetable broth
    and seasoning mix
¼ teaspoon paprika
¼ teaspoon ground cumin
    Dash pepper
2 ounces uncooked couscous
    (dry precooked semolina)

*Braised
Vegetables with
Couscous*

*Bell Pepper, Tomato,
and Red Leaf Lettuce
Salad with Balsamic
Vinegar and Herbs*

Raspberry Sherbet

Herbal Tea

1 In 3-quart nonstick saucepan heat oil; add onions, carrot, celery, and zucchini and cook over high heat, stirring frequently, until onions are lightly browned, about 3 minutes.

2 Add *1¾ cups water,* the chick-peas, currants, broth mix, paprika, cumin, and pepper. Reduce heat to low, cover, and let simmer until carrot is tender, about 10 minutes.

3 Remove ½ cup of broth from chick-pea mixture and pour into small saucepan. Cook broth over high heat until mixture comes to a boil; stir in couscous. Cover saucepan and remove from heat. Let stand for 5 minutes.

4 To serve, on serving platter arrange couscous; top with chick-pea mixture.

EACH SERVING PROVIDES: 1 FAT; 2 PROTEINS; 2½ VEGETABLES; 1 BREAD; ¼ FRUIT; 5 OPTIONAL CALORIES

PER SERVING: 353 CALORIES; 13 G PROTEIN; 8 G FAT; 57 G CARBOHYDRATE; 97 MG CALCIUM; 649 MG SODIUM; 0 MG CHOLESTEROL; 8 G DIETARY FIBER (THIS FIGURE DOES NOT INCLUDE COUSCOUS; NUTRITION ANALYSIS NOT AVAILABLE)

REDUCED CHOLESTEROL AND FAT

MINIATURE FALAFEL WITH YOGURT SAUCE

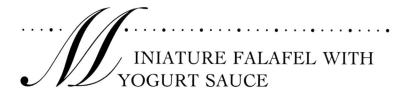

MAKES 2 SERVINGS, 6 FALAFEL EACH

1 ounce uncooked bulgur
   (cracked wheat)
¼ pound rinsed drained canned
   chick-peas
1 garlic clove, minced
1 teaspoon lemon juice
¼ teaspoon ground cumin

3 tablespoons seasoned dried
   bread crumbs
½ cup plain nonfat yogurt
2 tablespoons light sour cream
½ teaspoon granulated sugar
¼ teaspoon curry powder
   Dash pepper

1 In small saucepan bring *⅓ cup plus 2 teaspoons water* to a boil; stir in bulgur. Reduce heat to low, cover, and let simmer for 10 minutes. Remove from heat and let stand for 15 minutes. Drain and transfer to medium mixing bowl.

2 Preheat oven to 450°F. In food processor combine chick-peas, garlic, lemon juice, and cumin and process until mixture forms a smooth paste, about 2 minutes, scraping down sides of container as necessary. Add chick-pea mixture and bread crumbs to bulgur; mix well.

3 Shape chick-pea mixture into 12 equal balls and arrange on nonstick baking sheet. Bake for 15 minutes.

4 While falafel are baking, prepare yogurt sauce. Using a wire whisk, in small mixing bowl beat together yogurt, sour cream, sugar, curry powder, and pepper.

5 Serve falafel with yogurt sauce for dipping.

EACH SERVING PROVIDES: 1 PROTEIN; 1 BREAD; 60 OPTIONAL CALORIES

PER SERVING: 223 CALORIES; 11 G PROTEIN; 4 G FAT; 36 G CARBOHYDRATE; 155 MG CALCIUM; 457 MG SODIUM; 7 MG CHOLESTEROL; 6 G DIETARY FIBER

REDUCED CHOLESTEROL AND FAT

Miniature
Falafel with
Yogurt Sauce

Whole Wheat Pita

Romaine Lettuce,
Mushroom, and Cherry
Tomato Salad with
French Dressing

Baked Apple with
Brown Sugar and
Cinnamon

Coffee or Tea

SPINACH PIE

MAKES 4 SERVINGS

1 tablespoon plus 1 teaspoon
   olive *or* vegetable oil
1 cup chopped onions
1 cup diced red bell peppers
2 garlic cloves, minced
2 packages (10 ounces each)
   frozen chopped spinach,
   thawed and well drained

1 tablespoon all-purpose flour
1 cup low-fat milk (1% milk fat)
2 cups thawed frozen egg
   substitute
1 tablespoon grated Parmesan
   cheese
   Dash ground nutmeg
   Dash pepper

1 Preheat oven to 375°F. In 10-inch nonstick skillet heat oil; add onions, bell peppers, and garlic and cook over medium-high heat, stirring frequently, until onions are translucent, about 1 minute.

2 Add spinach and stir to combine; cook, stirring frequently, until moisture has evaporated, about 2 minutes.

3 Sprinkle with flour and stir quickly to combine; cook, stirring constantly, for 1 minute. Reduce heat to medium and gradually stir in milk. Cook, stirring frequently, until mixture thickens slightly, 1 to 2 minutes. Transfer to large mixing bowl and let cool slightly.

4 Add remaining ingredients to spinach mixture and stir to combine.

5 Spray an 8 × 8 × 2-inch baking pan with nonstick cooking spray and spread spinach mixture in pan. Bake until set, about 25 minutes.

EACH SERVING PROVIDES: ¼ MILK; 1 FAT; 2 PROTEINS; 3 VEGETABLES; 15 OPTIONAL CALORIES
PER SERVING: 184 CALORIES; 18 G PROTEIN; 6 G FAT; 17 G CARBOHYDRATE; 304 MG CALCIUM; 221 MG SODIUM; 3 MG CHOLESTEROL; 4 G DIETARY FIBER
REDUCED CHOLESTEROL, FAT AND SODIUM

Spinach Pie

*Baked Potato with
Light Sour Cream and
Chopped Chives*

*Tossed Salad with
Reduced-Calorie Italian
Dressing*

Pineapple Slices

*Coffee, Tea, or
Mineral Water*

SPINACH-STUFFED MUSHROOMS

Mushrooms tend to absorb water. The best way to clean them is to wipe them thoroughly with a damp paper towel.

MAKES 2 SERVINGS, 3 MUSHROOMS EACH

6 large mushrooms
2 teaspoons margarine
2 garlic cloves, minced
½ cup thawed and well-drained
    frozen chopped spinach
3 ounces feta cheese, crumbled

1 slice white bread (1 ounce),
    made into crumbs
1 tablespoon thawed frozen egg
    substitute
¼ teaspoon oregano leaves
    Dash pepper

1 Preheat oven to 375°F. Remove and chop stems of mushrooms, reserving caps.

2 In 9-inch nonstick skillet melt margarine; add garlic and cook over medium-high heat until softened, about 1 minute. Add chopped mushrooms and spinach and cook, stirring frequently, until moisture has evaporated, about 3 minutes.

3 Transfer spinach mixture to medium mixing bowl; add cheese, bread crumbs, egg substitute, oregano, and pepper and stir to combine.

4 Fill each reserved mushroom cap with an equal amount of spinach mixture and arrange in 1-quart casserole. Pour *2 tablespoons water* into bottom of casserole and bake until mushrooms are fork-tender and lightly browned, about 20 minutes.

EACH SERVING PROVIDES: 1 FAT; 2 PROTEINS; 2 VEGETABLES; ½ BREAD; 10 OPTIONAL CALORIES
PER SERVING: 229 CALORIES; 12 G PROTEIN; 14 G FAT; 17 G CARBOHYDRATE; 298 MG CALCIUM; 645 MG SODIUM; 38 MG CHOLESTEROL; 3 G DIETARY FIBER
REDUCED CHOLESTEROL

MICROWAVE FRITTATA

MAKES 2 SERVINGS

½ cup thawed frozen egg substitute
¼ cup evaporated skimmed milk
1 tablespoon light sour cream
¼ teaspoon dried salad herbs
Dash pepper
½ ounce garlic-and-herb-flavored cheese spread, broken into pieces

½ cup thoroughly washed and drained arugula *or* spinach leaves,* chopped
2 egg whites (at room temperature)
Dash cream of tartar
Dash ground nutmeg

1 Using a wire whisk, in medium mixing bowl beat together first 5 ingredients; add cheese spread and arugula and stir to combine.

2 Using mixer on high speed, in medium mixing bowl beat egg whites and cream of tartar until soft peaks form. Using a rubber scraper, stir ⅓ of the beaten egg whites into the arugula mixture. Gradually fold in the remaining beaten egg whites.

3 Spray 9-inch microwavable pie plate with nonstick cooking spray. Spread arugula mixture in pie plate.

4 Microwave on Medium-High (70%) for 3 minutes. Using rubber scraper, stir outer portion of arugula mixture toward center of pie plate. Microwave on Medium (50%) for 3 minutes. Rotate pie plate ¼ turn and microwave on Low (30%) for 2 minutes. Let stand for 2 minutes to complete cooking process.

5 Invert frittata onto serving platter and sprinkle with nutmeg.

EACH SERVING PROVIDES: ¼ MILK; 1 PROTEIN; ⅛ VEGETABLE; 55 OPTIONAL CALORIES
PER SERVING: 107 CALORIES; 13 G PROTEIN; 3 G FAT; 7 G CARBOHYDRATE; 129 MG CALCIUM; 210 MG SODIUM; 11 MG CHOLESTEROL; 0.4 G DIETARY FIBER
REDUCED CHOLESTEROL AND FAT

* ½ cup fresh arugula *or* spinach will yield about 2 tablespoons cooked.

Microwave Frittata

Cooked Sliced Mushrooms and Chopped Onion

Croissant with Reduced-Calorie Raspberry Spread

Strawberries

Café au Lait (coffee with warm milk)

EGETARIAN LOAF

This satisfying dish can be eaten at room temperature. Include a leftover serving in a brown-bag lunch.

MAKES 4 SERVINGS

2 teaspoons peanut oil
2 cups shredded carrots
1 cup finely chopped onions
1 cup finely chopped celery
1 cup finely chopped red bell peppers
1 cup finely chopped mushrooms
1 garlic clove, minced
¾ pound rinsed drained canned chick-peas

½ cup thawed frozen egg substitute
⅓ cup plus 2 teaspoons seasoned dried bread crumbs
1 tablespoon chopped fresh Italian (flat-leaf) parsley
Dash ground cumin

Vegetarian Loaf

French Bread with Reduced-Calorie Margarine

Cooked Cauliflower Florets

Mixed Green Salad with Reduced-Calorie French Dressing

Coffee, Tea, or Mineral Water

1   Preheat oven to 375°F. In 9-inch nonstick skillet heat oil; add carrots, onions, celery, peppers, mushrooms, and garlic and cook over medium-high heat, stirring frequently, until peppers are softened, about 5 minutes. Set aside and let cool slightly.

2   Using a fork, in large mixing bowl mash chick-peas. Add vegetable mixture, egg substitute, bread crumbs, parsley, and cumin and stir to combine thoroughly.

3   Spray a 9 × 5-inch nonstick loaf pan with nonstick cooking spray and press vegetable mixture into pan. Bake until edges of loaf come away from sides of pan, 25 to 30 minutes. Let loaf cool in pan for 5 minutes.

4   To serve, invert loaf onto serving platter.

EACH SERVING PROVIDES: ½ FAT; 2 PROTEINS; 3 VEGETABLES; ½ BREAD
PER SERVING: 230 CALORIES; 11 G PROTEIN; 5 G FAT; 35 G CARBOHYDRATE; 91 MG CALCIUM; 554 MG SODIUM; 1 MG CHOLESTEROL; 8 G DIETARY FIBER
REDUCED CHOLESTEROL AND FAT

FISH

LEANER THAN MEAT OR CHICKEN, LOW IN CALORIES, HIGH IN protein, good for the heart—it seems the accolades are never ending for those water-dwelling creatures we call fish. Also known as brain food, consumption of fish is on the rise as people have smartened up and realized the health benefits of eating fish two to three times a week, especially as a natural source of Omega-3 fatty acids, known to aid in reduction of cholesterol levels. And although we're eating more fish, we're not just talking fillet of sole. There are so many types of fresh and frozen fish available at supermarkets and fish markets alike, there's no reason not to make it a regular part of your diet. Besides, it even cooks up fast! Oysters with Herb Butter are ready in just 20 minutes, and we all know the reputation they've earned. Whether or not you believe in the oyster's power as an aphrodisiac, you can still enjoy them as a fabulous first course. Buttery Italian-Style Clams serves one as does Fillet Amandine. Why not enjoy them together for a fish extravaganza? Sandwiches are also fair game, as Open-Face Smoked Salmon Sandwich gets a kick from cream cheese and garlic. Curried Tuna Pita becomes a new lunch-bag favorite and our recipe for Salmon Cakes works just as well with tuna. Oriental Shrimp and Scallops and Teriyaki Fish show how Asian seasoning complements seafood.

OYSTERS WITH HERB BUTTER

MAKES 2 SERVINGS

1 tablespoon whipped butter, softened
2 teaspoons chopped fresh dill
2 teaspoons margarine, softened
1 teaspoon grated lime peel

Dash thyme leaves
Dash crushed red pepper flakes
12 medium oysters, scrubbed

1 Preheat barbecue or gas grill on high for 10 minutes. In small serving bowl combine all ingredients except oysters; set aside.

2 Arrange oysters on rack and cook until shells open, 5 to 8 minutes.

3 To serve, arrange open oysters on serving platter and serve with butter mixture.

EACH SERVING PROVIDES: 1 FAT; 1 PROTEIN; 25 OPTIONAL CALORIES

PER SERVING: 109 CALORIES; 4 G PROTEIN; 9 G FAT; 3 G CARBOHYDRATE; 35 MG CALCIUM; 148 MG SODIUM; 42 MG CHOLESTEROL; DIETARY FIBER DATA NOT AVAILABLE

Variation: Oysters with Herb Margarine—Omit butter and add 1 tablespoon lime juice. In Serving Information omit Optional Calories.

PER SERVING: 76 CALORIES; 4 G PROTEIN; 5 G FAT; 3 G CARBOHYDRATE; 35 MG CALCIUM; 110 MG SODIUM; 31 MG CHOLESTEROL; DIETARY FIBER DATA NOT AVAILABLE

REDUCED SODIUM

BUTTERY ITALIAN-STYLE CLAMS

MAKES 1 SERVING

½ cup chopped onion
2 tablespoons dry vermouth *or*
  dry white table wine
2 tablespoons lemon juice
1 tablespoon whipped butter

2 garlic cloves, thinly sliced
1 teaspoon olive oil
1 dozen littleneck clams,*
  scrubbed

1 In an 8 × 8 × 2-inch microwavable baking dish combine all ingredients except clams. Cover and microwave on High (100%) for 2 minutes.

2 In same baking dish arrange clams with hinged side of each clam toward edge of dish, leaving a space between each. Cover and microwave on Medium (50%) for 2 minutes. Rotate casserole ½ turn; cover and microwave on High for 3 minutes. Let stand for 1 minute.

3 Serve clams with onion mixture.

EACH SERVING PROVIDES: 1 FAT; 1 PROTEIN; 1 VEGETABLE; 75 OPTIONAL CALORIES
PER SERVING: 265 CALORIES; 16 G PROTEIN; 14 G FAT; 13 G CARBOHYDRATE; 91 MG CALCIUM; 152 MG SODIUM; 59 MG CHOLESTEROL; 1 G DIETARY FIBER

* One dozen littleneck clams will yield about 2 ounces cooked seafood.

Variation: Italian-Style Clams—Omit whipped butter. In Serving Information decrease Optional Calories to 25.

PER SERVING: 197 CALORIES; 16 G PROTEIN; 6 G FAT; 13 G CARBOHYDRATE; 89 MG CALCIUM; 74 MG SODIUM; 39 MG CHOLESTEROL; 1 G DIETARY FIBER
REDUCED SODIUM

Buttery Italian-Style Clams

Corn on the Cob with Reduced-Calorie Margarine

Cooked Broccoli Florets and Red Bell Pepper Strips

Tossed Salad with Red Wine Vinegar and Herbs

Cranberry Spritzer (cranberry juice cocktail and club soda)

CALLOP SEVICHE

The lime juice marinade does the "cooking" in this unique dish. A perfect way to keep the kitchen cool on a hot summer day.

Scallop Seviche

French Bread with Reduced-Calorie Margarine

Strawberries

Iced Coffee

MAKES 2 SERVINGS

¼ pound bay *or* sea scallops (cut into quarters)
¼ cup diced red onion
¼ cup diced celery
¼ cup red bell pepper strips
¼ cup green bell pepper strips
¼ cup freshly squeezed lime juice

1 medium tomato, blanched, peeled, seeded, and chopped
1 garlic clove, minced
2 small bay leaves, broken in half
Dash ground red pepper
Dash black pepper

1 In medium glass or stainless-steel mixing bowl place all ingredients, stirring to combine. Cover and refrigerate at least 3 hours or overnight.

2 Remove and discard bay leaves before serving.

EACH SERVING PROVIDES: 1 PROTEIN; 2 VEGETABLES
PER SERVING: 91 CALORIES; 11 G PROTEIN; 1 G FAT; 11 G CARBOHYDRATE; 42 MG CALCIUM; 112 MG SODIUM; 19 MG CHOLESTEROL; 2 G DIETARY FIBER
REDUCED CHOLESTEROL, FAT AND SODIUM

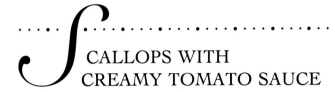

SCALLOPS WITH CREAMY TOMATO SAUCE

MAKES 2 SERVINGS

2 teaspoons olive *or* vegetable oil
5 ounces bay *or* sea scallops (cut into quarters)
1 cup sliced mushrooms
1 garlic clove, minced
1 teaspcon all-purpose flour
½ cup low-fat milk (1% milk fat)

¼ cup dry white table wine
1 tablespoon chopped fresh basil *or* ½ teaspoon basil leaves
1 teaspoon tomato paste
Dash pepper
1 cup cooked fettuccine (hot)

1 In 10-inch nonstick skillet heat oil; add scallops and cook over medium-high heat, turning occasionally, until lightly browned, about 3 minutes. Transfer to plate; set aside.

2 In same skillet combine mushrooms and garlic and cook over medium-high heat, stirring frequently, until mushrooms are softened, about 2 minutes. Sprinkle with flour and stir quickly to combine. Stir in remaining ingredients except fettuccine. Reduce heat to low and cook, stirring constantly, until mixture thickens, about 3 minutes.

3 Return scallops to skillet; turn to coat with sauce and cook until heated through, about 1 minute.

4 To serve, arrange fettuccine on serving platter; top with scallop mixture.

EACH SERVING PROVIDES: ¼ MILK; 1 FAT; 1 PROTEIN; 1 VEGETABLE; 1 BREAD; 30 OPTIONAL CALORIES
PER SERVING: 273 CALORIES; 19 G PROTEIN; 7 G FAT; 29 G CARBOHYDRATE; 118 MG CALCIUM; 175 MG SODIUM; 52 MG CHOLESTEROL; 2 G DIETARY FIBER

REDUCED FAT AND SODIUM

Scallops with Creamy Tomato Sauce

Cooked Sliced Zucchini and Pearl Onions

Red Leaf Lettuce, Cucumber, and Cauliflower Salad with Reduced-Calorie French Dressing

Mandarin Orange Sections with Shredded Coconut

White Wine Spritzer (dry white wine and club soda)

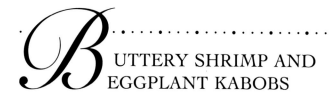

BUTTERY SHRIMP AND EGGPLANT KABOBS

MAKES 2 SERVINGS, 1 KABOB EACH

1 tablespoon whipped butter, melted
1 tablespoon chopped fresh basil
2 teaspoons olive oil
2 garlic cloves, minced
1 teaspoon lemon juice
Dash pepper

7 ounces shelled and deveined large shrimp
½ cup halved eggplant slices
Lettuce, basil sprigs, and lemon wedges for garnish (optional)

1 In medium glass or stainless-steel mixing bowl combine all ingredients except shrimp and eggplant and stir to combine; add shrimp and eggplant and turn to coat. Cover and refrigerate at least 1 hour or overnight.

2 Preheat barbecue or gas grill on high for 10 minutes. Onto each of two 12-inch or four 6-inch metal or presoaked bamboo skewers alternately thread half of the shrimp and eggplant.

3 Place kabobs on rack. Cook, turning kabobs occasionally and basting with marinade, until shrimp turn pink, 4 to 6 minutes. Garnish with lettuce, basil, and lemon as desired.

EACH SERVING PROVIDES: 1 FAT; 1¼ PROTEINS; ½ VEGETABLE; 25 OPTIONAL CALORIES

PER SERVING: 191 CALORIES; 21 G PROTEIN; 10 G FAT; 4 G CARBOHYDRATE; 78 MG CALCIUM; 188 MG SODIUM; 161 MG CHOLESTEROL; 0.3 G DIETARY FIBER

Variation: Shrimp and Eggplant Kabobs—Omit butter. In Serving Information omit Optional Calories.

PER SERVING: 157 CALORIES; 21 G PROTEIN; 6 G FAT; 4 G CARBOHYDRATE; 77 MG CALCIUM; 149 MG SODIUM; 151 MG CHOLESTEROL; 0.3 G DIETARY FIBER

REDUCED SODIUM

Buttery Shrimp and Eggplant Kabobs

Cooked Brown Rice with Pearl Onions

Grilled Zucchini Halves

Sliced Mushrooms and Diced Red Onion on Romaine Lettuce Leaves with Italian Dressing

White Wine Spritzer (dry white wine and club soda)

SHRIMP PURLOO

Sometimes called Shrimp Pilaw, Pelos, Pilau, or Purloo, this Charleston, South Carolina, specialty combines shrimp and rice and is worth a try.

2 teaspoons olive *or* vegetable oil
1 cup diced onions
2 ounces uncooked long-grain rice
2 cups thawed frozen okra, sliced

5 ounces shelled and deveined
    medium shrimp
Dash ground red pepper

1 In 9-inch nonstick skillet heat oil; add onions and cook over medium-high heat, stirring frequently, until translucent, about 2 minutes. Stir in rice and cook, stirring frequently, until onion is lightly browned, about 2 minutes.

2 Remove skillet from heat; stir in *2 cups water* and bring mixture to a boil. Reduce heat to low, cover, and let simmer until rice is tender, about 15 minutes.

3 Add okra and shrimp and stir to combine. Cook, uncovered, over medium-high heat, stirring occasionally, until shrimp turn pink, about 5 minutes. Stir in pepper.

EACH SERVING PROVIDES: 1 FAT; 1 PROTEIN; 3 VEGETABLES; 1 BREAD
PER SERVING: 302 CALORIES; 21 G PROTEIN; 7 G FAT; 43 G CARBOHYDRATE; 233 MG CALCIUM; 114 MG SODIUM; 108 MG CHOLESTEROL; 8 G DIETARY FIBER
REDUCED FAT AND SODIUM

Shrimp Purloo

Refrigerated Buttermilk Flaky Biscuit with Reduced-Calorie Margarine

Cooked Carrot Sticks

Tossed Salad with Balsamic Vinegar and Herbs

Reduced-Calorie Cherry Gelatin with Dairy Whipped Topping

Coffee or Tea

FILLET AMANDINE

MAKES 1 SERVING

¼ ounce (1 tablespoon) sliced
    almonds
1 teaspoon reduced-calorie
    margarine (tub)

1 teaspoon lemon juice
1 flounder *or* sole fillet (3
    ounces)

1. In 9-inch microwavable pie plate combine almonds and margarine; microwave on High (100%) for 1 minute, stirring once halfway through cooking, until almonds are toasted. Stir in lemon juice.

2. Arrange fish in bottom of pie plate and top with almond mixture. Microwave on High for 3 minutes, rotating plate ½ turn halfway through cooking. Let stand for 1 minute before serving.

EACH SERVING PROVIDES: 1 FAT; 1¼ PROTEINS
PER SERVING: 137 CALORIES; 17 G PROTEIN; 7 G FAT; 2 G CARBOHYDRATE; 35 MG CALCIUM; 107 MG SODIUM; 41 MG CHOLESTEROL; 0.3 G DIETARY FIBER
REDUCED SODIUM

ROILED FLOUNDER FILLETS

MAKES 2 SERVINGS

1 tablespoon lemon juice
2 teaspoons olive oil
2 flounder fillets (¼ pound each)
1 medium tomato, blanched, peeled, seeded, and chopped

2 tablespoons finely chopped fresh dill *or* 1 teaspoon dillweed

1. Preheat broiler. In small bowl combine lemon juice and oil. Arrange fillets on nonstick baking sheet. Brush each fillet with ¼ of the lemon-oil mixture. Broil for 2 minutes.

2. Add tomato and dill to the remaining lemon-oil mixture and stir to combine. Carefully turn fillets over and top each with half of the tomato-dill mixture. Broil until fish flakes easily when tested with a fork, 3 to 4 minutes.

EACH SERVING PROVIDES: 1 FAT; 1½ PROTEINS; 1 VEGETABLE
PER SERVING: 159 CALORIES; 22 G PROTEIN; 6 G FAT; 4 G CARBOHYDRATE; 35 MG CALCIUM; 100 MG SODIUM; 54 MG CHOLESTEROL; 1 G DIETARY FIBER
REDUCED SODIUM

Broiled Flounder Fillets

Fast-Cooking Whole-Grain Brown Rice with Sliced Mushrooms

Cooked Brussels Sprouts

Bibb Lettuce, Radicchio (red chicory), and Tomato Salad with Buttermilk Dressing

Reduced-Calorie Butterscotch Pudding

Coffee or Tea

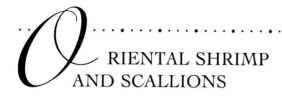

ORIENTAL SHRIMP AND SCALLIONS

Six ingredients combine to make this simple skillet supper. Serve with cooked rice, stir-fried vegetables, and tea for a complete meal.

MAKES 2 SERVINGS

1 teaspoon peanut oil
7 ounces shelled and deveined
  large shrimp
1 cup sliced scallions (green
  onions), cut into 3-inch
  pieces

¼ cup canned ready-to-serve low-
  sodium chicken broth
2 teaspoons hoisin sauce
½ teaspoon cornstarch
  Radish for garnish (optional)

1 In 10-inch nonstick skillet heat oil; add shrimp and cook over high heat, stirring frequently, until shrimp begin to turn pink, about 2 minutes. Add scallions and cook, stirring frequently, until tender, about 2 minutes.

2 Using a wire whisk, in small mixing bowl combine remaining ingredients, whisking to dissolve cornstarch. Stir into shrimp mixture and cook, stirring constantly, until mixture thickens, about 1 minute. Garnish with radish.

EACH SERVING PROVIDES: ½ FAT; 1¼ PROTEINS; 1 VEGETABLE; 20 OPTIONAL CALORIES
PER SERVING: 151 CALORIES; 22 G PROTEIN; 4 G FAT; 6 G CARBOHYDRATE; 83 MG CALCIUM; 326 MG SODIUM; 151 MG CHOLESTEROL; 1 G DIETARY FIBER
REDUCED FAT

*Oriental Shrimp
and Scallions*

*Cooked Rice with Sliced
Mushrooms*

*Tossed Salad with
Italian Dressing*

*Cinnamon-Spiced
Orange Wedges*

Coffee or Tea

TERIYAKI FISH

Red snapper or sole fillets can be substituted for flounder in this recipe.

MAKES 1 SERVING

2 teaspoons teriyaki sauce
2 teaspoons seasoned rice
   vinegar
¼ teaspoon grated pared
   gingerroot
¼ pound flounder fillet

¼ cup chopped drained canned
   water chestnuts
2 tablespoons finely diced red *or*
   green bell pepper
¼ teaspoon cornstarch

1 In shallow glass or stainless-steel mixing bowl combine *2 teaspoons water*, the teriyaki sauce, vinegar, and gingerroot; add fish and turn to coat with marinade. Cover and refrigerate for 20 minutes or overnight.

2 Preheat broiler. Spray broiler pan with nonstick cooking spray; arrange fish in broiling pan, reserving marinade. Broil until fish flakes easily when tested with a fork, about 5 minutes.

3 While fish is broiling, prepare sauce: Heat small nonstick skillet; add water chestnuts and pepper and cook over medium-high heat, stirring frequently, until pepper is slightly softened, about 1 minute.

4 Add cornstarch to reserved marinade, stirring to dissolve cornstarch. Stir into water chestnut mixture; cook, stirring constantly, until mixture comes to a boil. Continue to cook, stirring constantly, for 1 minute.

5 To serve, arrange fish on plate; top with water chestnut mixture.

EACH SERVING PROVIDES: 1½ PROTEINS; ¼ VEGETABLE; 30 OPTIONAL CALORIES
PER SERVING: 150 CALORIES; 22 G PROTEIN; 1 G FAT; 11 G CARBOHYDRATE; 26 MG CALCIUM; 616 MG SODIUM; 54 MG CHOLESTEROL; 0.2 G DIETARY FIBER (THIS FIGURE DOES NOT INCLUDE WATER CHESTNUTS; NUTRITION ANALYSIS NOT AVAILABLE)
REDUCED FAT

Teriyaki Fish

*Baked Potato with
Light Sour Cream*

*Cooked Sliced
Asparagus Spears*

*Sliced Mushrooms,
Alfalfa Sprouts, and
Cherry Tomatoes on
Torn Iceberg Lettuce
Leaves with Reduced-
Calorie Caesar
Dressing*

Peach Slices

Coffee or Tea

ORANGE-SOY FLOUNDER

MAKES 2 SERVINGS

¼ cup diagonally sliced scallions
  (green onions)
2 tablespoons seasoned rice
  vinegar
2 tablespoons reduced-sodium
  soy sauce
2 tablespoons thawed frozen
  concentrated orange juice
1½ teaspoons peanut *or* vegetable
  oil

1 garlic clove, minced
1 teaspoon minced pared
  gingerroot
1 teaspoon minced seeded chili
  pepper
½ teaspoon Chinese sesame oil
2 flounder fillets (3 ounces
  each)

Orange-Soy
Flounder

Cooked Rice with Diced
Red Bell Pepper

Cooked Snow Peas
(Chinese pea pods) and
Sliced Water Chestnuts
with Teriyaki Sauce

Kumquats

Tea with Honey

1 In 1-quart shallow microwavable casserole combine all ingredients except flounder. Microwave on High (100%) for 1 minute; stir to combine.

2 Arrange fillets in a single layer over scallion mixture. Cover and microwave on High for 2 minutes, rotating casserole ½ turn halfway through cooking. Cover and microwave on High for 1 minute. Let stand for 1 minute, until fish is opaque and flakes easily when tested with a fork.

EACH SERVING PROVIDES: 1 FAT; 1 PROTEIN; ¼ VEGETABLE; ½ FRUIT

PER SERVING: 182 CALORIES; 18 G PROTEIN; 6 G FAT; 15 G CARBOHYDRATE; 35 MG CALCIUM; 760 MG SODIUM; 41 MG CHOLESTEROL; 0.5 G DIETARY FIBER

REDUCED FAT

LEMON-THYME TROUT IN FOIL

MAKES 2 SERVINGS

2 teaspoons margarine
1 teaspoon dry white table wine
1 teaspoon finely chopped shallot
　　or onion
½ teaspoon freshly squeezed
　　lemon juice
¼ teaspoon grated lemon peel
9-ounce dressed trout (head and
　　tail removed), split in half

4 thyme sprigs *or* ⅛ teaspoon
　　thyme leaves, divided
2 lemon slices
　　Dash pepper

1　Preheat barbecue or gas grill on high for 10 minutes. In small mixing bowl combine margarine, wine, shallot, lemon juice, and lemon peel.

2　Spray two 16-inch-long pieces of heavy-duty foil with nonstick cooking spray; arrange a trout half, skin side down, in center of each piece of foil. Spread each with half of the margarine mixture; top with half of the thyme, the lemon slices, and the pepper.

3　Enclose fish in foil, folding edges to seal. Set packets on rack and cook for 8 to 10 minutes. Remove from grill and let stand for 2 minutes.

4　To serve, carefully remove packets from grill and pierce top of each packet to release steam. Open packets and transfer trout to serving platter; top with any remaining liquid from foil packets.

EACH SERVING PROVIDES: 1 FAT; 1½ PROTEINS; 2 OPTIONAL CALORIES
PER SERVING: 143 CALORIES; 15 G PROTEIN; 8 G FAT; 1 G CARBOHYDRATE; 35 MG CALCIUM; 82 MG SODIUM; 41 MG CHOLESTEROL; TRACE DIETARY FIBER
REDUCED SODIUM

*Lemon-Thyme
Trout in Foil*

*Baked Potato with
Light Sour Cream and
Chopped Scallions*

*Cooked Asparagus
Spears sprinkled with
Toasted Sesame Seed*

*Red Bell Pepper Strips,
Sliced Cucumber,
Grated Carrot, and
Seasoned Croutons on
Green Leaf Lettuce
with Reduced-Calorie
Thousand Island
Dressing*

Coffee or Tea

BUTTERY SCROD SAUTÉ

MAKES 2 SERVINGS

1 tablespoon plus 1½ teaspoons
   all-purpose flour
Dash pepper
5 ounces scrod fillet
1 tablespoon whipped butter

2 teaspoons olive *or* vegetable oil
2 tablespoons dry vermouth *or* dry
   white table wine
1 tablespoon rinsed drained capers
1 tablespoon lemon juice

1 On sheet of wax paper combine flour and pepper. Dredge fish in flour mixture, coating both sides; set aside.

2 In 10-inch nonstick skillet heat butter and oil until butter is melted; add fish and cook over medium-high heat, turning once, until fish is cooked through and flakes easily when tested with a fork, 3 to 4 minutes on each side. Transfer fish to serving platter; set aside and keep warm.

3 To same skillet add vermouth, capers, and lemon juice and bring to a boil. Reduce heat to low and let simmer, scraping pan drippings from bottom of pan, for 2 minutes. Pour over fish.

EACH SERVING PROVIDES: 1 FAT; 1 PROTEIN; ¼ BREAD; 40 OPTIONAL CALORIES

PER SERVING: 170 CALORIES; 13 G PROTEIN; 9 G FAT; 5 G CARBOHYDRATE; 16 MG CALCIUM; 190 MG SODIUM; 41 MG CHOLESTEROL; 0.2 G DIETARY FIBER (THIS FIGURE DOES NOT INCLUDE CAPERS; NUTRITION ANALYSIS NOT AVAILABLE)

Variation: Scrod Sauté—Omit whipped butter from recipe. In Serving Information decrease Optional Calories to 15.

PER SERVING: 131 CALORIES; 13 G PROTEIN; 5 G FAT; 5 G CARBOHYDRATE; 15 MG CALCIUM; 151 MG SODIUM; 31 MG CHOLESTEROL; 0.2 DIETARY FIBER (THIS FIGURE DOES NOT INCLUDE CAPERS; NUTRITION ANALYSIS NOT AVAILABLE)

REDUCED SODIUM

Buttery Scrod Sauté

Cooked Brown Rice with Sliced Mushrooms

Cooked Brussels Sprouts

Tomato and Red Onion Slices on Spinach Leaves with Reduced-Calorie Italian Dressing

Reduced-Calorie Chocolate Pudding with Whipped Topping

Coffee, Tea, or Mineral Water

GRILLED TUNA STEAKS AEGEAN

MAKES 2 SERVINGS

4 large plum tomatoes, cut
  lengthwise into quarters
2 medium onions, peeled and cut
  into wedges
¼ cup freshly squeezed lemon
  juice
2 tablespoons chopped fresh
  Italian (flat-leaf) parsley,
  divided

2 garlic cloves, minced
  Dash pepper
2 boneless tuna steaks (5 ounces
  each)
1 tablespoon olive *or* vegetable
  oil

1 Preheat barbecue or gas grill on high for 10 minutes.

2 In large glass or stainless-steel mixing bowl combine tomatoes, onions,
   lemon juice, 1 tablespoon parsley, the garlic, and pepper. Add tuna to
   vegetable mixture and turn to coat. Let marinate at room temperature
   for 10 minutes.

3 Spray rack with nonstick cooking spray; arrange tuna on rack, reserving
   vegetable mixture, and cook for 4 minutes.

4 On sheet of foil arrange vegetable mixture and top with oil. Fold edges
   of foil up slightly.

5 Turn tuna over and set foil-wrapped vegetables on rack. Cook until tuna
   flakes easily when tested with a fork and vegetables are tender, about
   4 minutes.

6 To serve, arrange tuna on serving platter; top with vegetable mixture
   and sprinkle with remaining parsley.

EACH SERVING PROVIDES: 1½ FATS; 1¾ PROTEINS; 3 VEGETABLES

PER SERVING: 316 CALORIES; 35 G PROTEIN; 14 G FAT; 12 G CARBOHYDRATE; 34 MG
CALCIUM; 67 MG SODIUM; 54 MG CHOLESTEROL; 2 G DIETARY FIBER

REDUCED SODIUM

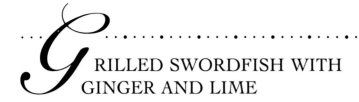

GRILLED SWORDFISH WITH GINGER AND LIME

MAKES 2 SERVINGS
(SHOWN WITH SUMMER VEGETABLE KABOBS; SEE PAGE 200)

2 teaspoons chopped fresh
cilantro (Chinese parsley) *or*
Italian (flat-leaf) parsley,
divided
2 teaspoons freshly squeezed lime
juice
2 garlic cloves, minced, divided

1 teaspoon grated pared
gingerroot, divided
2 boneless swordfish steaks (¼
pound each)
2 teaspoons margarine, softened
Lime wedges and parsley for
garnish (optional)

1 In shallow glass or stainless-steel mixing bowl combine 1 teaspoon cilantro, the lime juice, half of the garlic, and half of the gingerroot; mix well. Add swordfish to gingerroot–lime juice mixture and turn to coat. Cover and refrigerate for at least 1 hour or overnight.

2 Preheat barbecue or gas grill on high for 10 minutes. In small bowl combine remaining cilantro, garlic, gingerroot, and the margarine; mix well.

3 Spray rack with nonstick cooking spray; arrange swordfish on rack and cook until fish is cooked through and flakes easily when tested with a fork, about 2 minutes on each side.

4 To serve, transfer swordfish steaks to serving platter and top each with half of the margarine mixture. Serve garnished with lime and parsley.

EACH SERVING PROVIDES: 1 FAT; 1½ PROTEINS

PER SERVING: 181 CALORIES; 23 G PROTEIN; 9 G FAT; 2 G CARBOHYDRATE; 12 MG CALCIUM; 148 MG SODIUM; 44 MG CHOLESTEROL; DIETARY FIBER DATA NOT AVAILABLE

REDUCED SODIUM

*Grilled Swordfish
with Ginger and Lime*

*Cooked Rice with
Cooked Sliced
Mushrooms*

*Cooked Sliced Yellow
Squash*

*Blueberries sprinkled
with Confectioners'
Sugar*

*White Wine Spritzer
(dry white wine and
club soda)*

BROILED SWORDFISH OLIVADA

For extra flavor use Gaeta or Calamata olives in this recipe.

MAKES 2 SERVINGS

6 large black olives, pitted and minced

1 tablespoon reduced-calorie Dijon-style vinaigrette dressing (30 calories per tablespoon)

1 tablespoon chopped fresh basil *or* ½ teaspoon basil leaves

1 teaspoon freshly squeezed lemon juice

1 teaspoon tomato paste

½ pound boneless swordfish steak

1 Preheat broiler. In small mixing bowl combine all ingredients except swordfish.

2 Arrange swordfish on nonstick baking sheet and broil until fish turns opaque, 2 to 3 minutes. Turn swordfish over; spread olive mixture over swordfish and broil until fish is opaque and flakes easily when tested with a fork, 2 to 3 minutes.

EACH SERVING PROVIDES: ½ FAT; 1½ PROTEINS; 15 OPTIONAL CALORIES
PER SERVING: 171 CALORIES; 23 G PROTEIN; 7 G FAT; 2 G CARBOHYDRATE; 25 MG CALCIUM; 327 MG SODIUM; 44 MG CHOLESTEROL; 0.5 DIETARY FIBER

Broiled Swordfish Olivada

Succotash (cooked whole-kernel corn and green lima beans)

Tossed Salad with Olive Oil, Balsamic Vinegar, and Herbs

Honeydew Melon Wedge

Coffee, Tea, or Mineral Water

RED SNAPPER WITH PESTO SAUCE

MAKES 2 SERVINGS

2 red snapper fillets (¼ pound each)
1 tablespoon cracker meal
¼ cup chopped seeded tomato
1 tablespoon dry white table wine

2 tablespoons Pesto (see page 22)
3 large pitted black olives, sliced

1 On sheet of wax paper dredge fish in cracker meal, coating both sides.

2 Spray 9-inch nonstick skillet with nonstick cooking spray and cook fish over medium-high heat until it is golden and flakes easily when tested with a fork, about 3 minutes on each side. Transfer to serving platter; set aside and keep warm.

3 In same skillet combine tomato and wine and cook over medium-high heat, stirring frequently, for 2 minutes. Stir in remaining ingredients and cook until sauce is thoroughly heated, about 1 minute. Spoon sauce over fish.

EACH SERVING (INCLUDING PESTO) PROVIDES: 1¾ FATS; 1¾ PROTEINS; ¼ VEGETABLE; 30 OPTIONAL CALORIES
PER SERVING: 244 CALORIES; 27 G PROTEIN; 11 G FAT; 7 G CARBOHYDRATE; 177 MG CALCIUM; 233 MG SODIUM; 46 MG CHOLESTEROL; 0.5 G DIETARY FIBER

Red Snapper with Pesto Sauce

Cooked Noodles with Reduced-Calorie Margarine and Poppy Seed

Cooked Sliced Yellow Squash

Red Leaf Lettuce, Mushroom, and Cherry Tomato Salad with Red Wine Vinegar and Herbs

Reduced-Calorie Orange Gelatin with Whipped Topping

Coffee, Tea, or Mineral Water

SALMON CAKES

Serve with tartar sauce and lemon wedges. Drained canned tuna (packed in water) can be substituted.

MAKES 1 SERVING, 2 FISH CAKES

¼ cup finely chopped onion
¼ cup finely chopped celery
¼ cup finely chopped red bell
    pepper
3 slices reduced-calorie oat bread
    (40 calories per slice), made
    into crumbs, divided
2 ounces drained canned salmon
    (packed in water)

2 tablespoons thawed frozen egg
    substitute
½ teaspoon Worcestershire sauce
    Dash hot sauce
    Dash pepper

> *Salmon Cakes with Tartar Sauce*
>
> *Cooked Brussels Sprouts*
>
> *Tomato Slices and Sliced Mushrooms on Boston Lettuce Leaves with Blue Cheese Dressing*
>
> *Coffee or Tea*

1 Spray 9-inch nonstick skillet with nonstick cooking spray and heat; add onion, celery, and bell pepper and cook over medium-high heat, stirring frequently, until onion is softened, about 2 minutes. Transfer to medium mixing bowl.

2 Add all but ⅓ cup bread crumbs, the salmon, egg substitute, Worcestershire sauce, hot sauce, and pepper to vegetable mixture; using a fork, mix well. Shape mixture into 2 equal patties.

3 On sheet of wax paper dredge each patty in reserved bread crumbs, coating both sides.

4 Wipe skillet with paper towel. Spray skillet with nonstick cooking spray and heat. Add fish patties to skillet and cook over medium heat until browned, about 5 minutes on each side.

EACH SERVING PROVIDES: 2½ PROTEINS; 1½ VEGETABLES; 1½ BREADS
PER SERVING: 240 CALORIES; 22 G PROTEIN; 5 G FAT; 33 G CARBOHYDRATE; 234 MG CALCIUM; 664 MG SODIUM; 22 MG CHOLESTEROL; 3 G DIETARY FIBER
REDUCED CHOLESTEROL AND FAT

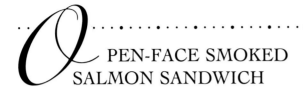 PEN-FACE SMOKED SALMON SANDWICH

MAKES 2 SERVINGS

2 ounces smoked salmon, diced
1½ ounces garlic-and-herb-
    flavored cheese spread
2 tablespoons light cream
    cheese, softened

2 slices pumpernickel bread
    (1 ounce each), toasted
2 teaspoons chopped red onion

1   In small mixing bowl combine salmon, cheese spread, and cream cheese.

2   Spread half of the salmon mixture on each slice of bread; top each with half of the onion.

EACH SERVING PROVIDES: 2 PROTEINS; 1 BREAD; 35 OPTIONAL CALORIES
PER SERVING: 202 CALORIES; 12 G PROTEIN; 10 G FAT; 18 G CARBOHYDRATE; 48 MG CALCIUM; 544 MG SODIUM; 35 MG CHOLESTEROL; 2 G DIETARY FIBER
REDUCED CHOLESTEROL

Open-Face
Smoked Salmon
Sandwich

Spinach Leaves with
Cherry Tomatoes, Red
Onion Slices, and
Italian Dressing

Apple Wedges

Club Soda with Lime
Wedge

 URRIED TUNA PITA

MAKES 1 SERVING

2 ounces drained canned tuna
    (packed in water)
2 tablespoons diced celery
2 tablespoons shredded carrot
2 tablespoons plain low-fat yogurt

1 tablespoon dried currants
2 teaspoons curry powder
    Dash pepper
1 small pita (1 ounce)

1. In medium mixing bowl combine all ingredients except pita, mixing well.

2. Using a sharp knife, cut ¼ of the way around edge of pita; open to form a pocket. Fill pocket with tuna mixture.

EACH SERVING PROVIDES: 1 PROTEIN; ½ VEGETABLE; 1 BREAD; ½ FRUIT, 15 OPTIONAL CALORIES

PER SERVING: 227 CALORIES; 22 G PROTEIN; 2 G FAT; 31 G CARBOHYDRATE; 101 MG CALCIUM; 424 MG SODIUM; 26 MG CHOLESTEROL; 3 G DIETARY FIBER

REDUCED FAT

SEAFOOD LOUIE SALAD

MAKES 2 SERVINGS

2 ounces thawed frozen imitation crabmeat, cut into cubes	1 teaspoon Worcestershire sauce
¼ cup finely chopped scallions (green onions)	1 teaspoon red wine vinegar
¼ cup finely chopped celery	1 teaspoon lemon juice Dash white pepper
1 tablespoon plus 1 teaspoon reduced-calorie mayonnaise	2 cups shredded lettuce
2 teaspoons ketchup	12 cherry tomatoes, cut into quarters
	½ cup thinly sliced cucumber

Seafood Louie Salad

Crispbreads with Brie Cheese

Pink Grapefruit with Cinnamon-Sugar Topping

Club Soda with Lime Slice

1. In medium mixing bowl combine crabmeat, scallions, celery, mayonnaise, ketchup, Worcestershire sauce, vinegar, lemon juice, and pepper. Cover and refrigerate until ready to serve.

2. To serve, line serving platter with lettuce. Toss crabmeat mixture and arrange on lettuce. Decoratively arrange tomato quarters and cucumber slices around crabmeat mixture.

EACH SERVING PROVIDES: 1 FAT; ½ PROTEIN; 4 VEGETABLES; 5 OPTIONAL CALORIES

PER SERVING: 95 CALORIES; 6 G PROTEIN; 3 G FAT; 11 G CARBOHYDRATE; 64 MG CALCIUM; 207 MG SODIUM; 12 MG CHOLESTEROL; 2 G DIETARY FIBER

REDUCED CHOLESTEROL AND FAT

POULTRY

NOTHING SEEMS MORE VERSATILE THAN POULTRY, THOUGH IF you've ever heard your family wail "Not chicken, again," you may have forgotten what else you can do with this bird. In recent years, the popularity of poultry has inspired a whole new generation of products that make enjoying chicken or turkey even easier and allow for more creativity in the kitchen. Ground chicken, ground turkey, chicken breasts, and turkey cutlets as well as turkey sausage give us an inexhaustible array of poultry options. Ground chicken is transformed into Swedish Meatballs and Savory Muffin Tarts. Company suppers call for Grilled Cornish Hens with Corn Relish. An Italian Turkey Sausage Platter takes a turn on the grill, as does Tropical Barbecue featuring bananas, mango, and turkey cutlets. Let your guests mind the coals while you fix a side dish or salad. Home alone? Turkey Patty Melt or Chicken Caesar Sandwich on a kaiser roll make fast, delicious meals. Ground Chicken Stir-Fry maintains true Oriental flavor while Chicken Mornay is cheesy with Parmesan and Swiss. Both are ready in just 15 minutes! When you're cooking for one, Chicken in Creamy Fruit Sauce will make you feel as though you've had dinner and dessert. Stock up on poultry products so you can sauté a breast in wine with herbs for a quick dinner, grill chicken or turkey burgers, or add some sausage to your breakfast omelet. With these poultry recipes, you won't have the urge to chicken out and order in!

BLACK BEAN DRUMSTICKS

MAKES 4 SERVINGS

1 pound chicken drumsticks
1 tablespoon plus 1 teaspoon
    black bean sauce
1 tablespoon plus 1 teaspoon
    vegetable oil
1 tablespoon plus 1 teaspoon
    balsamic *or* red wine vinegar

1 teaspoon reduced-sodium soy
    sauce
1 garlic clove, minced
    Dash crushed red pepper flakes
1 medium red bell pepper, seeded
    and cut lengthwise into strips

1 Pull skin away from meat on drumsticks, leaving skin attached to ends of drumsticks; set aside.

2 In shallow glass or stainless-steel mixing bowl (large enough to hold drumsticks in a single layer) combine black bean sauce, oil, vinegar, soy sauce, garlic, and crushed red pepper; add drumsticks and turn to coat. Cover and refrigerate, turning occasionally, for at least 4 hours or overnight.

3 Preheat barbecue or gas grill on medium-high for 10 minutes. Remove drumsticks from marinade, reserving marinade. Pull skin over meat on drumsticks and arrange on rack; cook, turning occasionally, for 20 minutes.

4 Dip bell pepper strips in reserved marinade and arrange on rack with drumsticks. Cook, brushing pepper strips and drumsticks with remaining marinade, until pepper strips are browned and drumsticks are tender, about 10 minutes. Remove and discard skin from drumsticks.

EACH SERVING PROVIDES: 2 PROTEINS; ½ VEGETABLE; 50 OPTIONAL CALORIES
PER SERVING: 152 CALORIES; 17 G PROTEIN; 8 G FAT; 3 G CARBOHYDRATE; 11 MG CALCIUM; 342 MG SODIUM; 53 MG CHOLESTEROL; 0.4 G DIETARY FIBER
REDUCED SODIUM

*Black Bean
Drumsticks*

*Stir-Fried Snow Peas
(Chinese pea pods)
with Red Bell Pepper
Strips and Sliced
Water Chestnuts*

*Tossed Salad with
Olive Oil, Red Wine
Vinegar, and Herbs*

*Tea with Lemon
Wedge*

GREEK CHICKEN

MAKES 2 SERVINGS

1 tablespoon lemon juice
2 teaspoons olive oil
2 garlic cloves, minced
1 teaspoon chopped fresh oregano
   or ¼ teaspoon oregano leaves

7 ounces chicken cutlets, thinly
   sliced
Dash pepper

1 In medium glass or stainless-steel mixing bowl place first 4 ingredients, stirring to combine. Add chicken and turn to coat with marinade. Cover and refrigerate for at least 1 hour or overnight.

2 Spray 9-inch nonstick skillet with nonstick cooking spray; add chicken to skillet, reserving marinade, and cook over high heat until chicken is no longer pink, about 1½ minutes on each side.

3 Add reserved marinade and pepper to skillet and bring to a boil; cook for 1 minute.

EACH SERVING PROVIDES: 1 FAT; 2½ PROTEINS

PER SERVING: 156 CALORIES; 23 G PROTEIN; 6 G FAT; 2 G CARBOHYDRATE; 20 MG CALCIUM; 67 MG SODIUM; 58 MG CHOLESTEROL; TRACE DIETARY FIBER

REDUCED SODIUM

Greek Chicken

Cooked Rice with Sliced Mushrooms

Cooked Chopped Spinach

Red Bell Pepper Rings, Shredded Red Cabbage, and Iceberg Lettuce with Blue Cheese Dressing

Lemon Sherbet

Tea with Cinnamon Stick

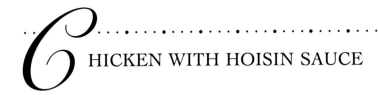

CHICKEN WITH HOISIN SAUCE

MAKES 4 SERVINGS

¼ cup canned ready-to-serve low-sodium chicken broth
2 tablespoons hoisin sauce
2 teaspoons reduced-sodium soy sauce
1 teaspoon rice wine vinegar
½ teaspoon granulated sugar
Dash ground white pepper
1 pound chicken thighs, skinned
Greens, ½ small orange, sliced, and orange rind twists for garnish

1 In gallon-size sealable plastic bag combine all ingredients except chicken thighs. Add chicken; seal bag, squeezing out air, and turn bag to coat chicken with marinade. Refrigerate at least 1 hour, turning bag occasionally.

2 Spray rack in broiling pan with nonstick cooking spray. Preheat broiler. Drain and reserve marinade. Place chicken on rack. Broil chicken, brushing with reserved marinade and turning occasionally, until juices are clear when meat is pricked with a fork, 15 to 20 minutes. Garnish with greens, ½ small orange, and orange rind twists.

EACH SERVING PROVIDES: 2 PROTEINS; 20 OPTIONAL CALORIES
PER SERVING: 142 CALORIES; 15 G PROTEIN; 6 G FAT; 5 G CARBOHYDRATE; 15 MG CALCIUM; 374 MG SODIUM; 54 MG CHOLESTEROL; .5 G DIETARY FIBER. WITH ORANGE, ADD 10 CALORIES PER SERVING

CHICKEN MORNAY

MAKES 2 SERVINGS

7 ounces chicken cutlets
1 cup White Sauce (see page 94)
½ ounce Parmesan cheese, grated

½ ounce reduced-fat Swiss
cheese, shredded

1   Spray 9-inch nonstick skillet with nonstick cooking spray and heat; add
    chicken and cook over medium-high heat until no longer pink, about 1
    minute on each side. Transfer to serving platter; set aside and keep
    warm.

2   In 1-quart nonstick saucepan cook White Sauce over low heat, stirring
    frequently, until heated, about 3 minutes. Stir in cheeses and cook,
    stirring constantly, until cheeses are melted, about 1 minute. Pour over
    chicken.

EACH SERVING (INCLUDING WHITE SAUCE) PROVIDES: ½ MILK; 1 FAT; 3 PROTEINS;
¼ BREAD; 35 OPTIONAL CALORIES
PER SERVING: 305 CALORIES; 33 G PROTEIN; 14 G FAT; 11 G CARBOHYDRATE; 350 MG
CALCIUM; 419 MG SODIUM; 83 MG CHOLESTEROL; 0.2 G DIETARY FIBER

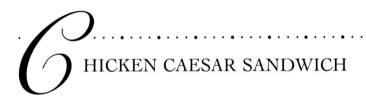

CHICKEN CAESAR SANDWICH

MAKES 1 SERVING

1 semolina *or* kaiser roll (1½
   ounces), cut in half
   horizontally
1 tablespoon reduced-calorie
   Caesar salad dressing (4
   calories per tablespoon),
   divided

¼ cup torn lettuce
2 ounces sliced cooked chicken
3 tomato slices

1 Brush cut side of each half of roll with ½ teaspoon salad dressing. In small mixing bowl combine remaining salad dressing and lettuce and toss to coat.

2 Onto bottom half of roll arrange chicken, lettuce, and tomato; top with remaining half of roll.

EACH SERVING PROVIDES: 2 PROTEINS; 1½ VEGETABLES; 1½ BREADS; 4 OPTIONAL CALORIES

PER SERVING: 253 CALORIES; 21 G PROTEIN; 6 G FAT; 28 G CARBOHYDRATE; 40 MG CALCIUM; 499 MG SODIUM; 52 MG CHOLESTEROL; 1 G DIETARY FIBER

REDUCED FAT

CHICKEN IN CREAMY FRUIT SAUCE

MAKES 1 SERVING

1 teaspoon olive oil *or* vegetable oil
¼ pound chicken cutlet, cut into thin strips
¼ cup sliced onion
¼ cup sliced mushrooms
½ garlic clove, minced
¼ cup canned ready-to-serve low-sodium chicken broth

2 tablespoons plus 2 teaspoons apricot nectar
3 dried apricot halves, cut into strips
1 tablespoon golden raisins
1 teaspoon Dijon-style mustard
1 tablespoon light sour cream

1 In 9-inch nonstick skillet heat oil; add chicken and cook over medium-high heat, stirring occasionally, until chicken is browned on all sides, about 3 minutes. Add onion, mushrooms, and garlic, and cook, stirring frequently, until onion is translucent, about 2 minutes.

2 Add remaining ingredients, except sour cream, and stir to combine; bring mixture to a boil. Reduce heat to low, add sour cream, and let simmer until flavors blend, about 5 minutes.

EACH SERVING PROVIDES: 1 FAT; 3 PROTEINS; 1 VEGETABLE; 1½ FRUITS; 35 OPTIONAL CALORIES

PER SERVING: 299 CALORIES; 30 G PROTEIN; 9 G FAT; 26 G CARBOHYDRATE; 39 MG CALCIUM; 242 MG SODIUM; 71 MG CHOLESTEROL; 2 G DIETARY FIBER

REDUCED FAT AND SODIUM

Chicken in Creamy Fruit Sauce

Cooked Fettuccine sprinkled with Grated Parmesan Cheese

Cooked Broccoli Spears

Red Bell Pepper Strips, Sliced Cucumber, and Grated Carrot on Bibb Lettuce Leaves with Reduced-Calorie French Dressing

Coffee or Tea

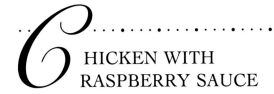

CHICKEN WITH RASPBERRY SAUCE

MAKES 1 SERVING

1 teaspoon olive *or* vegetable oil
¼ pound skinned and boned
    chicken breast
1 thoroughly washed leek, cut
    into strips (white portion
    and some green)
½ cup sliced shiitake *or* white
    mushrooms

¼ cup canned ready-to-serve low-
    sodium chicken broth
1 tablespoon raspberry liqueur
½ teaspoon cornstarch
¼ cup raspberries

*Chicken with
Raspberry Sauce*

Cooked Rice

*Romaine Lettuce, Red
Cabbage, and Tomato
Salad with Reduced-
Calorie Italian
Dressing*

Light White Wine

1 In 9-inch nonstick skillet heat oil; add chicken and cook over medium-high heat until browned, about 3 minutes on each side. Add leeks and mushrooms and cook, stirring occasionally, until leeks are tender-crisp, about 3 minutes.

2 In 1-cup liquid measure combine remaining ingredients except raspberries, stirring to dissolve cornstarch. Stir into skillet and cook, stirring constantly, until mixture comes to a boil. Reduce heat to low and let simmer until flavors blend, about 1 minute.

3 Using a slotted spoon, transfer chicken and vegetables to serving platter; set aside and keep warm. Add raspberries to skillet and cook until heated through, about 1 minute. Spoon raspberry mixture over chicken.

EACH SERVING PROVIDES: 1 FAT; 3 PROTEINS; 2 VEGETABLES; 85 OPTIONAL CALORIES
PER SERVING: 274 CALORIES; 29 G PROTEIN; 7 G FAT; 19 G CARBOHYDRATE; 52 MG CALCIUM; 99 MG SODIUM; 66 MG CHOLESTEROL; 3 G DIETARY FIBER
REDUCED FAT AND SODIUM

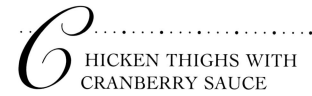

CHICKEN THIGHS WITH CRANBERRY SAUCE

MAKES 4 SERVINGS

⅓ cup cranberry juice cocktail
3 tablespoons barbecue sauce
2 garlic cloves, sliced
4 boneless chicken thighs (¼ pound each), skinned

2 teaspoons vegetable oil
1 cup chopped onions
1 cup diced green bell peppers
1 teaspoon cornstarch

1 In shallow glass or stainless-steel mixing bowl place cranberry juice cocktail, barbecue sauce, and garlic, stirring to combine. Add chicken and turn to coat with marinade. Cover and refrigerate for 30 minutes or overnight.

2 Preheat barbecue or gas grill on medium for 10 minutes. Remove chicken from marinade, reserving marinade. Arrange a sheet of heavy-duty foil on rack and place chicken on foil. Cook, turning frequently, until cooked through, about 15 minutes.

3 While chicken is cooking prepare cranberry sauce: In 9-inch nonstick skillet heat oil; add onions and peppers and cook over medium-high heat, stirring occasionally, until onions are translucent, about 1 minute.

4 Add cornstarch to reserved marinade, stirring to dissolve cornstarch. Stir into onion-pepper mixture; cook, stirring constantly, until mixture comes to a boil. Reduce heat to low and let simmer until flavors blend, about 5 minutes.

5 To serve, arrange chicken on serving platter; top with sauce.

EACH SERVING PROVIDES: ½ FAT; 3 PROTEINS; 1 VEGETABLE; ¼ FRUIT; 15 OPTIONAL CALORIES

PER SERVING: 243 CALORIES; 23 G PROTEIN; 12 G FAT; 10 G CARBOHYDRATE; 27 MG CALCIUM; 173 MG SODIUM; 81 MG CHOLESTEROL; 1 G DIETARY FIBER

REDUCED SODIUM

---

*Chicken Thighs
with Cranberry Sauce*

*Baked Sweet Potato
with Reduced-Calorie
Margarine*

*Cauliflower Florets
sprinkled with Grated
Parmesan Cheese*

*Bibb Lettuce, Radish,
and Cherry Tomato
Salad with Red Wine
Vinegar and Herbs*

Coffee or Tea

SKILLET CHICKEN AND FENNEL

MAKES 2 SERVINGS

1 tablespoon plus 1½ teaspoons
    all-purpose flour, divided
Dash pepper
¼ pound skinned and boned
    chicken breast, sliced
2 teaspoons olive *or* vegetable
    oil, divided
½ ounce pignolias (pine nuts)
1 cup sliced fennel

1 cup sliced onions
½ cup canned ready-to-serve low-
    sodium chicken broth
2 tablespoons dry vermouth *or*
    dry white table wine
½ medium tomato, seeded and
    sliced
Fennel sprigs for garnish
    (optional)

1 On sheet of wax paper combine 1 tablespoon flour and the pepper. Dredge chicken in flour mixture.

2 In 9-inch nonstick skillet heat 1½ teaspoons oil; add chicken and cook over medium-high heat, turning occasionally, until browned, about 1 minute. Transfer chicken to a plate; set aside.

3 In same skillet cook pignolias over low heat, stirring constantly, until lightly browned, about 1 minute. Transfer to plate with chicken.

4 In same skillet heat remaining oil; add fennel and onions and cook over medium-high heat, stirring occasionally, until onions are translucent, about 2 minutes. Sprinkle with remaining flour and stir quickly to combine; continuing to stir, gradually add broth and vermouth and cook until mixture comes to a boil.

5 Reduce heat to low; return chicken and pignolias to skillet. Let simmer until mixture thickens and flavors blend, about 4 minutes. Stir in tomato; cook 1 minute longer. Garnish with fennel sprigs.

EACH SERVING PROVIDES: 1½ FATS; 1¾ PROTEINS; 2½ VEGETABLES; ¼ BREAD; 25 OPTIONAL CALORIES

PER SERVING: 226 CALORIES; 18 G PROTEIN; 10 G FAT; 15 G CARBOHYDRATE; 59 MG CALCIUM; 109 MG SODIUM; 33 MG CHOLESTEROL; 2 G DIETARY FIBER (THIS FIGURE DOES NOT INCLUDE PIGNOLIAS; NUTRITION ANALYSIS NOT AVAILABLE)

REDUCED SODIUM

*Skillet Chicken and
Fennel*

*Whole Wheat Roll
with Reduced-Calorie
Margarine*

*Cooked Carrot Sticks
sprinkled with Toasted
Sesame Seed*

*Tomato Wedges,
Chopped Scallion, and
Cauliflower Florets on
Boston Lettuce Leaves
with Balsamic Vinegar
and Herbs*

*Sliced Peaches and
Blueberries*

*Iced Tea with Lemon
Wedge*

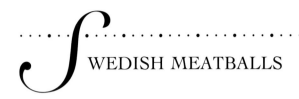

SWEDISH MEATBALLS

Our new version of Swedish Meatballs uses chicken for a lighter touch.

MAKES 4 SERVINGS

1 tablespoon plus 1 teaspoon
   reduced-calorie margarine
¼ cup minced shallots
2 slices white bread, cut into
   cubes
1 cup evaporated skimmed milk,
   divided
¾ pound ground lean chicken
1 egg, lightly beaten

½ teaspoon salt
¼ teaspoon pepper
¼ cup plus 2 tablespoons all-
   purpose flour, divided
1 cup canned ready-to-serve low-
   sodium chicken broth
1 tablespoon low-sodium
   Worcestershire sauce

1 In 12-inch nonstick skillet melt 2 teaspoons margarine; add shallots and cook, stirring frequently, until tender, about 2 minutes. Set aside. In large mixing bowl toss together bread cubes and ½ cup milk; let stand for 5 minutes until milk is absorbed.

2 Add shallots, chicken, egg, salt, and pepper to bowl; combine all ingredients. Shape into 32 equal balls. On large sheet of wax paper place ¼ cup flour. Roll each ball in flour, coating evenly.

3 In same skillet, melt 1 teaspoon of the remaining margarine. Add half the meatballs; cook, turning occasionally, until browned, 10 to 12 minutes. Using a slotted spoon, remove meatballs to a large plate. Repeat with remaining margarine and meatballs.

4 Using a wire whisk, in small mixing bowl beat together broth, remaining milk, flour, and the Worcestershire sauce until flour is dissolved. Stir broth mixture into skillet, scraping up any remaining particles from bottom of skillet. Bring to a boil; reduce heat to low and let simmer until sauce thickens, about 5 minutes. Return meatballs to skillet; cook 5 minutes until heated through.

EACH SERVING PROVIDES: ½ MILK; ½ FAT; 2½ PROTEINS; ⅛ VEGETABLE; 1 BREAD, 10 OPTIONAL CALORIES

PER SERVING: 315 CALORIES; 25 G PROTEIN; 12 G FAT; 26 G CARBOHYDRATE; 234 MG CALCIUM; 569 MG SODIUM; 127 MG CHOLESTEROL; 1 G DIETARY FIBER

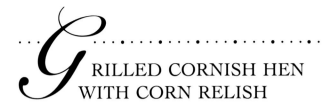

GRILLED CORNISH HEN WITH CORN RELISH

MAKES 2 SERVINGS

1 tablespoon white wine vinegar
2 teaspoons honey
1 garlic clove, minced
1 teaspoon Dijon-style mustard
¼ teaspoon celery seed
1 Cornish hen (about 1 pound*),
    cut in half and pounded

2 teaspoons vegetable oil
¼ cup diced red *or* green bell
    pepper
¼ cup frozen whole-kernel corn
¼ teaspoon cornstarch

1 In shallow glass or stainless-steel mixing bowl (large enough to hold hen halves in a single layer) combine vinegar, honey, garlic, mustard, and celery seed; add hen halves and turn to coat. Cover and refrigerate, turning occasionally, at least 1 hour or overnight.

2 Preheat barbecue or gas grill on medium-high for 10 minutes. Arrange hen halves on rack, reserving marinade, and cook, turning occasionally, until tender, about 30 minutes. Transfer to serving platter; set aside and keep warm.

3 In 1-quart nonstick saucepan heat oil; add pepper and cook over medium-high heat, stirring frequently, for 1 minute. Add reserved marinade and corn and bring to a boil; cook for 5 minutes.

4 In small bowl combine cornstarch and *1 teaspoon water,* stirring to dissolve cornstarch; add to corn mixture and cook, stirring constantly, until mixture thickens, about 1 minute.

5 Remove and discard skin from hen halves. Serve hen halves with corn relish on the side.

EACH SERVING PROVIDES: 1 FAT; 3 PROTEINS; ¼ VEGETABLE; ¼ BREAD; 20 OPTIONAL CALORIES
PER SERVING: 253 CALORIES; 25 G PROTEIN; 11 G FAT; 12 G CARBOHYDRATE; 22 MG CALCIUM; 150 MG SODIUM; 76 MG CHOLESTEROL; 1 G DIETARY FIBER
REDUCED SODIUM

* A 1-pound hen will yield about 6 ounces cooked poultry.

Grilled Cornish Hen with Corn Relish

Refrigerated Buttermilk Flaky Biscuit with Margarine

Sliced Tomatoes sprinkled with Chopped Fresh Basil

Lemon Sherbet

Iced Tea

ARROZ CON POLLO

MAKES 4 SERVINGS

2 teaspoons olive oil
4 skinned and boned chicken
    breasts (3 ounces each)
4 ounces long-grain white rice
½ cup chopped onion
1½ cups canned crushed tomatoes
1 cup chopped jarred roasted
    red pepper
1 cup canned ready-to-serve
    low-sodium chicken broth

¼ cup chopped fresh parsley
1 teaspoon chopped fresh
    rosemary *or* ¼ teaspoon
    rosemary leaves
¼ teaspoon salt
1 cup thawed frozen peas
    Coarsely ground black pepper
    Rosemary sprigs and lemon
    wedges for garnish

1 In 12-inch nonstick skillet heat oil. Add chicken and cook, turning once, until browned, 5 to 7 minutes. Transfer chicken to a plate; set aside. In same skillet, combine rice and onion. Cook until rice is translucent, about 2 minutes.

2 Stir in tomatoes, roasted red pepper, broth, parsley, rosemary, and salt. Return chicken to skillet; cover and let simmer for 25 minutes. Stir in peas and cook until rice is tender, about 5 minutes.

3 To serve, arrange chicken-rice mixture on serving platter; sprinkle with ground pepper to taste and garnish with rosemary sprigs and lemon wedges.

EACH SERVING PROVIDES: ½ FAT; 2 PROTEINS; 1½ VEGETABLES; 1½ BREADS; 10 OPTIONAL CALORIES.

PER SERVING: 291 CALORIES; 26 G PROTEIN; 4 G FAT; 36 G CARBOHYDRATE; 63 MG CALCIUM; 406 MG SODIUM; 49 MG CHOLESTEROL; 3 G DIETARY FIBER

SAVORY MUFFIN TARTS

MAKES 4 SERVINGS, 1 TART EACH

¼ pound cooked ground chicken
2 ounces reduced-sodium ham, diced
2 tablespoons grated Parmesan cheese
2 tablespoons chopped scallion (green onion)

Dash pepper
¾ cup buttermilk baking mix
½ cup skim *or* nonfat milk
½ cup thawed frozen egg substitute
1½ ounces part-skim mozzarella cheese, shredded

Savory Muffin Tarts

Zucchini Sticks and Red Bell Pepper Strips

Blueberry Yogurt (plain low-fat yogurt with blueberries)

Coffee, Tea, or Mineral Water

1 Preheat oven to 350°F. Spray four 4½ × 1¼-inch disposable aluminum foil tart pans with nonstick cooking spray.

2 In medium mixing bowl place chicken, ham, Parmesan cheese, scallion, and pepper, stirring to combine. Divide into prepared tart pans.

3 Using a wire whisk, in same mixing bowl beat together the baking mix, milk, and egg substitute; pour evenly into each tart pan. Sprinkle each portion with ¼ of the mozzarella cheese.

4 Arrange tart pans on baking sheet and bake for 20 minutes (until a toothpick inserted in center comes out dry). Set tart pans on wire rack and let cool.

EACH SERVING PROVIDES: 2½ PROTEINS; 1 BREAD; 45 OPTIONAL CALORIES
PER SERVING: 223 CALORIES; 20 G PROTEIN; 8 G FAT; 17 G CARBOHYDRATE; 188 MG CALCIUM; 549 MG SODIUM; 42 MG CHOLESTEROL; 0.3 G DIETARY FIBER

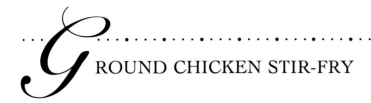

GROUND CHICKEN STIR-FRY

MAKES 2 SERVINGS

1½ teaspoons peanut *or* vegetable oil
1 to 2 dried hot chili peppers (optional)
5 ounces ground lean chicken
1 cup sliced onions
1 cup sliced mushrooms
1 cup red bell pepper strips

1 cup broccoli florets
1 garlic clove, minced
1 teaspoon minced pared gingerroot
1 cup canned ready-to-serve low-sodium chicken broth
1 teaspoon cornstarch
½ teaspoon Chinese sesame oil

Ground Chicken Stir-Fry

Cooked Cellophane Noodles

Mixed Green Salad with Red Wine Vinegar and Herbs

Raspberry Sherbet

Tea with Lemon and Honey

1 In 9-inch skillet or wok heat peanut oil; add chili peppers, if using, and cook over medium-high heat for 30 seconds. Using a slotted spoon, remove and discard chili peppers. If not using chili peppers, add chicken, onions, mushrooms, bell pepper, broccoli, garlic, and gingerroot to skillet and cook over high heat, stirring quickly and frequently, until chicken is no longer pink, 2 to 3 minutes.

2 In small mixing bowl combine broth, cornstarch, and sesame oil, stirring to dissolve cornstarch. Stir into chicken-vegetable mixture and cook, stirring constantly, until mixture comes to a boil. Reduce heat to low and let simmer until thoroughly heated, about 5 minutes.

EACH SERVING PROVIDES: 1 FAT; 2 PROTEINS; 4 VEGETABLES; 25 OPTIONAL CALORIES
PER SERVING: 240 CALORIES; 18 G PROTEIN; 12 G FAT; 16 G CARBOHYDRATE; 75 MG CALCIUM; 105 MG SODIUM; 59 MG CHOLESTEROL; 3 G DIETARY FIBER (THIS FIGURE DOES NOT INCLUDE BROCCOLI FLORETS; NUTRITION ANALYSIS NOT AVAILABLE)

REDUCED SODIUM

BUTTERY CHICKEN DIANE

Chicken gets a light coating of flour with a quick shake in a plastic bag. If you prefer, dredge the chicken in flour on a sheet of wax paper.

MAKES 2 SERVINGS

5 ounces chicken cutlets
1 tablespoon all-purpose flour
1 teaspoon margarine
1 teaspoon olive oil
½ cup sliced mushrooms
2 tablespoons chopped shallots *or* onion

1 garlic clove, minced
1 tablespoon chopped chives
1 tablespoon chopped fresh parsley
1 tablespoon brandy
1 tablespoon whipped butter
Dash white pepper

1   In plastic bag place chicken and flour; shake to coat chicken lightly with flour.

2   In 10-inch nonstick skillet heat margarine and oil until margarine is melted. Add chicken and cook over medium-high heat until lightly browned, about 2 minutes on each side. Transfer chicken to a plate and set aside.

3   In same skillet combine mushrooms, shallots, and garlic and sauté until mushrooms are lightly browned, about 1 minute. Add *¼ cup water,* the chives, parsley, brandy, butter, and pepper and cook, stirring frequently, until liquid is slightly reduced, about 1 minute.

4   Return chicken to skillet, cover, and cook until thoroughly heated, about 5 minutes.

EACH SERVING PROVIDES: 1 FAT; 2 PROTEINS; ½ VEGETABLE; 60 OPTIONAL CALORIES
PER SERVING: 196 CALORIES; 18 G PROTEIN; 9 G FAT; 6 G CARBOHYDRATE; 21 MG CALCIUM; 111 MG SODIUM; 52 MG CHOLESTEROL; 1 G DIETARY FIBER

Variation: Chicken Diane—Omit whipped butter. In Serving Information decrease Optional Calories to 35.

PER SERVING: 162 CALORIES; 18 G PROTEIN; 5 G FAT; 6 G CARBOHYDRATE; 20 MG CALCIUM; 71 MG SODIUM; 41 MG CHOLESTEROL; 1 G DIETARY FIBER
REDUCED SODIUM

Buttery Chicken Diane

Cooked Rice

Green Beans Amandine (cooked French-style green beans with slivered almonds)

Boston Lettuce, Tomato, and Celery Salad with Balsamic Vinegar and Herbs

Strawberries

Coffee or Tea

BRAISED CHICKEN

MAKES 4 SERVINGS

2 teaspoons olive oil	12 large pitted black olives, halved
1½ pounds chicken parts	½ cup canned ready-to-serve low-sodium chicken broth
10 ounces red potatoes, scrubbed and cubed	2 tablespoons dry white table wine
1 cup coarsely chopped red bell peppers	½ teaspoon thyme leaves
4 garlic cloves, minced	

1   In 12-inch nonstick skillet heat oil; add chicken and cook, turning once, until browned, 6 to 8 minutes. Remove chicken to plate; set aside. Add potatoes, bell pepper, and garlic; cook, stirring frequently, for 5 minutes.

2   Return chicken to skillet. Stir in remaining ingredients; bring to a boil. Reduce heat to low; cover and simmer, spooning liquid over chicken frequently, until chicken is tender, 25 to 30 minutes. Remove and discard skin before eating.

EACH SERVING PROVIDES: 1 FAT; 2 PROTEINS; ½ VEGETABLE; ½ BREAD; 10 OPTIONAL CALORIES.

PER SERVING: 220 CALORIES; 19 G PROTEIN; 8 G FAT; 16 G CARBOHYDRATE; 31 MG CALCIUM; 178 MG SODIUM; 50 MG CHOLESTEROL; 2 G DIETARY FIBER

CHICKEN TOAST

MAKES 4 SERVINGS, 5 TRIANGLES EACH

½ pound skinned and boned chicken breast, cut into pieces
¾ cup drained canned water chestnuts, sliced
1 medium carrot, cut into 1-inch pieces
1 egg white
2 tablespoons minced scallion (green onion)
2 teaspoons cornstarch

½ teaspoon granulated sugar
½ teaspoon ground ginger
⅛ teaspoon ground white pepper
5 slices thin white bread (1 ounce each)
2 tablespoons plus 2 teaspoons reduced-calorie margarine (tub), divided
Kale and mache leaves and carrot curl for garnish

1 In work bowl of food processor combine all ingredients except bread, margarine, and garnish; process until very smooth.

2 Cut each slice of bread into 4 triangles. Spread tops and sides of triangles with equal amounts of chicken mixture.

3 In 12-inch nonstick skillet melt half of the margarine. Place half of the triangles spread-side down in skillet. Cook 4 minutes until golden; turn and cook 2 minutes longer. Transfer to serving platter; set aside and keep warm. Repeat procedure with remaining margarine and triangles. To serve, garnish with kale, mache, and carrot curl.

EACH SERVING PROVIDES: 1 FAT; 1½ PROTEINS; ½ VEGETABLE; 1½ BREADS; 15 OPTIONAL CALORIES
PER SERVING: 230 CALORIES; 17 G PROTEIN; 7 G FAT; 25 G CARBOHYDRATE; 45 MG CALCIUM; 319 MG SODIUM; 41 MG CHOLESTEROL; 1 G DIETARY FIBER

BROILED TURKEY PATTY

MAKES 1 SERVING

½ teaspoon olive *or* vegetable oil
1 tablespoon finely chopped onion
1 tablespoon finely chopped red *or* green bell pepper
¼ pound ground turkey
3 tablespoons seasoned dried bread crumbs
2 teaspoons grated Parmesan cheese

2 teaspoons ketchup
2 teaspoons thawed frozen egg substitute
2 teaspoons part-skim ricotta cheese
1 teaspoon Worcestershire sauce
Dash pepper
Dash poultry seasoning

Broiled Turkey Patty

Whole Wheat Pita

Tomato Slices, Red Onion Slices, and Shredded Lettuce

Cooked Cauliflower Florets sprinkled with Toasted Sesame Seed

Diet Soda

1   In small nonstick skillet heat oil; add onion and bell pepper and cook, stirring occasionally, until onion is translucent, about 30 seconds. Remove from heat; set aside.

2   Preheat broiler. In small mixing bowl combine remaining ingredients; add onion mixture and mix well. Shape into a patty.

3   Spray rack in broiling pan with nonstick cooking spray and arrange patty on rack. Broil 6 inches from heat source for 6 to 7 minutes; turn patty over and broil until thoroughly cooked, 3 to 4 minutes.

EACH SERVING PROVIDES: ½ FAT; 3 PROTEINS; ¼ VEGETABLE; 1 BREAD; 55 OPTIONAL CALORIES

PER SERVING: 317 CALORIES; 27 G PROTEIN; 13 G FAT; 21 G CARBOHYDRATE; 121 MG CALCIUM; 967 MG SODIUM; 90 MG CHOLESTEROL; 1 G DIETARY FIBER

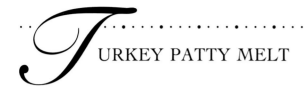

TURKEY PATTY MELT

MAKES 1 SERVING

3 ounces ground turkey
¼ cup minced mushrooms
1 tablespoon plus 1½ teaspoons
   seasoned dried bread crumbs
1 egg white
1 teaspoon reduced-calorie
   mayonnaise

⅛ teaspoon Italian seasoning
½ cup thinly sliced onion
¾ ounce reduced-fat Swiss cheese
2 slices reduced-calorie rye
   bread, toasted
1 teaspoon mustard

1 In medium mixing bowl combine turkey, mushrooms, bread crumbs, egg white, mayonnaise, and Italian seasoning. Shape into a patty and set aside.

2 Spray 9-inch nonstick skillet with nonstick cooking spray and heat; add onion and cook over medium-high heat, stirring frequently, for 1 minute. Reduce heat to medium and cook, stirring occasionally, until onion is browned, about 4 minutes. Transfer to a plate; set aside and keep warm.

3 Wipe skillet with paper towel. Spray skillet with nonstick cooking spray and heat. Add patty and cook over medium heat until bottom is lightly browned, about 5 minutes. Turn patty over and cook for 4 minutes. Top patty with cheese, cover, and cook until cheese begins to melt, about 1 minute.

4 To serve, spread one side of each slice of bread with half of the mustard. Top one slice of bread with the onion and patty; top with remaining slice of bread. Cut sandwich in half.

EACH SERVING PROVIDES: ½ FAT; 3 PROTEINS; 1½ VEGETABLES; 1½ BREADS; 20 OP-TIONAL CALORIES

PER SERVING: 366 CALORIES; 30 G PROTEIN; 14 G FAT; 34 G CARBOHYDRATE; 263 MG CALCIUM; 742 MG SODIUM; 74 MG CHOLESTEROL; 5 G DIETARY FIBER

Turkey Patty Melt

Carrot-Cabbage Salad
(shredded carrot and
cabbage with reduced-
calorie buttermilk
dressing)

Reduced-Calorie
Butterscotch Pudding
with Whipped Topping

Coffee, Tea, or
Mineral Water

ITALIAN TURKEY-
SAUSAGE PLATTER

MAKES 2 SERVINGS

5 ounces sweet Italian turkey
    sausage links, cut in half
    lengthwise
1 medium red bell pepper,
    seeded and cut into quarters
1 medium green bell pepper,
    seeded and cut into quarters

4 large Spanish onion slices
    (¼ inch thick)
½ teaspoon Italian seasoning,
    divided
1 medium tomato, cut in half

1   Preheat barbecue or gas grill on medium for 10 minutes. Spray rack
with nonstick cooking spray. Arrange sausage, peppers, and onion on
rack and spray with nonstick cooking spray; sprinkle with half of the
Italian seasoning. Arrange tomato halves, cut-side down, on rack. Cook
sausage and vegetables until lightly browned, about 5 minutes.

2   Turn sausage and vegetables over; sprinkle with remaining Italian seasoning. Cook until vegetables are browned and sausage is no longer
pink, about 4 minutes.

EACH SERVING PROVIDES: 2 PROTEINS; 4 VEGETABLES
PER SERVING: 164 CALORIES; 13 G PROTEIN; 8 G FAT; 11 G CARBOHYDRATE; 18 MG
CALCIUM; 509 MG SODIUM; 50 MG CHOLESTEROL; 2 G DIETARY FIBER (THIS FIGURE
DOES NOT INCLUDE SPANISH ONION; NUTRITION ANALYSIS NOT AVAILABLE)
REDUCED CHOLESTEROL

*Italian Turkey-
Sausage Platter*

*Italian Bread with
Reduced-Calorie
Margarine*

*Zucchini au Gratin
(baked sliced zucchini
with seasoned dried
bread crumbs)*

*Red Leaf Lettuce,
Tomato, and Sprout
Salad with Reduced-
Calorie Italian
Dressing*

Lemon Sorbet

Club Soda

TURKEY MARSALA

MAKES 2 SERVINGS

1 tablespoon all-purpose flour, divided
Dash pepper
7 ounces turkey cutlets, cut into 6 pieces

2 teaspoons margarine
¼ cup canned ready-to-serve low-sodium chicken broth
2 tablespoons dry marsala wine

1 On sheet of wax paper combine 2 teaspoons flour and the pepper; dredge turkey in flour mixture, lightly coating both sides.

2 In 9-inch nonstick skillet melt margarine; add turkey and sauté over medium-high heat until cooked through, about 3 minutes on each side. Transfer turkey to serving platter; set aside and keep warm.

3 In same skillet, over medium-high heat, sprinkle remaining flour over pan drippings and stir quickly to combine. Add broth and wine and cook, stirring constantly, until mixture thickens, about 1 minute. Spoon mixture over turkey.

EACH SERVING PROVIDES: 1 FAT; 2½ PROTEINS; 35 OPTIONAL CALORIES
PER SERVING: 188 CALORIES; 24 G PROTEIN; 6 G FAT; 5 G CARBOHYDRATE; 15 MG CALCIUM; 119 MG SODIUM; 62 MG CHOLESTEROL; 0.1 G DIETARY FIBER

REDUCED SODIUM

Turkey Marsala

*Cooked Noodles
sprinkled with
Poppy Seed*

*Cooked Asparagus
Spears*

*Chilled Cooked
Artichoke Hearts with
Cherry Tomato Halves,
Alfalfa Sprouts, and
Reduced-Calorie Italian
Dressing on Shredded
Lettuce*

*Peach Slices sprinkled
with Ground
Cinnamon*

Coffee or Tea

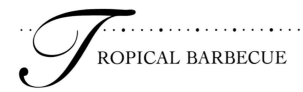

TROPICAL BARBECUE

MAKES 2 SERVINGS

3 tablespoons barbecue sauce
2 thin turkey cutlets (3 ounces each)
½ small mango (about ¼ pound with rind, without pit), pared and cut into thick slices

½ medium banana (about 3 ounces), peeled and diagonally sliced
½ cup medium mushrooms
4 medium scallions (green onions)

Tropical Barbecue

Cooked Rice with Reduced-Calorie Margarine

Cooked French-Style Green Beans with Sliced Mushrooms

Reduced-Calorie Strawberry-Flavored Gelatin

Iced Tea with Mint Sprig

1 Preheat barbecue or gas grill on medium for 10 minutes. In 9-inch pie plate combine barbecue sauce and *1 tablespoon water;* add turkey and turn to coat with sauce. Transfer turkey to a plate and set aside. Add remaining ingredients to sauce and turn to coat.

2 Spray rack with nonstick cooking spray. Place turkey, fruits, and vegetables on rack and cook, basting with barbecue sauce and turning once, until fruits and vegetables are browned and turkey is no longer pink, about 5 minutes.

EACH SERVING PROVIDES: 2 PROTEINS; ¾ VEGETABLE; 1 FRUIT; 25 OPTIONAL CALORIES
PER SERVING: 187 CALORIES; 22 G PROTEIN; 2 G FAT; 21 G CARBOHYDRATE; 41 MG CALCIUM; 251 MG SODIUM; 53 MG CHOLESTEROL; 2 G DIETARY FIBER
REDUCED FAT AND SODIUM

TURKEY-SAUSAGE CASSEROLE

This sensational casserole is sure to please! Serve over a bed of cooked noodles.

MAKES 2 SERVINGS

½ cup diced onion
2 teaspoons margarine
½ cup sliced carrot
½ cup frozen peas
½ cup low-fat milk (1% milk fat)
1 tablespoon plus 1½ teaspoons all-purpose flour

1 packet instant chicken broth and seasoning mix
Dash pepper
¼ pound fully cooked smoked turkey sausage links, sliced
1½ teaspoons chopped fresh parsley

1   In 2-quart microwavable casserole combine onion and margarine. Cover and microwave on High (100%) for 2 minutes, stirring once halfway through cooking, until onion is translucent.

2   Add carrot and peas; cover and microwave on High for 2 minutes, stirring once halfway through cooking, until peas are thoroughly heated.

3   Using a wire whisk, in medium mixing bowl beat together *½ cup water,* the milk, flour, broth mix, and pepper. Add to vegetable mixture and stir to combine. Microwave on High for 4 minutes, stirring vigorously halfway through cooking, until mixture thickens.

4   Add sausage and parsley and stir to combine. Microwave on High for 3 minutes, stirring every minute, until sausage is thoroughly heated.

EACH SERVING PROVIDES: ¼ MILK; 1 FAT; 2 PROTEINS; 1 VEGETABLE; ¾ BREAD; 5 OPTIONAL CALORIES
PER SERVING: 249 CALORIES; 15 G PROTEIN; 13 G FAT; 19 G CARBOHYDRATE; 114 MG CALCIUM; 1,066 MG SODIUM; 41 MG CHOLESTEROL; 3 G DIETARY FIBER
REDUCED CHOLESTEROL

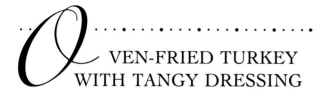

OVEN-FRIED TURKEY WITH TANGY DRESSING

MAKES 1 SERVING

Oven-Fried Turkey with Tangy Dressing

Applesauce

Oatmeal-Raisin Cookies

Herbal Tea

1 tablespoon plus 1½ teaspoons plain dried bread crumbs
1 teaspoon grated Parmesan cheese
1 teaspoon chopped fresh Italian (flat-leaf) parsley
¼ teaspoon paprika
1 tablespoon thawed frozen egg substitute
3 ounces turkey cutlet, cut into 2 × ½-inch pieces

2 tablespoons plain low-fat yogurt
1 tablespoon reduced-calorie creamy Italian dressing (25 calories per tablespoon)
Dash pepper
½ cup torn lettuce leaves
¼ cup diagonally sliced carrot
¼ cup sliced mushrooms

1 Preheat oven to 400°F. On sheet of wax paper combine bread crumbs, cheese, parsley, and paprika. Pour egg substitute into small mixing bowl; dip turkey pieces into egg substitute, then into crumb mixture, coating all sides.

2 Spray nonstick baking sheet with nonstick cooking spray. Arrange turkey pieces on baking sheet and bake until turkey is tender and coating is crisp, about 10 minutes. Set aside and let cool.

3 Using a wire whisk, in small mixing bowl beat together yogurt, Italian dressing, and pepper.

4 To serve, on serving plate arrange lettuce, carrot, and mushrooms; top with turkey and yogurt dressing.

EACH SERVING PROVIDES: 2¼ PROTEINS; 2 VEGETABLES; ½ BREAD; 50 OPTIONAL CALORIES

PER SERVING: 214 CALORIES; 26 G PROTEIN; 5 G FAT; 15 G CARBOHYDRATE; 131 MG CALCIUM; 335 MG SODIUM; 56 MG CHOLESTEROL; 2 G DIETARY FIBER

REDUCED FAT AND SODIUM

ROAST TURKEY SANDWICH

MAKES 1 SERVING

2 teaspoons reduced-calorie mayonnaise

1½ teaspoons rinsed drained capers

1 teaspoon Dijon-style mustard

¼ teaspoon honey

1 kaiser roll (1½ ounces), cut in half horizontally

2 ounces sliced roast turkey

3 tomato slices

2 lettuce leaves

1 large red onion slice

Roast Turkey Sandwich

Red Bell Pepper Strips and Cucumber Slices

Cherries

Coffee or Tea

1 In small bowl combine first 4 ingredients; spread evenly on cut side of each roll half.

2 Arrange remaining ingredients on bottom half of roll; top with remaining half of roll.

EACH SERVING PROVIDES: 1 FAT; 2 PROTEINS; 2 VEGETABLES; 1½ BREADS; 5 OPTIONAL CALORIES

PER SERVING: 285 CALORIES; 22 G PROTEIN; 7 G FAT; 32 G CARBOHYDRATE; 55 MG CALCIUM; 627 MG SODIUM; 48 MG CHOLESTEROL; 2 G DIETARY FIBER (THIS FIGURE DOES NOT INCLUDE CAPERS; NUTRITION ANALYSIS NOT AVAILABLE)

REDUCED CHOLESTEROL AND FAT

MEAT

FOR THOSE OF US WHO GREW UP IN MEAT AND POTATO HOUSE-holds, it seems as though a lot has changed. While common health sense seems to dictate that meat every day *won't* keep the doctor away, today's leaner cuts of pork and beef cook quicker and are more healthful, making it easier to enjoy our favorite dishes without the guilt. Marinated Pork Tenderloin and Beef Stew remind us of the good old days. Lamb Kabobs celebrate Middle Eastern flavor; try them served with a tangy cucumber salad for a light summer repast. If you love chili like we love chili, you'll love Chili Tostadas, Chili Enchiladas, and Cheese-Topped Chili. They're all made from one basic recipe, which you can make ahead and freeze, then thaw to use as needed. Dinner for two? Peppered Steak with cognac sounds fancy but takes just 15 minutes to prepare, as does Veal Sauté with Sun-Dried Tomatoes. A glass of wine, crusty French bread, and time to prepare a special dessert, you'll have the makings of a memorable evening. Reduced-sodium ham is the healthy basis for Fettuccine with Ham and Mushrooms as well as Open-Face Ham-and-Cheese Sandwich, updated with raisin bread, strawberries, and Brie. Skillet Knockwurst with Sauer-kraut doesn't sound as ambitious when you know you'll use ready-made sauerkraut in a bag. Veal Sausage–Stuffed Peppers are a natural to take to work; the peppers are nature's containers. So, regale the return of meat.

VEAL SAUSAGE–STUFFED PEPPERS

MAKES 2 SERVINGS, 1 PEPPER EACH

¼ cup chopped onion
2 teaspoons vegetable oil
¾ cup cooked long-grain rice
2½ ounces cooked veal sausage,
　　crumbled
2 tablespoons thawed frozen
　　egg substitute
1 tablespoon plus 1½ teaspoons
　　seasoned dried bread
　　crumbs

2 teaspoons chopped fresh
　　Italian (flat-leaf) parsley
Dash pepper
2 medium red *or* green bell
　　peppers

*Veal Sausage–
Stuffed Peppers*

*Cherry Tomatoes and
Whole Mushrooms*

Pear

*Coffee, Tea, or
Mineral Water*

1 In 2-quart microwavable casserole combine onion and oil and stir to coat; cover and microwave on High (100%) for 1½ minutes, until onion is translucent. Add remaining ingredients except bell peppers and stir to combine.

2 Cut a thin slice from stem end of each pepper, reserving slices. Remove and discard seeds and membranes from peppers. Spoon half of the sausage mixture into each pepper and top each with a reserved pepper slice.

3 In same casserole arrange stuffed peppers; add *¼ cup water*. Cover and microwave on High for 10 minutes, until peppers are fork-tender. Let stand for 2 minutes before serving.

EACH SERVING PROVIDES: 1 FAT; 1½ PROTEINS; 2¼ VEGETABLES; 1 BREAD
PER SERVING: 255 CALORIES; 14 G PROTEIN; 8 G FAT; 32 G CARBOHYDRATE; 36 MG CALCIUM; 662 MG SODIUM; 37 MG CHOLESTEROL; 2 G DIETARY FIBER
REDUCED FAT

VEAL PARMIGIANA

To reduce the cost of this dish, substitute chicken or turkey cutlets for the veal.

MAKES 2 SERVINGS

1 tablespoon thawed frozen egg
   substitute
7 ounces veal cutlets
3 tablespoons seasoned dried
   bread crumbs

¼ cup tomato sauce
¾ ounce part-skim mozzarella
   cheese, shredded

1 In shallow mixing bowl beat together egg substitute and *1 tablespoon water*. Dip veal cutlets in egg substitute mixture, coating all sides. On sheet of wax paper dredge veal cutlets in bread crumbs, coating both sides.

2 Spray 9-inch nonstick skillet with nonstick cooking spray and heat; add cutlets and cook over medium heat until golden, about 3 minutes on each side.

3 Top each cutlet with half of the tomato sauce and cheese. Cover skillet and cook until cheese is melted, about 1 minute.

EACH SERVING PROVIDES: 3 PROTEINS; ¼ VEGETABLE; ½ BREAD; 10 OPTIONAL CALORIES

PER SERVING: 189 CALORIES; 26 G PROTEIN; 4 G FAT; 10 G CARBOHYDRATE; 90 MG CALCIUM; 606 MG SODIUM; 84 MG CHOLESTEROL; 1 G DIETARY FIBER

REDUCED FAT

Veal Parmigiana

Cooked Spinach Linguine with Grated Parmesan Cheese

Cooked Sliced Zucchini and Yellow Squash

Romaine Lettuce, Mushroom, and Carrot Salad with Italian Dressing

Honeydew Melon Wedge

Red Wine

VEAL SAUTÉ WITH SUN-DRIED TOMATOES

Small cubes of veal cook in minutes, keeping the preparation time needed for this recipe to a minimum. Perfect with crunchy French bread.

MAKES 2 SERVINGS

8 sun-dried tomato halves (not packed in oil), cut into strips
2 teaspoons olive oil
1 cup sliced onions
1 cup sliced mushrooms
1 garlic clove, minced
5 ounces boneless veal, cut into small cubes

2 tablespoons dry vermouth *or* dry white table wine
1 tablespoon Dijon-style mustard
2 tablespoons light sour cream
Chopped fresh parsley for garnish (optional)

1 In small mixing bowl combine tomatoes and *¼ cup boiling water;* set aside to soften.

2 In 9-inch nonstick skillet heat oil; add onions, mushrooms, and garlic and cook over medium-high heat until onion is translucent, about 1 minute. Add veal and cook, stirring, until veal is no longer pink, about 3 to 4 minutes.

3 Drain tomatoes. Add tomatoes, vermouth, and mustard to veal mixture and stir to combine. Reduce heat to low and let simmer until flavors blend, about 3 minutes. Stir in sour cream. Garnish with parsley.

EACH SERVING PROVIDES: 1 FAT; 2 PROTEINS; 4 VEGETABLES; 40 OPTIONAL CALORIES
PER SERVING: 258 CALORIES; 18 G PROTEIN; 12 G FAT; 18 G CARBOHYDRATE; 47 MG CALCIUM; 290 MG SODIUM; 63 MG CHOLESTEROL; 4 G DIETARY FIBER

Variation: Veal Sauté—Omit sun-dried tomatoes from recipe. In Serving Information decrease Vegetables to 2.

EACH SERVING PROVIDES: 225 CALORIES; 17 G PROTEIN; 12 G FAT; 10 G CARBOHYDRATE; 35 MG CALCIUM; 276 MG SODIUM; 63 MG CHOLESTEROL; 2 G DIETARY FIBER
REDUCED SODIUM

Veal Sauté with Sun-Dried Tomatoes

Cooked Fettuccine

Cooked Sliced Green Beans sprinkled with Grated Romano Cheese

Tossed Salad with French Dressing

Reduced-Calorie Cherry-Flavored Gelatin with Whipped Topping

Coffee, Tea, or Mineral Water

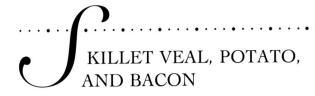

SKILLET VEAL, POTATO, AND BACON

MAKES 1 SERVING

1 teaspoon olive *or* vegetable oil
¼ pound veal sausage links, sliced
½ cup sliced onion
¼ cup sliced celery
¼ cup diced green bell pepper
¼ pound cooked small red potatoes, cut into quarters

2 tablespoons apple cider vinegar
¼ ounce (about 1½ teaspoons) bacon bits (made from real bacon)
½ teaspoon granulated sugar

1 In 9-inch nonstick skillet heat oil; add sausage and cook over medium-high heat, stirring occasionally, until browned, about 5 minutes.

2 Add onion, celery, and pepper and cook, stirring frequently, until pepper is tender-crisp, about 2 minutes. Reduce heat to low; add remaining ingredients and stir to combine. Cover and let simmer until flavors blend, about 5 minutes.

EACH SERVING PROVIDES: 1 FAT; 3 PROTEINS; 2 VEGETABLES; 1 BREAD; 55 OPTIONAL CALORIES
PER SERVING: 386 CALORIES; 28 G PROTEIN; 16 G FAT; 33 G CARBOHYDRATE; 52 MG CALCIUM; 1,004 MG SODIUM; 99 MG CHOLESTEROL; 4 G DIETARY FIBER

Variation: Skillet Veal and Potato—Omit bacon bits. In Serving Information decrease Optional Calories to 10.

PER SERVING: 345 CALORIES; 25 G PROTEIN; 13 G FAT; 32 G CARBOHYDRATE; 51 MG CALCIUM; 891 MG SODIUM; 93 MG CHOLESTEROL; 4 G DIETARY FIBER

Skillet Veal, Potato, and Bacon

Cooked Green Beans and Sliced Mushrooms

Green Leaf Lettuce, Tomato, and Green Bell Pepper Salad with Reduced-Calorie Italian Dressing

Reduced-Calorie Butterscotch Pudding with Whipped Topping and Cinnamon

Coffee or Tea

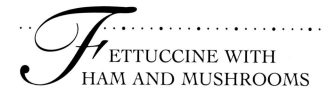ETTUCCINE WITH HAM AND MUSHROOMS

Save time by using fresh fettuccine in this recipe. It cooks in minutes.

MAKES 2 SERVINGS

2 teaspoons margarine
½ cup sliced shiitake *or* white mushrooms
1 tablespoon finely chopped shallot *or* onion
3 ounces julienne-cut reduced-sodium ham
1 cup thoroughly washed and drained spinach leaves,* chopped

¾ cup canned ready-to-serve low-sodium chicken broth
1 teaspoon cornstarch
2 tablespoons chopped fresh basil *or* 1 teaspoon basil leaves
Dash ground nutmeg
Dash pepper
1½ cups cooked fettuccine (hot)

1 In 9-inch nonstick skillet melt margarine; add mushrooms and shallot and cook over medium-high heat, stirring frequently, until mushrooms are softened, about 3 minutes.

2 Add ham and spinach to mushroom mixture and cook, stirring occasionally, until spinach is wilted, about 1 minute.

3 In 1-cup liquid measure combine broth and cornstarch, stirring to dissolve cornstarch. Stir broth mixture, basil, nutmeg, and pepper into ham-mushroom mixture. Reduce heat to medium and cook, stirring constantly, until mixture thickens, 1 to 2 minutes.

4 Add fettuccine and toss to combine.

EACH SERVING PROVIDES: 1 FAT; 1½ PROTEINS; ¾ VEGETABLE; 1½ BREADS; 20 OPTIONAL CALORIES

PER SERVING: 288 CALORIES; 17 G PROTEIN; 9 G FAT; 35 G CARBOHYDRATE; 66 MG CALCIUM; 429 MG SODIUM; 62 MG CHOLESTEROL; 4 G DIETARY FIBER

REDUCED FAT

* 1 cup fresh spinach yields about ¼ cup cooked.

Fettuccine with Ham and Mushrooms

Cooked Yellow Squash and Carrot Sticks

Cherry Tomato, Alfalfa Sprout, and Boston Lettuce Salad with Reduced-Calorie Italian Dressing

Raspberries with Whipped Topping

Light White Wine

MARINATED PORK TENDERLOIN

Marinating is the secret to preparing this dish, which is short on work but long on flavor.

MAKES 6 SERVINGS
(SHOWN WITH CREAMY MASHED POTATOES; SEE PAGE 214)

2 tablespoons teriyaki sauce
2 tablespoons dark corn syrup
2 tablespoons lemon juice
2 tablespoons dry sherry
2 tablespoons seasoned rice vinegar
2 garlic cloves, minced
1 teaspoon minced pared gingerroot
1½ pounds lean pork tenderloin, thinly sliced

1 tablespoon olive *or* vegetable oil
1 cup sliced mushrooms
1 cup sliced scallions (green onions)
1 cup shredded carrots
1 teaspoon cornstarch

1 In glass or stainless-steel mixing bowl combine teriyaki sauce, corn syrup, lemon juice, sherry, vinegar, garlic, and gingerroot; add pork and turn to coat with marinade. Cover and refrigerate at least 1 hour or overnight.

2 Preheat broiler. Arrange pork on rack in broiling pan, reserving marinade. Broil until done to taste, about 5 minutes on each side.

3 While pork is broiling, prepare vegetables. In 1-quart saucepan heat oil; add mushrooms, scallions, and carrots and cook over medium-high heat, stirring occasionally, until mushrooms are lightly browned, about 5 minutes. Add cornstarch to reserved marinade, stirring to dissolve cornstarch; stir into vegetable mixture. Bring mixture to a boil. Reduce heat to low and let simmer for 2 minutes.

4 To serve, arrange pork on serving platter and top with vegetable mixture.

EACH SERVING PROVIDES: ½ FAT; 3 PROTEINS; 1 VEGETABLE; 25 OPTIONAL CALORIES
PER SERVING: 220 CALORIES; 26 G PROTEIN; 6 G FAT; 13 G CARBOHYDRATE; 28 MG CALCIUM; 339 MG SODIUM; 79 MG CHOLESTEROL; 1 G DIETARY FIBER
REDUCED FAT AND SODIUM

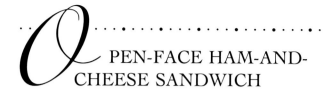

OPEN-FACE HAM-AND-CHEESE SANDWICH

MAKES 1 SERVING

1 teaspoon country Dijon-style mustard
½ teaspoon honey
2 slices raisin bread
1 ounce reduced-sodium ham, thinly sliced

¾ ounce Brie cheese (rind removed)
½ cup strawberries, sliced

In small bowl combine mustard and honey. Spread half of mixture on each slice of bread, then top each slice with half of the ham and cheese. Decoratively arrange half of the strawberries on each bread slice. Cut each slice of bread in half diagonally.

EACH SERVING PROVIDES: 2 PROTEINS; 2 BREADS; ½ FRUIT; 10 OPTIONAL CALORIES
PER SERVING: 283 CALORIES; 14 G PROTEIN; 9 G FAT; 36 G CARBOHYDRATE; 88 MG CALCIUM; 689 MG SODIUM; 38 MG CHOLESTEROL; 2 G DIETARY FIBER (THIS FIGURE DOES NOT INCLUDE RAISIN BREAD; NUTRITION ANALYSIS NOT AVAILABLE)
REDUCED CHOLESTEROL AND FAT

Open-Face Ham-and-Cheese Sandwich

Bibb Lettuce, Belgian Endive, and Red Cabbage Salad with French Dressing

Chocolate Chip Ice Cream

Iced Tea

GRILLED STEAK AND ONIONS WITH MUSHROOM SAUCE

When the weather turns warm, cook this outdoors on the grill.

MAKES 1 SERVING

5 ounces porterhouse steak (trimmed of excess fat)
Dash pepper
3 large Spanish onion slices (½ inch thick each)
1 teaspoon olive *or* vegetable oil
1 cup mushroom caps

1 small garlic clove, minced
¼ cup canned ready-to-serve beef broth
2 tablespoons dry sherry
½ teaspoon cornstarch
Italian parsley for garnish (optional)

1 Preheat broiler. Sprinkle steak with pepper; set aside.

2 Spray onion slices with nonstick cooking spray and arrange on rack in broiling pan. Broil, turning frequently, until onion slices are lightly browned. Transfer to plate; set aside and keep warm.

3 Set steak on rack in broiling pan and broil until done to taste, about 3 to 4 minutes on each side.

4 While steak is broiling prepare mushroom sauce: In 9-inch nonstick skillet heat oil; add mushrooms and garlic and cook over medium-high heat, stirring frequently, until mushrooms are browned, about 2 minutes.

5 In 1-cup liquid measure combine remaining ingredients, stirring to dissolve cornstarch. Stir broth mixture into mushroom mixture; continuing to stir, cook until mixture comes to a boil. Reduce heat to low and let simmer until mixture thickens, about 1 minute.

6 To serve, arrange steak on plate with onion slices; top with sauce and garnish with parsley as desired.

EACH SERVING PROVIDES: 1 FAT; 3 PROTEINS; 3½ VEGETABLES; 40 OPTIONAL CALORIES
PER SERVING: 337 CALORIES; 27 G PROTEIN; 14 G FAT; 17 G CARBOHYDRATE; 40 MG CALCIUM; 278 MG SODIUM; 68 MG CHOLESTEROL; 1 G DIETARY FIBER
REDUCED SODIUM

Grilled Steak and Onions with Mushroom Sauce

Cooked Brown Rice with Sliced Scallions

Cooked Sliced Yellow Squash

Spinach–Cherry Tomato Salad with Imitation Bacon Bits and Reduced-Calorie Buttermilk Dressing

Watermelon Wedge

PEPPERED STEAK

MAKES 2 SERVINGS

1 teaspoon cracked peppercorns
5 ounces boneless sirloin steak
1 tablespoon cognac

2 tablespoons half-and-half
  (blend of milk and cream)
¼ teaspoon all-purpose flour

1 Preheat broiler. Press half of the peppercorns into each side of steak until they adhere. Arrange steak on rack in broiling pan and broil until medium-rare, about 2 minutes on each side, or until done to taste. Transfer steak to serving platter and keep warm.

2 In small saucepan cook cognac over high heat until reduced by two-thirds, about 2 minutes.

3 Using a wire whisk, in small bowl combine half-and-half and flour, stirring to dissolve flour; stir into cognac. Reduce heat to medium and cook until mixture thickens, about 2 minutes. Slice steak in half and top with sauce.

EACH SERVING PROVIDES: 2 PROTEINS; 45 OPTIONAL CALORIES
PER SERVING: 152 CALORIES; 18 G PROTEIN; 6 G FAT; 2 G CARBOHYDRATE; 27 MG CALCIUM; 44 MG SODIUM; 56 MG CHOLESTEROL; 0.3 G DIETARY FIBER
REDUCED SODIUM

Peppered Steak

*Cooked Sliced Red
Potatoes topped with
Light Sour Cream and
Chopped Chives*

*Cooked French-Style
Green Beans with
Sliced Almonds*

*Tossed Salad with
Reduced-Calorie French
Dressing*

*Sliced Strawberries and
Kiwi Fruit Salad*

Coffee or Tea

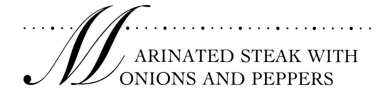

MARINATED STEAK WITH ONIONS AND PEPPERS

MAKES 2 SERVINGS

¼ cup chopped fresh cilantro (Chinese parsley) or Italian (flat-leaf) parsley
¼ cup lime juice (no sugar added)
1 tablespoon seeded and minced jalapeño pepper
2 garlic cloves, minced
 Dash pepper

½ pound boneless sirloin steak
2 teaspoons olive or vegetable oil
1 cup diced onions
½ cup diced red bell pepper
½ cup diced green bell pepper
½ cup canned ready-to-serve beef broth
½ teaspoon cornstarch

1 In glass or stainless-steel pie plate combine cilantro, lime juice, jalapeño pepper, garlic, and pepper; add steak and turn several times to coat with marinade.

2 Preheat barbecue or gas grill on high for 10 minutes. Arrange steak on rack, reserving marinade, and cook until rare, 2 to 3 minutes on each side, or until done to taste.

3 While steak is cooking prepare onion-pepper mixture: In 9-inch nonstick skillet heat oil; add onions and bell peppers and cook, stirring frequently, until onions are translucent, about 1 minute.

4 Add broth and cornstarch to reserved marinade, stirring to dissolve cornstarch. Stir into onion-pepper mixture and cook, stirring constantly, until mixture comes to a boil. Reduce heat to low and let simmer until flavors blend, about 3 minutes.

5 To serve, arrange steak on serving platter and top with onion-pepper mixture.

EACH SERVING PROVIDES: 1 FAT; 3 PROTEINS; 2 VEGETABLES; 15 OPTIONAL CALORIES
PER SERVING: 266 CALORIES; 28 G PROTEIN; 11 G FAT; 13 G CARBOHYDRATE; 45 MG CALCIUM; 386 MG SODIUM; 76 MG CHOLESTEROL; 2 G DIETARY FIBER
REDUCED SODIUM

Marinated Steak with Onions and Peppers

Baked Potato with Light Sour Cream and Chives

Cooked Sliced Carrots

Iceberg Lettuce, Tomato, and Radicchio (red chicory) Salad with Reduced-Calorie Italian Dressing

Coffee or Tea

# ROAST BEEF HERO SANDWICH

MAKES 1 SERVING

1 tablespoon light sour cream
1 tablespoon prepared horseradish
1 tablespoon finely chopped
   scallion
1 teaspoon reduced-calorie
   mayonnaise
1 club roll (2 ounces), cut in half
   horizontally

2 lettuce leaves
2 thin tomato slices
2 ounces thinly sliced roast beef
   Cucumber slices and bell pepper
   strips for garnish (optional)

Roast Beef Hero Sandwich

Cucumber and Bell Pepper

Coleslaw

Watermelon

Club Soda

1   In small mixing bowl combine sour cream, horseradish, scallion, and mayonnaise, mixing well.

2   On bottom half of roll arrange lettuce, tomato, roast beef, and sour cream mixture; cover with top half of roll. Secure with toothpicks and cut sandwich in half. Serve with cucumber and bell pepper as desired.

EACH SERVING PROVIDES: ½ FAT; 2 PROTEINS; 1 VEGETABLE; 2 BREADS; 25 OPTIONAL CALORIES

PER SERVING: 335 CALORIES; 24 G PROTEIN; 9 G FAT; 38 G CARBOHYDRATE; 55 MG CALCIUM; 436 MG SODIUM; 54 MG CHOLESTEROL; 2 G DIETARY FIBER

REDUCED FAT

BEEF STEW

Reheat leftover stew in the morning and tote to the office in a wide-mouth vacuum container for a great tasting lunch when you're away from home.

MAKES 4 SERVINGS

1 tablespoon plus 1 teaspoon
    vegetable oil
1 cup chopped onions
1 cup sliced carrots
2 tablespoons all-purpose flour
1½ cups light beer
1 tablespoon Dijon-style
    mustard

1 tablespoon red wine vinegar
¼ teaspoon thyme leaves
5 ounces pared all-purpose
    potato, thinly sliced
½ pound cubed cooked beef
    (½-inch pieces)
½ teaspoon browning sauce
    Dash pepper

> *Beef Stew*
>
> *French Bread with
> Reduced-Calorie
> Margarine*
>
> *Orange*
>
> *Coffee, Tea, or
> Mineral Water*

1 In 3-quart saucepan heat oil; add onions and carrots and cook over high heat, stirring frequently, until onions are translucent, about 2 to 3 minutes. Sprinkle flour over onion mixture and stir quickly to combine; cook, stirring constantly, for 1 minute.

2 Add beer, *½ cup water,* the mustard, vinegar, and thyme; stir to combine and bring mixture to a boil. Reduce heat to low; add potato and let simmer until potato is tender, 15 to 20 minutes.

3 Add beef, browning sauce, and pepper and stir to combine. Cook until beef is heated through, about 2 minutes.

EACH SERVING PROVIDES: 1 FAT; 2 PROTEINS; 1 VEGETABLE; ¼ BREAD; 40 OPTIONAL CALORIES
PER SERVING: 244 CALORIES; 18 G PROTEIN; 8 G FAT; 17 G CARBOHYDRATE; 30 MG CALCIUM; 170 MG SODIUM; 46 MG CHOLESTEROL; 2 G DIETARY FIBER
REDUCED CHOLESTEROL AND SODIUM

MEXICAN BURGERS

Prepare the meat mixture, shape into patties, and refrigerate before you leave for work. They'll be ready for the grill when you get home from the office.

Mexican Burgers

Light Guacamole
Taco Chips

Cooked Wax Beans

Tossed Salad

Light Beer

MAKES 2 SERVINGS, 1 BURGER EACH
(SHOWN WITH ½ OUNCE TACO CHIPS AND LIGHT GUACAMOLE; SEE PAGE 20)

7 ounces lean ground beef
½ cup finely chopped onion
½ cup finely chopped green bell pepper
2 large plum tomatoes, blanched, peeled, seeded, and chopped
1 tablespoon chopped fresh cilantro (Chinese parsley) *or* Italian (flat-leaf) parsley

1 tablespoon seeded and chopped green chili pepper
1 garlic clove, minced
½ teaspoon ground cumin
½ teaspoon ground coriander

1 Preheat barbecue or gas grill on high for 10 minutes. In small mixing bowl combine all ingredients, mixing thoroughly. Shape mixture into 2 equal patties.

2 Arrange patties on rack and cook until medium-rare, 3 to 4 minutes on each side, or until done to taste.

EACH SERVING PROVIDES: 2½ PROTEINS; 2 VEGETABLES

PER SERVING: 255 CALORIES; 21 G PROTEIN; 15 G FAT; 8 G CARBOHYDRATE; 34 MG CALCIUM; 69 MG SODIUM; 70 MG CHOLESTEROL; 2 G DIETARY FIBER

REDUCED SODIUM

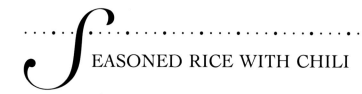

SEASONED RICE WITH CHILI

MAKES 2 SERVINGS

1 teaspoon margarine
2 ounces uncooked regular
  long-grain rice
½ cup canned ready-to-serve
  low-sodium chicken broth

¼ teaspoon curry powder
2 teaspoons chopped fresh
  Italian (flat-leaf) parsley
1½ cups thawed Chili (see
  below), heated

1 In 1-quart saucepan melt margarine; add rice and cook over medium heat, stirring frequently, for 1 minute. Add chicken broth and curry powder and bring to a boil. Reduce heat to low, cover, and let simmer until liquid is absorbed, about 20 minutes. Stir in parsley.

2 To serve, into each of 2 serving bowls arrange half of the rice mixture; top each portion with half of the Chili.

EACH SERVING (INCLUDING CHILI) PROVIDES: 1 FAT; 2 PROTEINS; 1½ VEGETABLES; 1 BREAD; 10 OPTIONAL CALORIES

PER SERVING: 311 CALORIES; 18 G PROTEIN; 8 G FAT; 40 G CARBOHYDRATE; 37 MG CALCIUM; 845 MG SODIUM; 38 MG CHOLESTEROL; 3 G DIETARY FIBER

REDUCED CHOLESTEROL AND FAT

CHILI

This simple dish is sure to please. Try it as is, with a biscuit or crackers, or in the following recipes.

YIELD: 7½ CUPS

1 tablespoon plus 2 teaspoons
  vegetable oil
2½ cups chopped onions
5 cups chunky salsa
10 ounces rinsed drained canned
  red kidney beans

15 ounces cooked sirloin steak,
  cut into ½-inch pieces
⅛ teaspoon pepper

1 In 4-quart saucepan heat oil; add onions and cook over medium heat, stirring occasionally, until softened, about 5 minutes.

2 Add salsa and beans and stir to combine. Reduce heat to low and let simmer until flavors blend, 20 to 25 minutes.

3 Add steak and pepper and stir to combine; cook until steak is heated through, about 10 minutes.

4 Store ¾-cup servings of Chili in resealable freezer bags or containers. Label and freeze for up to 1 month.

EACH ¾-CUP SERVING PROVIDES: ½ FAT; 2 PROTEINS; 1½ VEGETABLES

PER SERVING: 182 CALORIES; 16 G PROTEIN; 6 G FAT; 16 G CARBOHYDRATE; 25 MG CALCIUM; 808 MG SODIUM; 38 MG CHOLESTEROL; 3 G DIETARY FIBER (THIS FIGURE DOES NOT INCLUDE SALSA; NUTRITION ANALYSIS NOT AVAILABLE)

REDUCED CHOLESTEROL AND FAT

CHEESE-TOPPED CHILI

MAKES 2 SERVINGS

1½ cups thawed Chili (see opposite page), heated
¾ ounce reduced-fat Monterey Jack cheese, shredded

½ teaspoon Mexican seasoning
1 ounce corn chips

Cheese-Topped Chili

Cooked Rice

Tossed Salad with Reduced-Calorie Italian Dressing

Cantaloupe Chunks

Lemon-Lime Flavored Seltzer

1 Preheat broiler. Spray 1-quart flameproof casserole with nonstick cooking spray and place Chili in casserole. Sprinkle with cheese and Mexican seasoning.

2 Broil until cheese is melted, about 2 minutes. Serve with corn chips.

EACH SERVING (INCLUDING CHILI) PROVIDES: ½ FAT; 2½ PROTEINS; 1½ VEGETABLES; ½ BREAD; 40 OPTIONAL CALORIES

PER SERVING: 291 CALORIES; 20 G PROTEIN; 13 G FAT; 24 G CARBOHYDRATE; 136 MG CALCIUM; 1,014 MG SODIUM; 45 MG CHOLESTEROL; 3 G DIETARY FIBER

REDUCED CHOLESTEROL

CHILI TOSTADAS

MAKES 2 SERVINGS

2 tostada shells (1 ounce each)
1½ cups thawed Chili (see page 188), heated
1 cup shredded lettuce
1 medium tomato, diced

¼ medium avocado (about 2 ounces), pared and diced
2 tablespoons light sour cream
Scallion for garnish (optional)

1 Preheat oven to 375°F. On nonstick baking sheet arrange tostada shells and bake until browned, about 5 to 7 minutes.

2 Transfer tostada shells to serving platter; top each with half of the Chili, lettuce, tomato, avocado, and sour cream. Garnish with scallion.

EACH SERVING (INCLUDING CHILI) PROVIDES: 1½ FATS; 2 PROTEINS; 3½ VEGETABLES; 1 BREAD; 25 OPTIONAL CALORIES

PER SERVING: 392 CALORIES; 20 G PROTEIN; 19 G FAT; 37 G CARBOHYDRATE; 51 MG CALCIUM; 971 MG SODIUM; 43 MG CHOLESTEROL; 4 G DIETARY FIBER (THIS FIGURE DOES NOT INCLUDE TOSTADA SHELLS; NUTRITION ANALYSIS NOT AVAILABLE)

REDUCED CHOLESTEROL

CHILI ENCHILADAS

MAKES 2 SERVINGS, 1 ENCHILADA EACH

1½ cups thawed Chili (see page 188), heated

6 large black olives, pitted and sliced, divided

2 flour tortillas (6-inch diameter each)

¼ cup tomato sauce

¾ ounce reduced-fat Monterey Jack cheese, shredded

1 tablespoon grated Parmesan cheese

1 Preheat oven to 375°F. In small mixing bowl combine Chili and half of the olives; set aside.

2. Arrange tortillas on nonstick baking sheet and bake until softened, about 1 minute.

3 Onto center of each tortilla spoon ⅓ of the Chili mixture; fold tortillas over filling to enclose. In 1-quart casserole spread tomato sauce. Arrange enchiladas, seam-side down, in casserole; top with remaining Chili mixture. Sprinkle with cheeses and remaining olives.

4 Bake until enchiladas are thoroughly heated, about 10 minutes.

EACH SERVING (INCLUDING CHILI) PROVIDES: 1 FAT; 2½ PROTEINS; 1¾ VEGETABLES; 1 BREAD; 15 OPTIONAL CALORIES

PER SERVING: 318 CALORIES; 22 G PROTEIN; 12 G FAT; 31 G CARBOHYDRATE; 209 MG CALCIUM; 1,361 MG SODIUM; 47 MG CHOLESTEROL; 4 G DIETARY FIBER

REDUCED CHOLESTEROL

Chili Enchiladas

Cooked Sliced Green Beans

Shredded Carrot, Bell Pepper Strips, and Tomato Wedges on Shredded Lettuce with Red Wine Vinegar and Herbs

Fruit Salad with Toasted Shredded Coconut

Sangria

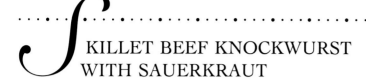

SKILLET BEEF KNOCKWURST WITH SAUERKRAUT

MAKES 2 SERVINGS

2 teaspoons margarine
2 beef knockwurst (3 ounces each), cut lengthwise into halves
1 tablespoon barbecue sauce
1 tablespoon duck sauce

1 tablespoon Dijon-style mustard
1 teaspoon sweet pickle relish
½ cup thinly sliced onion
1 cup rinsed drained sauerkraut*
¼ cup beer

1   In 9-inch nonstick skillet melt margarine; add knockwurst and cook over medium-high heat, turning occasionally, until lightly browned, 3 to 4 minutes. Transfer to plate; set aside.

2   In small bowl combine barbecue sauce, duck sauce, mustard, and relish; stir to combine and set aside.

3   To same skillet add onion and sauté over medium-high heat until softened, 1 to 2 minutes. Add sauerkraut, beer, and barbecue sauce mixture and stir until thoroughly combined. Return knockwurst to skillet. Reduce heat to low, cover, and cook, stirring occasionally, until flavors blend, 4 to 5 minutes.

EACH SERVING PROVIDES: 1 FAT; 3 PROTEINS; 1½ VEGETABLES; 30 OPTIONAL CALORIES
PER SERVING: 358 CALORIES; 11 G PROTEIN; 28 G FAT; 12 G CARBOHYDRATE; 36 MG CALCIUM; 1,486 MG SODIUM; 49 MG CHOLESTEROL; 2 G DIETARY FIBER
REDUCED CHOLESTEROL

Skillet Beef Knockwurst and Sauerkraut

Cooked Red Potatoes with Reduced-Calorie Margarine

Cooked Carrot Chunks sprinkled with Poppy Seed

Mixed Green Salad with Reduced-Calorie Buttermilk Dressing

Reduced-Calorie Butterscotch Pudding with Whipped Topping and Cinnamon

Club Soda with Lemon Wedge

* Use sauerkraut that is packaged in plastic bags and stored in the refrigerator section of the supermarket; it is usually crisper and less salty than the canned variety.

GRILLED RABBIT IN JUNIPER BERRY MARINADE

MAKES 2 SERVINGS

1 tablespoon gin
2 teaspoons vegetable oil
1 teaspoon lemon juice
1 teaspoon chopped shallot *or* onion

4 dried juniper berries, crushed
½ teaspoon grated lemon zest
⅛ teaspoon pepper
1 pound 2 ounces thawed frozen rabbit parts*

1 In shallow glass or stainless-steel mixing bowl (large enough to hold rabbit parts in a single layer) combine gin, oil, lemon juice, shallot, juniper berries, lemon zest, and pepper; add rabbit and turn to coat. Cover and refrigerate, turning occasionally, for at least 2 hours or overnight.

2 Preheat barbecue or gas grill on medium-high for 10 minutes. Arrange rabbit on rack, reserving marinade. Cook, turning occasionally and basting with reserved marinade, until rabbit is tender, about 30 minutes.

EACH SERVING PROVIDES: 1 FAT; 3 PROTEINS; 20 OPTIONAL CALORIES
PER SERVING: 191 CALORIES; 19 G PROTEIN; 10 G FAT; 1 G CARBOHYDRATE; 15 MG CALCIUM; 32 MG SODIUM; 54 MG CHOLESTEROL; TRACE DIETARY FIBER

Variation: Grilled Chicken in Juniper Berry Marinade—Substitute 1 pound 2 ounces chicken parts, skinned, for the rabbit

PER SERVING: 222 CALORIES; 25 G PROTEIN; 11 G FAT; 1 G CARBOHYDRATE; 15 MG CALCIUM; 74 MG SODIUM; 76 MG CHOLESTEROL; TRACE DIETARY FIBER

REDUCED SODIUM

* 1 pound 2 ounces rabbit parts will yield about 6 ounces boned cooked rabbit.

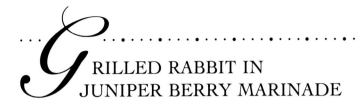

Grilled Rabbit in Juniper Berry Marinade

Corn on the Cob with Reduced-Calorie Margarine

Cooked Green Beans

Romaine Lettuce, Cucumber, and Alfalfa Sprout Salad with Buttermilk Dressing

Iced Coffee topped with Vanilla Ice Milk

LAMB KABOBS

MAKES 2 SERVINGS, 1 KABOB EACH

¼ cup plain low-fat yogurt
1 tablespoon chopped fresh mint
2 garlic cloves, minced
½ pound boneless lamb, cut into
    12 equal pieces

¼ cup whole peeled shallots *or*
    pearl onions
6 cherry tomatoes

1 In medium glass or stainless-steel mixing bowl combine first 3 ingredients; add lamb and turn to coat. Cover and refrigerate for at least 1 hour or overnight.

2 Preheat barbecue or gas grill on high for 10 minutes. Onto each of two 12-inch metal skewers alternately thread half of the lamb, shallots, and cherry tomatoes. Brush shallots and cherry tomatoes with yogurt mixture.

3 Arrange skewers on rack and cook, turning kabobs occasionally, until lamb is browned, about 8 minutes.

EACH SERVING PROVIDES: 3 PROTEINS; ¾ VEGETABLE; 15 OPTIONAL CALORIES
PER SERVING: 201 CALORIES; 26 G PROTEIN; 7 G FAT; 8 G CARBOHYDRATE; 79 MG CALCIUM; 90 MG SODIUM; 79 MG CHOLESTEROL; 1 G DIETARY FIBER

REDUCED SODIUM

Lamb Kabobs

Cooked Broad Noodles sprinkled with Poppy Seed

Cooked Spinach Leaves

Carrot, Cucumber, Red Cabbage, and Green Leaf Lettuce Salad with Buttermilk Dressing

Reduced-Calorie Vanilla Pudding topped with Banana Slices

Coffee or Tea

SIDE DISHES

WHILE THE SIDE DISH OFTEN PLAYS SECOND FIDDLE TO THE more glamorous, substantial main course, a smart cook knows the value of this part of the meal. A single vegetable, prepared with almonds, pignolias, lemon, or garlic adds flavor and dimension to your menu. More important, vegetables or whole grains add nutrient value to your feast, contain little or no fat, and can often be prepared while the main course is cooking. A pasta course not only rounds out a meal, it's an elegant extra in an era where many meals feature it as the main attraction. Try Pasta with Olive Pesto or Pasta Primavera, substituting your favorite veggies to customize these healthy dishes. Orzo Provençal is a change from rice pilaf and sits well side by side with chicken or fish, and especially lamb. Basic dishes like Oriental Rice can stretch a meal of leftovers. Take Easy Focaccia with Sun-Dried Tomatoes, an Italian pizzalike bread topped with herbs, add a protein-rich salad, and make a meal. What's easy about this bread is its refrigerated pizza-dough crust. Macaroni Salad pinch-hits as your contribution at the next picnic or barbecue. Summer Vegetable Kabobs with burgers or chicken make easy warm-weather meals. Gingersnap Yams will become a new holiday staple, and so will an updated version of a classic—Creamy Mashed Potatoes, made fluffy with light sour cream. And when you're cooking for one, who's more important than you? Broccoli with Pignolias and Peppers or Cheese 'n' Bacon–Topped Potato serve one and make your quick meal special. Choose a pasta and two vegetable side dishes and create a dinner that merits star billing!

VEGETABLE MEDLEY WITH CREAMY YOGURT SAUCE

Cook the vegetables for this tangy side dish ahead of time in your microwave oven. Keep them warm until serving time.

MAKES 2 SERVINGS

½ cup plain low-fat yogurt
¼ cup thawed frozen egg
    substitute
1 teaspoon lemon juice
½ teaspoon cornstarch
½ packet (about ½ teaspoon)
    instant chicken broth and
    seasoning mix

1 cup cooked broccoli florets
    (hot)
1 cup cooked sliced carrots (hot)
1 cup cooked cauliflower florets
    (hot)

1 Using a wire whisk, in small microwavable mixing bowl combine all ingredients except vegetables, mixing well.

2 Cover and microwave on Medium-High (70%) for 1 minute; beat vigorously with whisk. Cover and microwave on Medium (50%) for 1 minute; beat vigorously with whisk. Cover and microwave on Medium-Low (30%) for 1 minute; beat vigorously with whisk.

3 Arrange vegetables in serving bowl and top with yogurt sauce.

EACH SERVING PROVIDES: ½ PROTEIN; 3 VEGETABLES; 40 OPTIONAL CALORIES
PER SERVING: 123 CALORIES; 10 G PROTEIN; 1 G FAT; 20 G CARBOHYDRATE; 183 MG CALCIUM; 398 MG SODIUM; 3 MG CHOLESTEROL; 3 G DIETARY FIBER (THIS FIGURE DOES NOT INCLUDE BROCCOLI FLORETS; NUTRITION ANALYSIS NOT AVAILABLE)
REDUCED CHOLESTEROL AND FAT

$\mathcal{S}$PINACH SAUTÉ

Fresh spinach is often very sandy. To wash spinach thoroughly, place it in a clean kitchen sink and fill with cold water. The spinach will float to the top while the sand sinks to the bottom. Remove spinach from sink and repeat, if necessary.

MAKES 2 SERVINGS

1 teaspoon margarine
1 garlic clove, minced
4 cups thoroughly washed and drained spinach leaves,* chopped

1 ounce prosciutto (Italian-style ham) *or* reduced-sodium ham, cut into thin strips
½ ounce pignolias (pine nuts)

1 In 1-quart microwavable casserole combine margarine and garlic; cover and microwave on High (100%) for 1 minute, stirring once halfway through cooking.

2 Add remaining ingredients; cover and microwave on High for 3 minutes, stirring once every minute, until spinach is wilted.

EACH SERVING PROVIDES: 1 FAT; ¾ PROTEIN; 1 VEGETABLE
PER SERVING WITH PROSCIUTTO: 106 CALORIES; 8 G PROTEIN; 7 G FAT; 5 G CARBOHYDRATE; 117 MG CALCIUM; 421 MG SODIUM; 8 MG CHOLESTEROL; 3 G DIETARY FIBER (THIS FIGURE DOES NOT INCLUDE PIGNOLIAS; NUTRITION ANALYSIS NOT AVAILABLE)
WITH HAM: 101 CALORIES; 8 G PROTEIN; 7 G FAT; 6 G CARBOHYDRATE; 117 MG CALCIUM; 222 MG SODIUM; 8 MG CHOLESTEROL; 3 G DIETARY FIBER
REDUCED CHOLESTEROL

* 4 cups fresh spinach yield about 1 cup cooked spinach.

SUMMER VEGETABLE KABOBS

MAKES 2 SERVINGS, 2 KABOBS EACH
(SHOWN WITH GRILLED SWORDFISH WITH GINGER AND LIME; SEE
PAGE 134)

1½ cups cubed eggplant (1-inch cubes)

2 medium scallop (pattypan) squash (about 5 ounces each) *or* 8 whole baby squash, each cut into quarters

1 medium zucchini (about 5 ounces), cut crosswise into 8 equal slices

1 medium yellow squash (about 5 ounces), cut crosswise into 8 equal slices

8 medium mushrooms

8 cherry tomatoes

3 tablespoons hickory-flavored barbecue sauce

1 In large glass or stainless-steel mixing bowl combine vegetables. In small mixing bowl place barbecue sauce and *2 tablespoons water,* stirring to combine. Add to vegetables and stir to coat. Cover and refrigerate at least 30 minutes or overnight.

2 Preheat barbecue or gas grill on medium-high for 10 minutes. Onto each of four 10-inch or eight 6-inch metal skewers alternately thread ¼ of the eggplant, scallop squash, zucchini, yellow squash, mushrooms, and cherry tomatoes, reserving marinade.

3 Arrange kabobs on rack and cook for 5 minutes on each side, basting with reserved marinade.

EACH SERVING PROVIDES: 7⅛ VEGETABLES; 25 OPTIONAL CALORIES

PER SERVING: 192 CALORIES; 6 G PROTEIN; 1 G FAT; 22 G CARBOHYDRATE; 85 MG CALCIUM; 204 MG SODIUM; 0 MG CHOLESTEROL; 3 G DIETARY FIBER

REDUCED CHOLESTEROL AND FAT

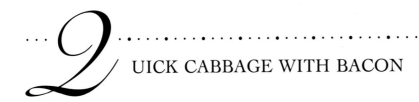

QUICK CABBAGE WITH BACON

Use leftovers to turn this into a main dish by adding cooked chicken or turkey. Reheat in the microwave oven for a no-fuss meal.

MAKES 4 SERVINGS

8 cups thinly sliced green
   cabbage
1 cup sliced onions
1 cup sliced red bell peppers
2 teaspoons olive *or* vegetable oil
1 garlic clove, minced

¼ cup canned ready-to-serve low-
   sodium chicken broth
1 tablespoon dry sherry
¼ ounce (about 1½ teaspoons)
   bacon bits (made from real
   bacon)

1   In 4-quart microwavable casserole place cabbage, onions, peppers, oil, and garlic and toss to combine. Cover and microwave on High (100%) for 5 minutes, until cabbage is wilted.

2   Add remaining ingredients and microwave on High for 5 minutes, until thoroughly heated. Toss again before serving.

EACH SERVING PROVIDES: ½ FAT; 5 VEGETABLES; 15 OPTIONAL CALORIES

PER SERVING: 92 CALORIES; 3 G PROTEIN; 4 G FAT; 13 G CARBOHYDRATE; 79 MG CALCIUM; 59 MG SODIUM; 2 MG CHOLESTEROL; 4 G DIETARY FIBER

Variation: Quick Cabbage—Omit bacon bits from recipe. In Serving Information decrease Optional Calories to 5.

PER SERVING: 82 CALORIES; 3 G PROTEIN; 3 G FAT; 13 G CARBOHYDRATE; 79 MG CALCIUM; 31 MG SODIUM; 0 MG CHOLESTEROL; 4 G DIETARY FIBER

REDUCED CHOLESTEROL AND SODIUM

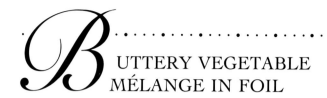

BUTTERY VEGETABLE MÉLANGE IN FOIL

MAKES 2 SERVINGS

1 small ear corn on the cob (5 inches long), husk and silk removed, and cut crosswise into 4 equal pieces
5-ounce baking potato, cut into 8 pieces
1 cup red bell pepper strips
1 cup sliced onions
1 cup diagonally sliced carrots
1 garlic clove, sliced
1 tablespoon whipped butter, melted
2 teaspoons olive oil
2 teaspoons lemon juice
1 tablespoon chopped fresh basil *or* 1 teaspoon basil leaves

1 Preheat barbecue or gas grill on high for 10 minutes. Fold two 24-inch-long pieces of heavy-duty foil in half crosswise; set aside.

2 In large mixing bowl combine corn, potato, pepper, onions, carrots, and garlic. In small bowl combine butter, oil, and lemon juice; pour over vegetable mixture and toss to coat.

3 In center of each sheet of foil arrange half of the vegetable mixture. Sprinkle half of the basil over each portion. Gather corners of foil and twist to seal.

4 Arrange packets on rack and cook until potato is tender, about 15 minutes.

5 Remove packets from grill and carefully pierce top of each packet to release steam. Open packets and arrange on serving platter.

EACH SERVING PROVIDES: 1 FAT; 3 VEGETABLES; 1 BREAD; 25 OPTIONAL CALORIES
PER SERVING: 235 CALORIES; 5 G PROTEIN; 9 G FAT; 36 G CARBOHYDRATE; 72 MG CALCIUM; 80 MG SODIUM; 10 MG CHOLESTEROL; 7 G DIETARY FIBER

Variation: Vegetable Mélange in Foil—Omit butter. In Serving Information omit Optional Calories.

PER SERVING: 201 CALORIES; 5 G PROTEIN; 6 G FAT; 36 G CARBOHYDRATE; 71 MG CALCIUM; 40 MG SODIUM; 0 MG CHOLESTEROL; 7 G DIETARY FIBER
REDUCED CHOLESTEROL AND SODIUM

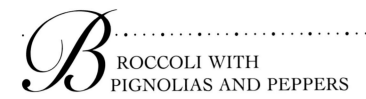

BROCCOLI WITH PIGNOLIAS AND PEPPERS

MAKES 1 SERVING

¼ ounce pignolias (pine nuts)
½ cup red bell pepper strips
¼ cup chopped onion

1 garlic clove, minced
2 cups broccoli florets

1   In 1-quart microwavable casserole microwave pignolias on High (100%) for 1 minute, stirring every 20 seconds, until toasted. Transfer pignolias to a plate; set aside.

2   In same casserole combine pepper, onion, and garlic; cover and microwave on High for 2 minutes, until onion is translucent. Add broccoli and *¼ cup water* and stir to combine; cover and microwave on High for 2 minutes, stirring once halfway through cooking, until broccoli is tender. Drain water and discard.

3   Return pignolias to casserole; stir to combine and let stand for 1 minute.

EACH SERVING PROVIDES: ½ FAT; ¼ PROTEIN; 5½ VEGETABLES
PER SERVING: 146 CALORIES; 12 G PROTEIN; 5 G FAT; 22 G CARBOHYDRATE; 132 MG CALCIUM; 65 MG SODIUM; 0 MG CHOLESTEROL; 1 G DIETARY FIBER (THIS FIGURE DOES NOT INCLUDE BROCCOLI FLORETS AND PIGNOLIAS; NUTRITION ANALYSIS NOT AVAILABLE)
REDUCED CHOLESTEROL, FAT AND SODIUM

MARINATED LEEKS

MAKES 2 SERVINGS

6 medium thoroughly washed leeks (white portion and some green), cut into halves lengthwise

2 teaspoons granulated sugar
2 teaspoons pickling spice
2 teaspoons apple cider vinegar
2 teaspoons lemon juice

1 In an 8 × 8 × 2-inch microwavable baking dish arrange leeks in a single layer; add *1 cup water,* cover, and microwave on High (100%) for 10 minutes, until tender. Drain leeks, reserving ¼ cup cooking liquid.

2 In small mixing bowl combine reserved cooking liquid and remaining ingredients; pour over leeks. Cover and refrigerate at least 1 hour or overnight.

EACH SERVING PROVIDES: 3 VEGETABLES; 20 OPTIONAL CALORIES
PER SERVING: 65 CALORIES; 1 G PROTEIN; 0.2 G FAT; 16 G CARBOHYDRATE; 47 MG CALCIUM; 17 MG SODIUM; 0 MG CHOLESTEROL; 1 G DIETARY FIBER
REDUCED CHOLESTEROL, FAT AND SODIUM

LIMA BEANS WITH TOMATOES

MAKES 2 SERVINGS

2 tablespoons finely chopped
   shallots *or* onion
1 teaspoon vegetable oil
1 cup frozen green lima beans
½ cup canned Italian tomatoes
   (reserve liquid), seeded and
   chopped

1 teaspoon chopped fresh thyme
   or ⅛ teaspoon thyme leaves
½ teaspoon cornstarch
   Dash pepper

1 In 1-quart microwavable casserole combine shallots and oil and stir to coat. Cover and microwave on High (100%) for 1 minute, until shallots are translucent.

2 Add lima beans, tomatoes, and thyme. Cover and microwave on High for 5 minutes, stirring once halfway through cooking, until mixture is thoroughly heated.

3 Using a wire whisk, in small mixing bowl combine reserved tomato liquid, *2 tablespoons water,* the cornstarch, and pepper. Stir into lima bean–tomato mixture. Cover and microwave on High for 1 minute, until mixture thickens slightly.

EACH SERVING PROVIDES: ½ FAT; ½ VEGETABLE; 1 BREAD; 3 OPTIONAL CALORIES
PER SERVING: 127 CALORIES; 6 G PROTEIN; 3 G FAT; 21 G CARBOHYDRATE; 40 MG CALCIUM; 146 MG SODIUM; 0 MG CHOLESTEROL; 11 G DIETARY FIBER
REDUCED CHOLESTEROL, FAT AND SODIUM

GLAZED JICAMA AND CARROT SAUTÉ

MAKES 2 SERVINGS

1½ cups julienne-cut pared jicama
1½ cups julienne-cut carrots
  2 tablespoons plus 2 teaspoons
    dry white table wine

1 tablespoon thawed frozen
    concentrated apple juice
    (no sugar added)
¼ teaspoon ground cumin

1 Spray 10-inch nonstick skillet with nonstick cooking spray; add jicama and carrots and cook over high heat, stirring frequently, for 3 minutes.

2 Reduce heat to medium. Add *½ cup water,* the wine, and apple juice concentrate; cover and cook for 2 minutes. Stir vegetable mixture; cover and cook until vegetables are tender, about 3 minutes. (If necessary, add additional water, 1 teaspoon at a time, to prevent vegetables from sticking.)

3 Stir in cumin and cook, uncovered, until vegetables are glazed, about 1 minute.

EACH SERVING PROVIDES: 3 VEGETABLES; ¼ FRUIT; 15 OPTIONAL CALORIES
PER SERVING: 105 CALORIES; 2 G PROTEIN; 1 G FAT; 20 G CARBOHYDRATE; 42 MG CALCIUM; 38 MG SODIUM; 0 MG CHOLESTEROL; 4 G DIETARY FIBER
REDUCED CHOLESTEROL, FAT AND SODIUM

EGGPLANT BOATS

MAKES 2 SERVINGS

1 small eggplant (about ¾ pound)
⅛ teaspoon salt
½ cup chopped onion
½ cup shredded carrot
1 teaspoon margarine
¾ cup plain nonfat yogurt
1½ teaspoons cornstarch

½ ounce almonds, finely chopped and divided
2 tablespoons dark raisins, chopped, divided
1 tablespoon plus 1½ teaspoons seasoned dried bread crumbs

1 Cut eggplant in half lengthwise. Remove pulp from each half, leaving ¼-inch-thick shells. Sprinkle inside of each shell evenly with salt and set aside. Dice eggplant pulp.

2 In 1-quart microwavable casserole combine diced eggplant, the onion, carrot, and margarine. Cover and microwave on High (100%) for 4 minutes, stirring once after 1 minute, until eggplant is tender.

3 Add yogurt and cornstarch to eggplant mixture in casserole and stir to combine. Cover and microwave on High for 1 minute, until mixture thickens. Add half of the almonds and 1 tablespoon plus 1 teaspoon raisins to the eggplant mixture and stir to combine. Set aside.

4 In small mixing bowl combine remaining almonds, remaining raisins, and the bread crumbs; set aside.

5 Fill each reserved eggplant shell with half of the eggplant mixture and sprinkle each with half of the almond mixture.

6 Set eggplant shells in 1-quart microwavable casserole. Cover and microwave on High for 9 minutes, rotating casserole ¼ turn every 3 minutes. Let stand for 2 minutes, until thoroughly heated.

EACH SERVING PROVIDES: ½ MILK; 1 FAT; ¼ PROTEIN; 3 VEGETABLES; ¼ BREAD; ½ FRUIT; 10 OPTIONAL CALORIES

PER SERVING: 223 CALORIES; 10 G PROTEIN; 6 G FAT; 35 G CARBOHYDRATE; 266 MG CALCIUM; 392 MG SODIUM; 2 MG CHOLESTEROL; 5 G DIETARY FIBER

REDUCED CHOLESTEROL AND FAT

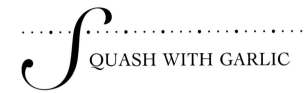

SQUASH WITH GARLIC

MAKES 1 SERVING

¾ cup sliced yellow squash
¾ cup sliced zucchini
1 teaspoon margarine
1 garlic clove, minced

½ teaspoon lemon juice
⅛ teaspoon oregano leaves
Dash pepper

1 In 1-quart microwavable casserole place all ingredients, tossing to combine.

2 Cover and microwave on High (100%) for 4 minutes, stirring once halfway through cooking. Let stand 1 minute, until squash is tender.

EACH SERVING PROVIDES: 1 FAT; 3 VEGETABLES

PER SERVING: 72 CALORIES; 2 G PROTEIN; 4 G FAT; 8 G CARBOHYDRATE; 46 MG CALCIUM; 51 MG SODIUM; 0 MG CHOLESTEROL; 2 G DIETARY FIBER

REDUCED CHOLESTEROL AND SODIUM

SPAGHETTI SQUASH

Bake this versatile vegetable and store the pulp in your freezer. We've included it in four tempting recipes. Try it as a salad, side dish, or entrée.

YIELD: 6 CUPS

1 spaghetti squash (about 3 pounds)

1 Cut squash in half lengthwise. Remove and discard seeds. In microwavable baking dish large enough to hold them, set squash halves, cut-side down. Add 1 cup water and microwave on High (100%) for 20 minutes, rotating casserole ½ turn every 5 minutes, until squash is tender.

2 Remove from oven and let squash stand for 5 minutes. Remove squash from water and let stand until cool enough to handle. Using a fork, scoop out pulp.

3 Store ½-cup servings of pulp in resealable plastic freezer bags or containers. Label and freeze for up to 1 month.

EACH ½-CUP SERVING PROVIDES: 1 VEGETABLE

PER SERVING: 53 CALORIES; 1 G PROTEIN; 1 G FAT; 11 G CARBOHYDRATE; 37 MG CALCIUM; 27 MG SODIUM; 0 MG CHOLESTEROL; DIETARY FIBER DATA NOT AVAILABLE

REDUCED CHOLESTEROL, FAT AND SODIUM

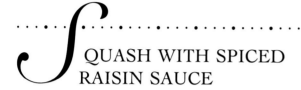

SQUASH WITH SPICED RAISIN SAUCE

The microwave oven bakes acorn squash in minutes for this delightfully sweet side dish.

MAKES 2 SERVINGS

1 pound acorn squash*	1 teaspoon maple syrup
2 tablespoons golden raisins	1 teaspoon cornstarch
½ cup apple juice (no sugar added)	¼ teaspoon ground cinnamon
	⅛ teaspoon ground allspice

1 Cut squash in half lengthwise and discard seeds and membranes. Set squash halves, cut-side up, in an 8 × 8 × 2-inch microwavable baking dish. Pour *¼ cup water* into dish, cover, and microwave on High (100%) for 5 minutes.

2 Fill cavity of each squash half with 1 tablespoon raisins.

3 In 1-cup liquid measure combine remaining ingredients, stirring to dissolve cornstarch. Pour half of mixture into each squash cavity. Cover and microwave on High for 2 minutes, until squash is fork-tender and liquid thickens.

EACH SERVING PROVIDES: ½ BREAD; 1 FRUIT; 15 OPTIONAL CALORIES

PER SERVING: 140 CALORIES; 2 G PROTEIN; 0.3 G FAT; 36 G CARBOHYDRATE; 74 MG CALCIUM; 9 MG SODIUM; 0 MG CHOLESTEROL; 7 G DIETARY FIBER

REDUCED CHOLESTEROL, FAT AND SODIUM

* A 1-pound acorn squash will yield about 7 ounces cooked squash.

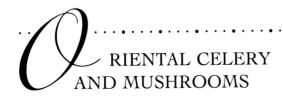

ORIENTAL CELERY AND MUSHROOMS

Add cooked shrimp, chicken, or turkey to this side dish and it becomes an entrée.

MAKES 2 SERVINGS

1 cup diagonally sliced celery
1 cup sliced shiitake *or* white
    mushrooms
½ cup thinly sliced onion

1 tablespoon reduced-sodium soy
    sauce
½ teaspoon cornstarch

1 Spray 1-quart microwavable casserole with nonstick cooking spray; add celery, mushrooms, onion, and *1 tablespoon water.* Cover and microwave on High (100%) for 4 minutes, stirring once halfway through cooking, until celery is tender.

2 Using a wire whisk, in small mixing bowl beat together *3 tablespoons water,* the soy sauce, and cornstarch, stirring to dissolve cornstarch. Add to vegetable mixture and stir to combine; cover and microwave on High for 1½ minutes, until mixture thickens.

EACH SERVING PROVIDES: 2½ VEGETABLES; 3 OPTIONAL CALORIES
PER SERVING: 39 CALORIES; 2 G PROTEIN; 0.3 G FAT; 8 G CARBOHYDRATE; 35 MG CALCIUM; 355 MG SODIUM; 0 MG CHOLESTEROL; 2 G DIETARY FIBER
REDUCED CHOLESTEROL AND FAT

WATERCRESS WITH SESAME SEED

MAKES 1 SERVING

1 teaspoon sesame seed
1 garlic clove, minced
¾ teaspoon peanut oil
2 cups thoroughly washed and
    drained watercress* (thick
    stems removed)
¼ teaspoon Chinese sesame oil

1   On small microwavable plate arrange sesame seed; microwave on High
    (100%) for 3 minutes. Set aside.

2   In 1-quart microwavable casserole combine garlic and peanut oil; cover
    and microwave on High for 1 minute.

3   Add watercress and *1 teaspoon water* to casserole; cover and microwave
    on High for 3 minutes, stirring once halfway through cooking. Add
    sesame seed and sesame oil and stir to combine.

EACH SERVING PROVIDES: 1 FAT; 1 VEGETABLE; 20 OPTIONAL CALORIES
PER SERVING: 69 CALORIES; 2 G PROTEIN; 6 G FAT; 3 G CARBOHYDRATE; 116 MG
CALCIUM; 29 MG SODIUM; 0 MG CHOLESTEROL; 2 G DIETARY FIBER
REDUCED CHOLESTEROL AND SODIUM

* 2 cups watercress yield about ½ cup cooked watercress.

YAM-STUFFED APPLES

MAKES 2 SERVINGS, 1 APPLE EACH

¼ pound yam *or* sweet potato, pared, diced
2 small Golden Delicious apples (¼ pound each)
1 tablespoon minced shallot *or* onion

2 teaspoons margarine
¼ teaspoon ground nutmeg *or* cinnamon
Mint sprig for garnish (optional)

1 In medium microwavable mixing bowl combine *2 cups water* and the yam. Microwave on High (100%) for 3 minutes.

2 Core apples, being careful not to cut through bottoms of apples. Scoop out pulp from each apple, leaving ¼-inch-thick shells and reserving pulp; set shells aside.

3 Add apple pulp and shallot to yam and microwave on High for 3 minutes. Drain yam-apple mixture, discarding cooking liquid. Add margarine and nutmeg and, using a fork, mash mixture until smooth.

4 Fill each apple shell with half of the yam-apple mixture. Set apple shells in an 8 × 8 × 2-inch microwavable baking dish, cover, and microwave on High for 4 minutes, until thoroughly heated. Garnish with mint sprig.

EACH SERVING PROVIDES: 1 FAT; ½ BREAD; 1 FRUIT
PER SERVING: 168 CALORIES; 1 G PROTEIN; 4 G FAT; 33 G CARBOHYDRATE; 21 MG CALCIUM; 50 MG SODIUM; 0 MG CHOLESTEROL; 5 G DIETARY FIBER
REDUCED CHOLESTEROL, FAT AND SODIUM

GINGERSNAP YAMS

MAKES 2 SERVINGS

½ pound pared yams *or* sweet
   potatoes, diced
2 tablespoons low-fat milk (1%
   milk fat), heated
½ ounce gingersnap cookies,
   made into crumbs

2 teaspoons margarine, melted
1½ teaspoons firmly packed light
   brown sugar

1　Preheat oven to 350°F. In 1½-quart saucepan add yams to boiling water; cook until fork-tender, about 15 minutes.

2　Drain yams, discarding cooking liquid; transfer to medium mixing bowl. Using electric mixer on low speed, beat yams until mashed; add milk and beat on medium speed until smooth and fluffy.

3　Spray 2-cup casserole with nonstick cooking spray; spread yam mixture in casserole; set aside.

4　In small mixing bowl combine remaining ingredients, mixing well. Sprinkle evenly over yam mixture. Bake until mixture is thoroughly heated, about 15 minutes.

EACH SERVING PROVIDES: 1 FAT; 1 BREAD; 60 OPTIONAL CALORIES
PER SERVING: 217 CALORIES; 3 G PROTEIN; 5 G FAT; 41 G CARBOHYDRATE; 48 MG CALCIUM; 104 MG SODIUM; 3 MG CHOLESTEROL; 4 G DIETARY FIBER
REDUCED CHOLESTEROL, FAT AND SODIUM

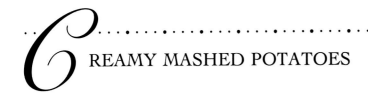

CREAMY MASHED POTATOES

Mashed potatoes with that old-fashioned taste, thanks to light sour cream.

MAKES 2 SERVINGS
(SHOWN WITH MARINATED PORK TENDERLOIN; SEE PAGE 178)

½ cup finely chopped onion
2 teaspoons reduced-calorie
   margarine (tub)
½ cup skim *or* nonfat milk

1½ ounces instant potato flakes
2 tablespoons light sour cream
Dash salt
Freshly ground pepper

In 2-cup microwavable casserole combine onion and margarine; microwave on High (100%) for 2 minutes, until margarine is melted. Stir in milk and *⅓ cup water.* Microwave on High for 2 minutes; stir in potato flakes and sour cream. Microwave on Medium (50%) for 2 minutes, stirring once halfway through cooking. Stir in salt and a few grinds fresh pepper.

EACH SERVING PROVIDES: ¼ MILK; ½ FAT; ½ VEGETABLE; 1 BREAD; 25 OPTIONAL CALORIES
PER SERVING: 154 CALORIES; 5 G PROTEIN; 4 G FAT; 25 G CARBOHYDRATE; 93 MG CALCIUM; 164 MG SODIUM; 6 MG CHOLESTEROL; 1 G DIETARY FIBER
REDUCED CHOLESTEROL, FAT AND SODIUM

LEMON POTATOES

Plan a Sunday outing that includes Lemon Potatoes in the picnic basket. Prepare ahead and store in a resealable plastic container.

MAKES 2 SERVINGS

2 teaspoons olive *or* vegetable oil
10 ounces red potatoes, cut into
  ¼-inch-thick slices
½ cup canned ready-to-serve
  reduced-sodium chicken
  broth

1 tablespoon lemon juice
1 teaspoon grated lemon peel
1 teaspoon chopped fresh parsley
1 garlic clove, minced
⅛ teaspoon pepper

1 In 12-inch nonstick skillet heat oil; arrange potatoes in a single layer in skillet and cook over medium-high heat until bottoms are browned, 3 to 4 minutes. Turn potatoes over and cook until other sides are browned, 3 to 4 minutes.

2 Add remaining ingredients to skillet and stir to combine. Reduce heat to low, cover, and let cook until potatoes are tender, about 5 minutes. Serve warm or chilled.

EACH SERVING PROVIDES: 1 FAT; 1 BREAD; 10 OPTIONAL CALORIES
PER SERVING: 165 CALORIES; 4 G PROTEIN; 5 G FAT; 27 G CARBOHYDRATE; 10 MG CALCIUM; 190 MG SODIUM; 0 MG CHOLESTEROL; 2 G DIETARY FIBER
REDUCED CHOLESTEROL, FAT AND SODIUM

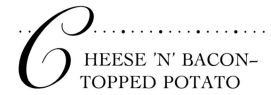

CHEESE 'N' BACON–TOPPED POTATO

MAKES 1 SERVING

5-ounce baking potato, scrubbed
¾ ounce reduced-fat Swiss cheese, shredded, divided
2 tablespoons plain low-fat yogurt

1 teaspoon chopped fresh chives
1 teaspoon reduced-calorie mayonnaise
1 teaspoon bacon bits (made from real bacon), divided
Dash pepper

1. Using tines of a fork, pierce potato in several places. Set potato on microwavable plate and microwave on High (100%) for 5 minutes, rotating plate ½ turn halfway through cooking. Let stand 1 minute, until potato is tender.

2. Cut potato in half lengthwise and, using a spoon, scoop out pulp from potato halves, leaving ¼-inch-thick shells; reserve shells.

3. In medium mixing bowl combine potato pulp, ½ ounce cheese, the yogurt, chives, mayonnaise, ½ teaspoon bacon bits, and the pepper, stirring to combine thoroughly. Spoon half of potato mixture into each reserved potato shell.

4. Sprinkle remaining cheese and bacon bits evenly over filled potato shells. Microwave on High for 1 minute, until cheese is melted.

EACH SERVING PROVIDES: ½ FAT; 1 PROTEIN; 1 BREAD; 45 OPTIONAL CALORIES
PER SERVING: 217 CALORIES; 13 G PROTEIN; 7 G FAT; 27 G CARBOHYDRATE; 334 MG CALCIUM; 127 MG SODIUM; 20 MG CHOLESTEROL; 3 G DIETARY FIBER

Variation: Cheese-Topped Potato—Omit bacon bits. In Serving Information decrease Optional Calories to 15.

PER SERVING: 204 CALORIES; 12 G PROTEIN; 6 G FAT; 27 G CARBOHYDRATE; 334 MG CALCIUM; 91 MG SODIUM; 18 MG CHOLESTEROL; 3 G DIETARY FIBER
REDUCED CHOLESTEROL, FAT AND SODIUM

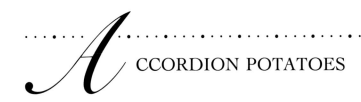

ACCORDION POTATOES

MAKES 2 SERVINGS, 2 POTATO HALVES EACH

2 baking potatoes (5 ounces each), cut in half lengthwise

2 teaspoons olive *or* vegetable oil, divided

2 teaspoons Italian seasoning, divided

2 tablespoons finely chopped red bell pepper

2 tablespoons grated Parmesan cheese

1 Preheat oven to 400°F. Set each potato half, cut-side down, on clean work surface. Cut each potato half crosswise into ¼-inch-thick slices, *making sure to cut only ¾ of the way through.* Transfer potato halves to nonstick baking sheet.

2 Brush each potato half with ¼ teaspoon oil and sprinkle each with ¼ teaspoon Italian seasoning. Bake until tender, about 30 minutes.

3 In small nonstick skillet heat remaining oil; add pepper and cook over medium-high heat, stirring frequently, until tender-crisp, about 30 seconds. Remove from heat; stir in remaining Italian seasoning and the cheese.

4 To serve, spoon pepper mixture evenly over each potato half.

EACH SERVING PROVIDES: 1 FAT; ⅛ VEGETABLE; 1 BREAD; 30 OPTIONAL CALORIES
PER SERVING: 175 CALORIES; 5 G PROTEIN; 6 G FAT; 25 G CARBOHYDRATE; 87 MG CALCIUM; 120 MG SODIUM; 4 MG CHOLESTEROL; 3 G DIETARY FIBER
REDUCED CHOLESTEROL AND SODIUM

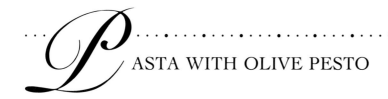

PASTA WITH OLIVE PESTO

MAKES 4 SERVINGS

½ cup firmly packed Italian (flat-leaf) parsley
¼ cup pimiento
10 small pimiento-stuffed green olives
¾ ounce Parmesan cheese, grated
½ ounce pignolias (pine nuts), toasted

2 teaspoons olive oil
1 teaspoon balsamic *or* red wine vinegar
1 small garlic clove
3 cups cooked small shell macaroni (hot)

1 In food processor combine all ingredients except macaroni and process until pureed, scraping down sides of work bowl as necessary.

2 Arrange macaroni in serving bowl; add pesto and toss well to coat.

EACH SERVING PROVIDES: 1 FAT; ¼ PROTEIN; ⅛ VEGETABLE; 1½ BREADS; 10 OPTIONAL CALORIES

PER SERVING: 225 CALORIES; 8 G PROTEIN; 7 G FAT; 32 G CARBOHYDRATE; 98 MG CALCIUM; 280 MG SODIUM; 4 MG CHOLESTEROL; 2 G DIETARY FIBER (THIS FIGURE DOES NOT INCLUDE PIMIENTO; NUTRITION ANALYSIS NOT AVAILABLE)

REDUCED CHOLESTEROL AND FAT

PASTA WITH CREAMY TOMATO SAUCE

MAKES 2 SERVINGS

1 teaspoon margarine
¼ cup minced onion
1 garlic clove, minced
½ cup canned Italian tomatoes
   (reserve liquid), seeded and
   chopped
2 tablespoons dry white table
   wine
¼ teaspoon dried Italian
   seasoning

⅓ cup plus 2 teaspoons part-skim
   ricotta cheese
¼ cup low-fat milk (1% milk fat)
2 cups cooked penne *or* ziti
   macaroni (hot)
½ ounce Parmesan cheese, grated
   and divided
   Dash pepper

1 In 9-inch nonstick skillet melt margarine; add onion and garlic and cook over medium-high heat, stirring occasionally, until softened, about 2 minutes.

2 Stir in tomatoes with reserved liquid, the wine, and Italian seasoning. Reduce heat to medium and cook, stirring occasionally, for 5 minutes.

3 In blender combine ricotta cheese and milk and process on high speed for 1 minute, scraping down sides of container as necessary.

4 Stir ricotta-cheese mixture into skillet. Add pasta, all but 1 teaspoon of the Parmesan cheese, and the pepper and toss to coat.

5 To serve, transfer pasta mixture to serving bowl and sprinkle with remaining Parmesan cheese.

EACH SERVING PROVIDES: ½ FAT; ¾ PROTEIN; ¾ VEGETABLE; 2 BREADS; 45 OPTIONAL CALORIES
PER SERVING: 355 CALORIES; 17 G PROTEIN; 9 G FAT; 49 G CARBOHYDRATE; 296 MG CALCIUM; 330 MG SODIUM; 21 MG CHOLESTEROL; 3 G DIETARY FIBER
REDUCED CHOLESTEROL AND FAT

BUCKWHEAT PASTA SALAD

MAKES 2 SERVINGS

1½ ounces uncooked buckwheat
    pasta (soba) *or* spaghetti
¼ cup diagonally sliced carrot
¼ cup sliced seeded pared
    cucumber
¼ cup sliced radishes
¼ cup diagonally sliced scallions
    (green onions), green
    portion only

1 tablespoon reduced-sodium
    soy sauce
1½ teaspoons dry sherry
1½ teaspoons peanut *or* vegetable
    oil
1 garlic clove, minced
½ teaspoon minced pared
    gingerroot
½ teaspoon Chinese sesame oil

1 In 1-quart microwavable casserole microwave *2 cups water* on High (100%) for 5 minutes, until water comes to a full boil. Stir in pasta; cover and microwave on High for 3 minutes. Stir in carrot and microwave on High for 2 minutes, until tender-crisp. Pour pasta-carrot mixture into colander and hold under running cold water to stop the cooking process; drain well.

2 Transfer pasta-carrot mixture to salad bowl; add remaining ingredients and toss to combine. Serve immediately or cover and refrigerate until chilled, about 30 minutes.

EACH SERVING PROVIDES: 1 FAT; 1 VEGETABLE; 1 BREAD; 3 OPTIONAL CALORIES
PER SERVING WITH BUCKWHEAT PASTA: 138 CALORIES; 4 G PROTEIN; 5 G FAT; 21 G CARBOHYDRATE; 29 MG CALCIUM; 479 MG SODIUM; 0 MG CHOLESTEROL; 1 G DIETARY FIBER (THIS FIGURE DOES NOT INCLUDE BUCKWHEAT PASTA; NUTRITION ANALYSIS NOT AVAILABLE)
WITH SPAGHETTI: 146 CALORIES; 4 G PROTEIN; 5 G FAT; 21 G CARBOHYDRATE; 26 MG CALCIUM; 312 MG SODIUM; 0 MG CHOLESTEROL; 2 G DIETARY FIBER

REDUCED CHOLESTEROL

PASTA PRIMAVERA

A wide assortment of vegetables can be used in this recipe. Be creative and come up with your own combinations.

MAKES 2 SERVINGS

2 teaspoons olive oil
6 medium asparagus spears, cut into 1-inch pieces
½ cup sliced yellow squash
½ cup diced red bell pepper
2 garlic cloves, minced
½ cup canned ready-to-serve low-sodium chicken broth
1 tablespoon chopped fresh parsley

1 tablespoon chopped fresh basil *or* ½ teaspoon basil leaves
1½ cups cooked thin spaghetti (hot)
1 tablespoon grated Parmesan cheese

1 In 10-inch nonstick skillet heat oil; add asparagus, squash, pepper, and garlic and cook over medium-high heat, stirring occasionally, until squash is softened, 1 to 2 minutes.

2 Stir in broth, parsley, and basil. Reduce heat to low, cover, and cook until asparagus is tender, about 5 minutes.

3 Add spaghetti to vegetable mixture and, using two forks, toss to combine. Transfer to serving bowl and sprinkle with cheese.

EACH SERVING PROVIDES: 1 FAT; 1½ VEGETABLES; 1½ BREADS; 25 OPTIONAL CALORIES
PER SERVING: 235 CALORIES; 9 G PROTEIN; 7 G FAT; 36 G CARBOHYDRATE; 76 MG CALCIUM; 65 MG SODIUM; 2 MG CHOLESTEROL; 3 G DIETARY FIBER
REDUCED CHOLESTEROL, FAT AND SODIUM

ORZO PROVENÇAL

MAKES 2 SERVINGS

½ cup shredded zucchini
½ medium tomato, diced
¼ cup diced red onion
1 tablespoon chopped fresh
    mint
1 tablespoon chopped fresh
    Italian (flat-leaf) parsley
1 tablespoon lemon juice

2 teaspoons olive oil
1 garlic clove, minced
   Dash pepper
2¼ ounces uncooked orzo (rice-
    shaped pasta), cooked
    according to package
    directions and drained

In medium mixing bowl place all ingredients except orzo and toss to combine.
Add orzo and stir to combine.

EACH SERVING PROVIDES: 1 FAT; 1¼ VEGETABLES; 1½ BREADS

PER SERVING: 181 CALORIES; 5 G PROTEIN; 5 G FAT; 29 G CARBOHYDRATE; 25 MG
CALCIUM; 9 MG SODIUM; 0 MG CHOLESTEROL; 2 G DIETARY FIBER

REDUCED CHOLESTEROL, FAT AND SODIUM

MACARONI SALAD

Yogurt, rather than mayonnaise, is the dressing for this salad. Enjoy great taste minus the fat.

MAKES 2 SERVINGS

1 cup cooked elbow macaroni, chilled
1 hard-cooked egg, finely chopped
¼ cup plain low-fat yogurt
2 tablespoons diced pimiento
1 tablespoon chopped scallion (green onion)
Dash pepper

In medium mixing bowl combine all ingredients, mixing well. Cover and refrigerate until flavors blend, at least 1 hour.

EACH SERVING PROVIDES: ½ PROTEIN; ⅛ VEGETABLE; 1 BREAD; 15 OPTIONAL CALORIES

PER SERVING: 159 CALORIES; 8 G PROTEIN; 4 G FAT; 23 G CARBOHYDRATE; 72 MG CALCIUM; 55 MG SODIUM; 108 MG CHOLESTEROL; 1 G DIETARY FIBER (THIS FIGURE DOES NOT INCLUDE PIMIENTO; NUTRITION ANALYSIS NOT AVAILABLE)

REDUCED FAT AND SODIUM

BROWN RICE PILAF

MAKES 4 SERVINGS

½ cup shredded carrot
½ cup chopped thoroughly washed leek (white portion and some green)
1 ounce sliced almonds
2 teaspoons margarine
4 ounces uncooked fast-cooking whole grain brown rice
⅓ cup apricot nectar
¼ cup dried currants *or* dark raisins
6 dried apricot halves (¾ ounce), thinly sliced

1 In 2-quart microwavable casserole combine vegetables, almonds, and margarine; microwave on High (100%) for 1 minute. Stir in *1 cup water,* the rice, and apricot nectar. Cover and microwave on High for 4 minutes.

2 Stir in fruits; cover and microwave on Medium (50%) for 5 minutes, stirring once halfway through cooking. Let stand for 5 minutes. Using a fork, fluff rice.

EACH SERVING PROVIDES: 1 FAT; ¼ PROTEIN; ½ VEGETABLE; 1 BREAD; 1 FRUIT
PER SERVING: 219 CALORIES; 5 G PROTEIN; 7 G FAT; 40 G CARBOHYDRATE; 43 MG CALCIUM; 44 MG SODIUM; 0 MG CHOLESTEROL; 3 G DIETARY FIBER
REDUCED CHOLESTEROL, FAT AND SODIUM

ORIENTAL RICE

MAKES 1 SERVING

½ cup sliced scallions (green onions), divided
1 garlic clove, minced
½ teaspoon grated pared gingerroot
1½ ounces uncooked quick-cooking rice

½ cup canned ready-to-serve low-sodium chicken broth
½ teaspoon seasoned rice vinegar

1 In 2-cup microwavable casserole combine ¼ cup scallions, the garlic, and gingerroot. Cover and microwave on High (100%) for 1 minute. Add rice and broth and stir to combine; cover and microwave on High for 6 minutes, stirring once every 2 minutes. Microwave on Medium (50%) for 6 minutes, stirring once every 2 minutes.

2 Add remaining scallions and the vinegar and stir to combine; let stand for 1 minute. Using a fork, fluff rice.

EACH SERVING PROVIDES: 1 VEGETABLE; 1½ BREADS; 20 OPTIONAL CALORIES
PER SERVING: 197 CALORIES; 5 G PROTEIN; 1 G FAT; 41 G CARBOHYDRATE; 43 MG CALCIUM; 47 MG SODIUM; 0 MG CHOLESTEROL; 2 G DIETARY FIBER
REDUCED CHOLESTEROL, FAT AND SODIUM

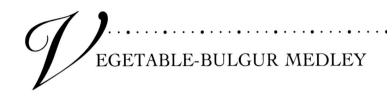

VEGETABLE-BULGUR MEDLEY

MAKES 4 SERVINGS

1 cup sliced shiitake *or* white
    mushrooms
1 cup chopped thoroughly
    washed leeks (white portion
    and some green)
1 tablespoon seeded and minced
    hot *or* mild chili pepper
2 garlic cloves, minced
2 teaspoons olive oil
¼ pound uncooked bulgur
    (cracked wheat)

2 large plum tomatoes, blanched,
    peeled, seeded, and cut into
    strips
1 ounce walnuts, toasted and
    chopped
1 teaspoon chopped fresh cilantro
    (Chinese parsley) *or* Italian
    (flat-leaf) parsley
1 teaspoon Mexican seasoning
1 teaspoon lime juice (no sugar
    added)

1 In 1-quart microwavable casserole combine mushrooms, leeks, pepper, garlic, and oil and stir to coat. Cover and microwave on High (100%) for 3 minutes, stirring once halfway through cooking, until mushrooms soften.

2 Add *1 cup water* and the bulgur and stir to combine; cover and microwave on High for 4 minutes, stirring once halfway through cooking. Add remaining ingredients and stir to combine; cover and let stand for 5 minutes.

EACH SERVING PROVIDES: 1 FAT; ¼ PROTEIN; 1½ VEGETABLES; 1 BREAD
PER SERVING: 193 CALORIES; 6 G PROTEIN; 7 G FAT; 30 G CARBOHYDRATE; 38 MG CALCIUM; 53 MG SODIUM; 0 MG CHOLESTEROL; 6 G DIETARY FIBER
REDUCED CHOLESTEROL AND SODIUM

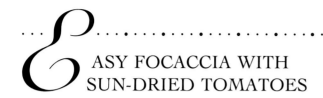

EASY FOCACCIA WITH SUN-DRIED TOMATOES

Pizza—without the sauce or cheese, but still a taste treat!

MAKES 10 SERVINGS, 1 SLICE EACH

10 sun-dried tomato halves (not packed in oil)
1 tablespoon plus 2 teaspoons olive oil, divided
4 garlic cloves, finely chopped
1 teaspoon rosemary leaves, divided

1 package refrigerated ready-to-bake pizza crust dough (10 ounces)
Dash pepper

1 In small bowl combine tomatoes with warm water to cover; set aside.

2 In small saucepan heat 1 teaspoon oil; add garlic and cook over medium-high heat until golden, about 1 minute. Remove from heat; set aside.

3 Preheat oven to 400°F. Drain tomatoes, discarding liquid. Cut tomatoes into thin strips. Add tomatoes, 1 tablespoon oil, and ½ teaspoon rosemary leaves to garlic-oil mixture and stir to combine.

4 On clean work surface unroll pizza crust dough. Spread tomato mixture over surface of pizza crust dough. Fold dough in half crosswise, then fold in half crosswise again.

5 On 12-inch round nonstick pizza pan arrange pizza crust dough. Using palms of hands and starting from center of dough, stretch dough to cover bottom of pan. Brush dough with remaining oil and sprinkle with remaining rosemary and the pepper.

6 Bake until dough is golden, about 10 minutes. Let cool slightly and cut into 10 equal slices.

EACH SERVING PROVIDES: ½ FAT; ½ VEGETABLE; 1 BREAD

PER SERVING: 102 CALORIES; 3 G PROTEIN; 3 G FAT; 15 G CARBOHYDRATE; 7 MG CALCIUM; 140 MG SODIUM; 0 MG CHOLESTEROL; 1 G DIETARY FIBER (THIS FIGURE DOES NOT INCLUDE PIZZA CRUST DOUGH; NUTRITION ANALYSIS NOT AVAILABLE)
REDUCED CHOLESTEROL, FAT AND SODIUM

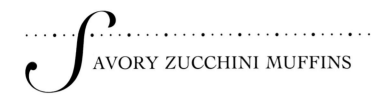

SAVORY ZUCCHINI MUFFINS

MAKES 6 SERVINGS, 2 MUFFINS EACH
(SHOWN WITH APPLE AND CHEDDAR CORN MUFFINS; SEE PAGE 4)

1½ cups shredded zucchini
1 cup all-purpose flour
¾ cup less 1 tablespoon whole
    wheat flour
¾ ounce reduced-fat Cheddar
    cheese, shredded
2 tablespoons granulated sugar
2 teaspoons double-acting
    baking powder
¼ teaspoon baking soda
¼ teaspoon pepper
⅛ teaspoon salt
½ cup plain low-fat yogurt
2 eggs
2 tablespoons vegetable oil
1 teaspoon dried *fines herbes*

1   Preheat oven to 350°F. In center of kitchen towel arrange zucchini; gather corners of towel to enclose zucchini and squeeze to remove excess liquid.

2   In large mixing bowl combine zucchini, flours, cheese, sugar, baking powder, baking soda, pepper, and salt; set aside.

3   Using a wire whisk, in small mixing bowl whisk together yogurt, eggs, oil, and *fines herbes*. Add yogurt mixture to flour mixture and stir until blended (*do not beat or overmix*).

4   Spray twelve 2½-inch-diameter muffin-pan cups with nonstick cooking spray. Fill each with an equal amount of batter (each will be about ⅔ full). Bake in middle of center oven rack for 20 minutes (until muffins are golden and a toothpick inserted in center comes out dry).

5   Set pan on wire rack and let cool slightly. Invert muffins onto wire rack and let cool.

EACH SERVING PROVIDES: 1 FAT; ½ PROTEIN; ½ VEGETABLE; 1½ BREADS; 30 OPTIONAL CALORIES

PER SERVING: 232 CALORIES; 8 G PROTEIN; 8 G FAT; 33 G CARBOHYDRATE; 158 MG CALCIUM; 283 MG SODIUM; 74 MG CHOLESTEROL; 2 G DIETARY FIBER

REDUCED FAT

DESSERTS

FOR THOSE OF US WHO ENJOY SOMETHING SWEET AT THE END of a meal, there is no greater pleasure than pondering dessert. Then there are people with a serious sweet tooth, for whom the best part of the meal *is* the dessert. The following pages feature all your favorites—puddings, tarts, strudels, meringues, chocolate—tempting treats to make hearts flutter with anticipation. What makes these desserts even more exciting is that many are prepared with few ingredients, ideal when you need a quick dessert or a treat for someone special. Orange Lace Cookies, made with seven ingredients, go from mixing bowl to cooling rack in less than a half hour. Seasonal homemade desserts make family celebrations memorable. Bring your hostess Pumpkin-Currant Bread, delicious for dessert or as a sweet table bread during the meal. The same goes for Banana Cake, a tasty way to put very ripe bananas to good use. What could be more traditional than a Holiday Fruit Cake? Packed in a colorful tin, it becomes part of a time-honored tradition. If you long for dessert at *every* meal, indulge in Carrot Muffins with Walnut-Cream Centers, cupcakelike creations that can be a special breakfast, too. To liven up your lunch bag, tote Buttery Raisin-Walnut Bars. They'll quell any afternoon cravings. Need an elegant yet easy fix? Black Forest Pie uses a ready-made graham cracker crust and frozen whipped topping. Individual Strawberry Shortcakes can be frozen to have on hand for unexpected guests. Phyllo Pirouette Cookies, made with only four ingredients, are impressive yet economical. Did someone say dessert? Love some.

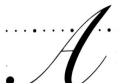

APPLE STRUDEL

MAKES 4 SERVINGS

¾ pound apples, cored, pared, and diced
2 tablespoons dark raisins
2 tablespoons granulated sugar
½ teaspoon apple pie spice
½ teaspoon cornstarch
¼ teaspoon grated lemon peel

6 frozen phyllo dough sheets (12 × 17 inches each), thawed*
2 tablespoons margarine, melted, divided
½ teaspoon confectioners' sugar

1 Preheat oven to 350°F. In medium mixing bowl place apples, raisins, granulated sugar, apple pie spice, cornstarch, and lemon peel; toss to combine.

2 On clean work surface unroll 1 sheet of phyllo dough. Cover remaining sheets of phyllo dough with plastic wrap or a slightly damp towel and set aside.

3 Using a pastry brush, brush 1 teaspoon margarine over unrolled sheet of phyllo dough. Repeat procedure, using remaining phyllo dough sheets and margarine, making a stack.

4 Spoon apple mixture over stacked phyllo dough sheets, leaving a 4-inch border on one wide side of stack and a 3-inch border on remaining sides. Fold borders over mixture. Starting from the wide side, roll jelly-roll fashion to enclose mixture. Using a paring knife, cut 4 slits in the top of the stacked phyllo dough to allow steam to escape.

5 Spray nonstick baking sheet with nonstick cooking spray and arrange strudel on baking sheet, seam-side down. Bake in middle of center oven rack for 20 minutes (until strudel is lightly browned). Cool on wire rack.

6 To serve, transfer strudel to serving platter and sprinkle evenly with confectioners' sugar.

EACH SERVING PROVIDES: 1½ FATS; 1 BREAD; 1 FRUIT; 35 OPTIONAL CALORIES
PER SERVING: 228 CALORIES; 3 G PROTEIN; 6 G FAT; 41 G CARBOHYDRATE; 11 MG CALCIUM; 194 MG SODIUM; 0 MG CHOLESTEROL; 2 G DIETARY FIBER (THIS FIGURE DOES NOT INCLUDE PHYLLO DOUGH; NUTRITION ANALYSIS NOT AVAILABLE)
REDUCED CHOLESTEROL, FAT AND SODIUM

* Phyllo dough must be thawed in the refrigerator for at least 8 hours, or overnight.

APPLE COFFEECAKE

MAKES 8 SERVINGS

1½ cups all-purpose flour
2 teaspoons double-acting
    baking powder
½ pound Golden Delicious *or*
    Granny Smith apples,
    cored, pared, and thinly
    sliced
⅓ cup plus 1 tablespoon
    granulated sugar, divided

1 tablespoon lemon juice
1 teaspoon ground cinnamon
2 tablespoons whipped butter
2 tablespoons plus 2 teaspoons
    margarine, divided
2 eggs
½ cup low-fat buttermilk (1%
    milk fat)

1 Preheat oven to 350°F. On sheet of wax paper sift together flour and baking powder; set aside.

2 In small mixing bowl place apples, 1 tablespoon sugar, the lemon juice, and cinnamon and stir to combine; set aside.

3 Using mixer on high speed, in large mixing bowl beat together butter and half of the margarine until combined; add remaining sugar and continue beating until light and fluffy. Beat in eggs. Reduce speed to low and gradually beat in flour mixture. Add buttermilk and beat until thoroughly combined.

4 Spray an 8 × 8 × 2-inch baking pan with nonstick cooking spray and spread batter evenly in pan. Arrange apple mixture in a single layer over batter. Dot apple mixture with remaining margarine. Bake in middle of center oven rack for 35 to 40 minutes (until a toothpick inserted into center comes out dry).

5 Set pan on wire rack and let cool at least 5 minutes.

EACH SERVING PROVIDES: 1 FAT; ¼ PROTEIN; 1 BREAD; ¼ FRUIT; 65 OPTIONAL CALORIES

PER SERVING: 215 CALORIES; 5 G PROTEIN; 7 G FAT; 33 G CARBOHYDRATE; 87 MG CALCIUM; 204 MG SODIUM; 59 MG CHOLESTEROL; 1 G DIETARY FIBER

BANANA CAKE

Bananas that are past their peak are perfect for this scrumptious cake.

MAKES 12 SERVINGS

2¼ cups cake flour, divided
½ cup granulated sugar
1 tablespoon double-acting baking powder
½ teaspoon baking soda
3 medium very ripe bananas (about 6 ounces each), peeled
½ cup less 2 teaspoons reduced-calorie margarine (tub)
½ cup thawed frozen egg substitute
1 teaspoon vanilla extract
¾ cup golden raisins, plumped and drained
2 ounces walnuts, finely chopped

1 Preheat oven to 375°F. Spray 9-inch round nonstick cake pan with nonstick cooking spray; sprinkle with 2 teaspoons flour, tilting pan so flour coats bottom and side. Remove excess flour and reserve.

2 In large mixing bowl combine all of the remaining flour, the sugar, baking powder, and baking soda; set aside. Using a fork, in medium mixing bowl mash bananas and margarine. Stir in egg substitute and vanilla.

3 Add banana mixture to flour mixture and stir to combine; stir in raisins and walnuts. Transfer batter to prepared pan. Bake in middle of center oven rack for 35 to 40 minutes (until cake is golden and a toothpick inserted in center comes out dry). Let cake cool in pan for 5 minutes. Remove cake from pan and set on wire rack to cool.

EACH SERVING PROVIDES: 1¼ FATS; ¼ PROTEIN; 1 BREAD; 1 FRUIT; 45 OPTIONAL CALORIES
PER SERVING: 226 CALORIES; 4 G PROTEIN; 7 G FAT; 39 G CARBOHYDRATE; 70 MG CALCIUM; 223 MG SODIUM; 0 MG CHOLESTEROL; 1 G DIETARY FIBER (THIS FIGURE DOES NOT INCLUDE CAKE FLOUR; NUTRITION ANALYSIS NOT AVAILABLE)
REDUCED CHOLESTEROL AND FAT

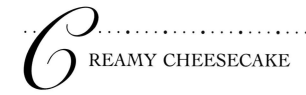

CREAMY CHEESECAKE

To make graham cracker crumbs in an instant, process graham crackers in a food processor.

MAKES 12 SERVINGS

30 graham crackers (2½-inch squares), made into crumbs
½ cup plus 2 teaspoons reduced-calorie margarine (tub), divided
1 ounce shelled almonds, toasted and finely ground
1½ cups part-skim ricotta cheese
1 cup thawed frozen egg substitute

½ cup granulated sugar
⅓ cup plus 2 teaspoons all-purpose flour
¼ cup light sour cream
3 tablespoons light cream cheese
1 teaspoon grated lemon peel

1 Preheat oven to 400°F. In medium mixing bowl combine graham cracker crumbs, ¼ cup plus 2 teaspoons margarine, and the almonds, mixing thoroughly.

2 Spray an 8-inch springform pan with nonstick cooking spray. Using the back of a spoon, press crumb mixture over bottom and up side of prepared pan. Bake in middle of center oven rack until crust is crisp and browned, about 5 minutes; set aside.

3 Reduce oven temperature to 325°F. In large mixing bowl combine remaining margarine, the ricotta cheese, egg substitute, sugar, flour, sour cream, cream cheese, and lemon peel. Using mixer on medium speed, beat until blended. Pour mixture over crust in springform pan and bake in middle of center oven rack for 30 minutes (until a knife inserted in center comes out dry).

4 Set pan on wire rack and let cool for 5 minutes. Remove side of pan and let cool completely. Cover and refrigerate until ready to serve.

EACH SERVING PROVIDES: 1¼ FATS; ¾ PROTEIN; 1 BREAD; 70 OPTIONAL CALORIES
PER SERVING: 232 CALORIES; 8 G PROTEIN; 11 G FAT; 27 G CARBOHYDRATE; 109 MG CALCIUM; 284 MG SODIUM; 13 MG CHOLESTEROL; 1 G DIETARY FIBER
REDUCED CHOLESTEROL

LEMON CHEESECAKE TARTS

MAKES 4 SERVINGS, 1 TART EACH

1 cup plain low-fat yogurt
3 tablespoons light cream cheese
1 envelope (four ½-cup servings)
  reduced-calorie instant vanilla
  pudding mix (25 calories per
  serving as packaged)

1 teaspoon grated lemon peel
4 graham cracker tart shells (¾
  ounce each)

1   In blender combine yogurt and cream cheese and process until smooth, about 30 seconds, scraping down sides of container as necessary. Add pudding mix and lemon peel and process until smooth, about 2 minutes. Scrape down sides of container and stir mixture to combine.

2   Into each tart shell spoon ¼ of the pudding mixture. Cover and refrigerate until set, about 1 hour.

EACH SERVING PROVIDES: ¼ MILK; ½ BREAD; 110 OPTIONAL CALORIES
PER SERVING: 184 CALORIES; 5 G PROTEIN; 8 G FAT; 24 G CARBOHYDRATE; 127 MG CALCIUM; 556 MG SODIUM; 9 MG CHOLESTEROL; 0 G DIETARY FIBER
REDUCED CHOLESTEROL

BLACK FOREST PIE

A ready-to-use graham cracker pie crust, purchased at your supermarket, simplifies preparation.

MAKES 8 SERVINGS

1½ cups plain low-fat yogurt
1 cup skim *or* nonfat milk
2 envelopes (four ½-cup servings each) reduced-calorie instant chocolate pudding mix (30 calories per serving as packaged)
48 fresh *or* thawed frozen pitted cherries (no sugar added), reserve 8 cherries for garnish

1 ready-to-use 9-inch graham cracker pie crust
½ cup thawed frozen dairy whipped topping

1 In blender process yogurt and milk until smooth; add pudding mix and process on high speed, scraping down sides of container as necessary until thick and smooth.

2 Transfer mixture to large mixing bowl; fold in cherries. Spread mixture in pie crust. Cover and refrigerate until firm, at least 3 hours or overnight.

3 To serve, decoratively spoon whipped topping onto pie; top with reserved cherries.

EACH SERVING PROVIDES: ¼ MILK; ½ BREAD; ½ FRUIT; 105 OPTIONAL CALORIES
PER SERVING: 214 CALORIES; 5 G PROTEIN; 7 G FAT; 33 G CARBOHYDRATE; 128 MG CALCIUM; 425 MG SODIUM; 3 MG CHOLESTEROL; 1 G DIETARY FIBER
REDUCED CHOLESTEROL AND FAT

PEAR TART

A mere six ingredients combine to make this elegant dessert.

MAKES 8 SERVINGS

1 refrigerated ready-to-bake
    9-inch pie crust
8 small Bartlett *or* Bosc pears
    (about 6 ounces each),
    cored, pared, and thinly
    sliced
1 tablespoon lemon juice

1 tablespoon honey
1 teaspoon granulated sugar
¼ teaspoon ground cardamom *or*
    ground cinnamon
    Mint sprig (optional) for
    garnish

1 Preheat oven to 450°F. Fit pie crust dough over bottom and up side of
   10-inch tart pan. Using tines of fork, prick bottom and sides of dough
   and flute edges, if desired. Bake in middle of center oven rack until crust
   is browned, about 10 minutes.

2 Decoratively arrange pear slices in tart pan; set aside.

3 In small saucepan combine lemon juice and honey; cook over low heat,
   stirring frequently, until honey is melted, about 1 minute.

4 Using a pastry brush, brush pear slices with honey mixture. Bake in
   middle of center oven rack for 15 minutes.

5 Turn oven control to broil. In small bowl combine sugar and cardamom;
   sprinkle evenly over pear slices. Broil until sugar caramelizes, 1 to 2
   minutes. Set tart on wire rack and let cool. Garnish with mint sprig.

EACH SERVING PROVIDES: ½ BREAD; 1 FRUIT; 60 OPTIONAL CALORIES

PER SERVING: 223 CALORIES; 2 G PROTEIN; 8 G FAT; 38 G CARBOHYDRATE; 18 MG
CALCIUM; 106 MG SODIUM; 0 MG CHOLESTEROL; 4 G DIETARY FIBER (THIS FIGURE
DOES NOT INCLUDE PIE CRUST; NUTRITION ANALYSIS NOT AVAILABLE)

REDUCED CHOLESTEROL AND SODIUM

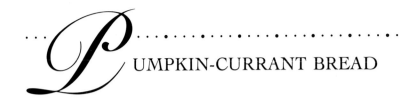

PUMPKIN-CURRANT BREAD

MAKES 12 SERVINGS

1 cup plus 2 tablespoons all-purpose flour
½ cup granulated sugar
2 tablespoons grated orange peel
1 teaspoon baking soda
½ teaspoon double-acting baking powder

1 cup canned pumpkin (no sugar added)
¾ cup thawed frozen egg substitute
¼ cup vegetable oil
¾ cup dried currants, plumped and drained
1½ ounces walnuts, chopped

1 Preheat oven to 375°F. In large mixing bowl combine flour, sugar, orange peel, baking soda, and baking powder; set aside.

2 In separate large mixing bowl combine pumpkin, egg substitute, and oil, stirring until blended. Add pumpkin mixture to flour mixture and stir until moistened. Add currants and walnuts and stir to combine.

3 Spray an 8½ × 4½ × 2½-inch nonstick loaf pan with nonstick cooking spray and transfer batter to pan. Bake in middle of center oven rack for 50 minutes (until golden and a toothpick inserted in center comes out dry). Set pan on wire rack and let cool.

EACH SERVING PROVIDES: 1¼ FATS; ¼ PROTEIN; ⅛ VEGETABLE; ½ BREAD; ½ FRUIT; 50 OPTIONAL CALORIES
PER SERVING: 177 CALORIES; 4 G PROTEIN; 7 G FAT; 27 G CARBOHYDRATE; 34 MG CALCIUM; 109 MG SODIUM; 0 MG CHOLESTEROL; 1 G DIETARY FIBER
REDUCED CHOLESTEROL AND SODIUM

CARROT MUFFINS WITH WALNUT-CREAM CENTERS

MAKES 12 SERVINGS, 1 MUFFIN EACH

2¼ cups all-purpose flour
⅓ cup plus 1 teaspoon
   granulated sugar, divided
2 teaspoons baking soda
1½ cups shredded carrots
⅔ cup less 2 teaspoons golden
   raisins, plumped and
   drained
¼ cup less 1 teaspoon
   margarine, softened
1 cup low-fat buttermilk (1%
   milk fat)

½ cup thawed frozen egg
   substitute
2 tablespoons thawed frozen
   concentrated orange juice
   (no sugar added)
1 teaspoon vanilla extract
⅓ cup plus 2 teaspoons light
   cream cheese
2 ounces walnuts, finely
   chopped
2 tablespoons light sour cream

1 Preheat oven to 350°F. Line twelve 2½-inch muffin-pan cups with paper baking cups; set aside.

2 In large mixing bowl combine flour, ⅓ cup sugar, and the baking soda, stirring to combine. Add carrots and raisins and stir to coat. Stir in margarine; set aside.

3 In small mixing bowl combine buttermilk, egg substitute, orange juice concentrate, and vanilla; stir into flour mixture. Fill each baking cup with an equal amount of batter (each will be about ⅔ full).

4 In separate small mixing bowl combine cream cheese, walnuts, sour cream, and remaining sugar. Top each portion of batter with an equal amount of cream cheese mixture. Bake in middle of center oven rack until golden brown, 20 to 25 minutes. Remove muffins from pan to wire rack and let cool.

EACH SERVING PROVIDES: 1¼ FATS; ¼ PROTEIN; ¼ VEGETABLE; 1 BREAD; ½ FRUIT; 65 OPTIONAL CALORIES

PER SERVING: 236 CALORIES; 6 G PROTEIN; 8 G FAT; 35 G CARBOHYDRATE; 55 MG CALCIUM; 260 MG SODIUM; 5 MG CHOLESTEROL; 2 G DIETARY FIBER

REDUCED CHOLESTEROL

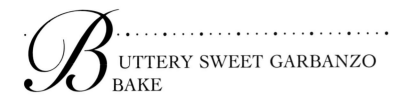

BUTTERY SWEET GARBANZO BAKE

MAKES 8 SERVINGS

1 ounce walnut pieces
¼ cup golden raisins
½ pound rinsed drained canned chick-peas
¼ cup granulated sugar
1 tablespoon plus 1 teaspoon sweet margarine
1 tablespoon sweet whipped butter

¼ teaspoon ground cinnamon
¼ teaspoon pumpkin pie spice
¼ cup thawed frozen egg substitute
3 egg whites (at room temperature)
½ teaspoon confectioners' sugar

1 Preheat oven to 350°F. In food processor process walnuts until finely ground, about 1 minute. Add raisins and, using an on-off motion, process until raisins are finely chopped. Add chick-peas and process until mixture forms a paste, about 2 minutes.

2 Add sugar, margarine, butter, cinnamon, and pumpkin pie spice to chick-pea mixture and process until combined, about 1 minute. Add egg substitute and process until blended, about 1 minute. Transfer to large mixing bowl.

3 Using mixer on high speed, in medium mixing bowl beat egg whites until stiff peaks form. Fold beaten whites, ⅓ at a time, into chick-pea mixture.

4 Spray 9-inch pie plate with nonstick cooking spray and transfer chick-pea mixture to pie plate. Bake in middle of center oven rack for 30 minutes (until a toothpick inserted in center comes out dry). Transfer to wire rack and let cool.

5 To serve, sprinkle with confectioners' sugar.

EACH SERVING PROVIDES: ¾ FAT; ¼ PROTEIN; ½ BREAD; ¼ FRUIT; 45 OPTIONAL CALORIES
PER SERVING: 131 CALORIES; 4 G PROTEIN; 6 G FAT; 16 G CARBOHYDRATE; 21 MG CALCIUM; 97 MG SODIUM; 3 MG CHOLESTEROL; 2 G DIETARY FIBER

Variation: Sweet Garbanzo Bake—Omit whipped butter and increase margarine to 2 tablespoons. In Serving Information increase Fat to 1 and decrease Optional Calories to 40.

PER SERVING: 131 CALORIES; 4 G PROTEIN; 6 G FAT; 16 G CARBOHYDRATE; 21 MG CALCIUM; 87 MG SODIUM; 0 MG CHOLESTEROL; 2 G DIETARY FIBER

REDUCED CHOLESTEROL AND SODIUM

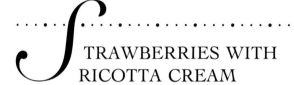

STRAWBERRIES WITH RICOTTA CREAM

We've called for strawberries in this recipe, but blueberries or peaches are delicious alternatives.

MAKES 2 SERVINGS

¼ cup part-skim ricotta cheese
2 tablespoons thawed frozen
   dairy whipped topping
1 tablespoon light cream cheese

½ teaspoon grated lemon peel
½ teaspoon grated orange peel
2 cups strawberries

1 Set sieve over small mixing bowl; press ricotta cheese through sieve. Add whipped topping, cream cheese, lemon peel, and orange peel to ricotta and stir to combine.

2 To serve, arrange half the strawberries and half the ricotta mixture in each of 2 dessert dishes.

EACH SERVING PROVIDES: ½ PROTEIN; 1 FRUIT; 30 OPTIONAL CALORIES
PER SERVING: 116 CALORIES; 5 G PROTEIN; 5 G FAT; 14 G CARBOHYDRATE; 116 MG CALCIUM; 85 MG SODIUM; 13 MG CHOLESTEROL; 4 G DIETARY FIBER
REDUCED CHOLESTEROL AND SODIUM

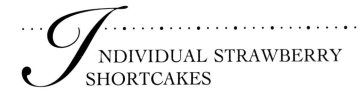

INDIVIDUAL STRAWBERRY SHORTCAKES

MAKES 6 SERVINGS, 1 SHORTCAKE EACH

1 cup plus 2 tablespoons all-purpose flour
1 tablespoon granulated sugar
1½ teaspoons double-acting baking powder
2 tablespoons margarine, cut into pieces
½ cup low-fat buttermilk (1% milk fat)

1½ cups strawberries, divided
½ cup thawed frozen dairy whipped topping
2 tablespoons light sour cream
Slivers of lime peel (optional) for garnish

1 Preheat oven to 425°F. Line six 2½-inch muffin-pan cups with paper baking cups; set aside.

2 In medium mixing bowl combine flour, sugar, and baking powder. Using a pastry blender, cut in margarine until mixture resembles coarse meal. Add buttermilk and stir until moistened.

3 Fill each baking cup with an equal amount of batter (each will be about ⅔ full). Bake in middle of center oven rack for 10 to 12 minutes (until cakes are golden and a toothpick inserted in center comes out dry). Remove cakes to wire rack and let cool.

4 When ready to serve, in food processor puree half of the strawberries; halve remaining strawberries and set aside. In small mixing bowl combine whipped topping and sour cream.

5 Remove paper baking cups from cakes. Cut each cake in half horizontally and spoon an equal amount of whipped topping mixture onto bottom half of each cake; top each with remaining half of cake. Onto 6 individual plates spoon an equal amount of pureed strawberries; set 1 shortcake on each plate, and top with an equal amount of sliced strawberry halves. Garnish with lime peel.

EACH SERVING PROVIDES: 1 FAT; 1 BREAD; ¼ FRUIT; 45 OPTIONAL CALORIES
PER SERVING: 172 CALORIES; 4 G PROTEIN; 6 G FAT; 26 G CARBOHYDRATE; 87 MG CALCIUM; 180 MG SODIUM; 2 MG CHOLESTEROL; 2 G DIETARY FIBER
REDUCED CHOLESTEROL AND SODIUM

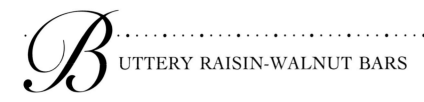

BUTTERY RAISIN-WALNUT BARS

Wrap bars individually and freeze for future snacking. Pack a frozen bar in your brown-bag lunch and it will thaw by noon.

MAKES 12 SERVINGS, 1 BAR EACH

2 cups less 2 tablespoons golden raisins, finely chopped

½ cup less 2 teaspoons granulated sugar, divided

1 teaspoon grated lemon peel

2 ounces walnuts, finely chopped

2¼ cups all-purpose flour, divided

1 teaspoon double-acting baking powder

¼ cup whipped butter

2 tablespoons plus 2 teaspoons margarine

½ cup thawed frozen egg substitute

¼ cup light sour cream

1 teaspoon vanilla extract

2 teaspoons ground cinnamon

1   Preheat oven to 350°F. In 1-quart saucepan combine raisins, *1 cup water*, 1 tablespoon sugar, and the lemon peel and cook over high heat until mixture comes to a boil. Reduce heat to low and let simmer until mixture thickens, 2 to 3 minutes. Stir in walnuts and 2 tablespoons flour; set aside and let cool.

2   On sheet of wax paper sift together remaining flour and the baking powder; set aside.

3   Using mixer on high speed in large mixing bowl, beat ⅓ cup sugar, the butter, and margarine until light and fluffy, about 3 minutes. Beat in egg substitute, until blended. Stir in sour cream and vanilla. Stir in flour mixture.

4   Spray a 13 × 9 × 2-inch nonstick baking pan with nonstick cooking spray. Divide dough in half; press half of dough over bottom of prepared pan. Spread raisin mixture in pan and top with remaining half of dough.

5   In small bowl combine remaining 1 tablespoon sugar and the cinnamon; sprinkle over dough. Bake in middle of center oven rack until golden,

25 to 30 minutes. Set pan on wire rack and let cool. Remove from pan and cut into 12 equal bars.

EACH SERVING PROVIDES: 1 FAT; ¼ PROTEIN; 1 BREAD; 1¼ FRUITS; 70 OPTIONAL CALORIES
PER SERVING: 274 CALORIES; 5 G PROTEIN; 9 G FAT; 45 G CARBOHYDRATE; 48 MG CALCIUM; 109 MG SODIUM; 9 MG CHOLESTEROL; 2 G DIETARY FIBER

Variation: Raisin-Walnut Bars—Substitute ⅓ cup reduced-calorie margarine (tub) for the whipped butter and margarine. In Serving Information decrease Optional Calories to 50.

PER SERVING: 251 CALORIES; 5 G PROTEIN; 7 G FAT; 45 G CARBOHYDRATE; 46 MG CALCIUM; 101 MG SODIUM; 2 MG CHOLESTEROL; 2 G DIETARY FIBER
REDUCED CHOLESTEROL, FAT AND SODIUM

PETIT FOUR PRUNES

MAKES 2 SERVINGS, 3 PRUNES EACH

¼ cup part-skim ricotta cheese
¼ ounce walnuts, finely chopped (about 1 tablespoon)
¼ ounce (about 2 teaspoons) mini semisweet chocolate chips

1 tablespoon light cream cheese
½ teaspoon grated orange peel
6 medium pitted prunes

In small mixing bowl combine all ingredients except prunes. Press center of each prune to indent and spoon an equal amount of cheese mixture into each indentation.

EACH SERVING PROVIDES: ¼ FAT; ½ PROTEIN; 1 FRUIT; 45 OPTIONAL CALORIES
PER SERVING: 147 CALORIES; 6 G PROTEIN; 7 G FAT; 18 G CARBOHYDRATE; 108 MG CALCIUM; 80 MG SODIUM; 13 MG CHOLESTEROL; 2 G DIETARY FIBER
REDUCED CHOLESTEROL AND SODIUM

ROSY CRANBERRY APPLESAUCE

Serve each portion of this tangy treat topped with whipped topping and sprinkled with cinnamon.

MAKES 2 SERVINGS, ABOUT ½ CUP EACH

1 small apple (about ¼ pound), cored, pared, and cubed
¾ cup applesauce (no sugar added)

½ cup cranberries
2 teaspoons firmly packed dark brown sugar

1   Spray 1-quart saucepan with nonstick cooking spray and heat; add apple and cook over medium-high heat, stirring frequently, for 1 minute.

2   Add applesauce, cranberries, *2 tablespoons water,* and the brown sugar and cook, stirring occasionally, until cranberries pop, about 10 minutes. Let cool slightly. Transfer to bowl; cover and refrigerate until ready to serve.

EACH SERVING PROVIDES: 1½ FRUITS; 20 OPTIONAL CALORIES

PER SERVING: 97 CALORIES; 0.3 G PROTEIN; 0.2 G FAT; 25 G CARBOHYDRATE; 10 MG CALCIUM; 3 MG SODIUM; 0 MG CHOLESTEROL; 2 G DIETARY FIBER (THIS FIGURE DOES NOT INCLUDE CRANBERRIES; NUTRITION ANALYSIS NOT AVAILABLE)

REDUCED CHOLESTEROL, FAT AND SODIUM

SUMMER FRUIT CRISP

Delicious served warm or chilled.

MAKES 8 SERVINGS

1 pound plums, pitted and sliced
1 pound nectarines, blanched, peeled, pitted, and sliced
¾ cup plus 1 teaspoon all-purpose flour, divided
2 tablespoons firmly packed light brown sugar
1 teaspoon ground cinnamon, divided
½ teaspoon grated lemon peel
2 tablespoons granulated sugar
2 tablespoons plus 2 teaspoons margarine

1 Preheat oven to 375°F. In medium mixing bowl combine plums and nectarines; add 1 teaspoon flour, the brown sugar, ½ teaspoon cinnamon, and the lemon peel and toss to combine.

2 Spray an 8 × 8 × 2-inch baking dish with nonstick cooking spray and arrange fruit mixture in dish.

3 In small bowl combine remaining flour, cinnamon, the granulated sugar, and margarine; sprinkle over fruit mixture. Bake until fruit mixture is bubbly, 25 to 30 minutes.

EACH SERVING PROVIDES: 1 FAT; ½ BREAD; 1 FRUIT; 30 OPTIONAL CALORIES
PER SERVING: 158 CALORIES; 2 G PROTEIN; 4 G FAT; 29 G CARBOHYDRATE; 14 MG CALCIUM; 46 MG SODIUM; 0 MG CHOLESTEROL; 2 G DIETARY FIBER
REDUCED CHOLESTEROL, FAT AND SODIUM

PEANUTTY PUDDING

MAKES 4 SERVINGS

¼ cup creamy peanut butter
2 cups skim *or* nonfat milk, divided
1 envelope (four ½-cup servings) reduced-calorie instant vanilla pudding mix (25 calories per serving as packaged)

2 tablespoons plus 2 teaspoons reduced-calorie strawberry spread (16 calories per 2 teaspoons)
¼ cup thawed frozen dairy whipped topping

1 In small microwavable mixing bowl microwave peanut butter on High (100%) for 30 seconds, until softened. Add 1 cup milk and stir to combine; microwave on High for 1 minute, stirring once halfway through cooking.

2 Transfer peanut butter mixture to large mixing bowl. Add remaining milk and the pudding mix and, using mixer on low speed, beat until blended, 1 to 2 minutes.

3 Into each of four 6-ounce dessert dishes pour ¼ of pudding mixture. Cover and refrigerate until pudding is set, at least 30 minutes.

4 To serve, in small microwavable mixing bowl microwave strawberry spread on High for 10 seconds, until melted. Top each pudding with 1 tablespoon whipped topping and 2 teaspoons strawberry spread.

EACH SERVING PROVIDES: ½ MILK; 1 FAT; 1 PROTEIN; 55 OPTIONAL CALORIES
PER SERVING: 193 CALORIES; 9 G PROTEIN; 10 G FAT; 20 G CARBOHYDRATE; 157 MG CALCIUM; 474 MG SODIUM; 2 MG CHOLESTEROL; 1 G DIETARY FIBER
REDUCED CHOLESTEROL

"BREAD AND BUTTER" PUDDING

Serve warm or chilled.

MAKES 4 SERVINGS

8 slices reduced-calorie white bread (40 calories per slice)
2 tablespoons plus 2 teaspoons reduced-calorie margarine (tub)
¼ cup dark raisins, divided
½ cup evaporated skimmed milk
½ cup low-fat milk (1% milk fat)

¼ cup thawed frozen egg substitute
2 tablespoons plus 2 teaspoons instant nonfat dry milk powder
1 tablespoon plus 1½ teaspoons granulated sugar
½ teaspoon vanilla extract

1 Preheat oven to 350°F. Spread both sides of each slice of bread with ½ teaspoon margarine. Arrange 4 bread slices in a stack and cut stack in half diagonally, making 8 triangles. Cut stack in opposite direction, making 8 more triangles. Repeat procedure with remaining bread slices, making 16 more triangles.

2 Spray 9-inch pie plate with nonstick cooking spray and arrange half of the bread triangles over bottom and up sides of plate, overlapping triangles slightly. Sprinkle half of the raisins over triangles. Repeat procedure using remaining bread triangles and topping with remaining raisins.

3 Using a wire whisk, in medium mixing bowl beat together remaining ingredients; pour over bread. Bake in middle of center oven rack for 40 minutes (until a knife inserted in center comes out dry).

EACH SERVING PROVIDES: ½ MILK; 1 FAT; ¼ PROTEIN; 1 BREAD; ½ FRUIT; 25 OPTIONAL CALORIES
PER SERVING: 214 CALORIES; 10 G PROTEIN; 5 G FAT; 37 G CARBOHYDRATE; 212 MG CALCIUM; 352 MG SODIUM; 3 MG CHOLESTEROL; 1 G DIETARY FIBER
REDUCED CHOLESTEROL AND FAT

ALMOND PUDDING

MAKES 4 SERVINGS

1 cup low-fat milk (1% milk fat)
½ cup evaporated skimmed milk
1 envelope (four ½-cup servings) reduced-calorie instant vanilla pudding mix (25 calories per serving as packaged)

¼ teaspoon almond extract
¼ cup light sour cream
⅓ cup thawed frozen dairy whipped topping, divided
1 ounce chopped dry-roasted almonds (no salt added), divided

1 In medium mixing bowl combine first four ingredients. Using mixer on low speed, beat until blended.

2 Using rubber scraper, fold in sour cream, ¼ cup whipped topping, and ½ ounce almonds.

3 Into each of four 6-ounce dessert dishes spoon ¼ of the pudding mixture. Top each portion with ¼ of the remaining whipped topping and almonds. Cover and refrigerate until set, about 30 minutes.

EACH SERVING PROVIDES: ½ MILK; ½ FAT; ¼ PROTEIN; 65 OPTIONAL CALORIES
PER SERVING: 161 CALORIES; 7 G PROTEIN; 8 G FAT; 17 G CARBOHYDRATE; 188 MG CALCIUM; 405 MG SODIUM; 9 MG CHOLESTEROL; 0.3 G DIETARY FIBER
REDUCED CHOLESTEROL

MELBA PUDDING

Use a sharp paring knife to peel the peaches for this scrumptious dessert.

MAKES 4 SERVINGS

2 cups skim *or* nonfat milk
1 envelope (four ½-cup
    servings) reduced-calorie
    instant vanilla pudding mix
    (25 calories per serving as
    packaged)

¾ pound peaches, peeled, pitted,
    and pureed
½ cup thawed frozen dairy
    whipped topping, divided
1½ cups raspberries (reserve 8
    raspberries for garnish)

1 Using milk, prepare pudding according to package directions; stir in peach puree and ¼ cup whipped topping.

2 Into each of four 6-ounce dessert dishes spoon ⅛ of the pudding mixture. Top each portion with ¼ of the raspberries, ¼ of the remaining pudding, 1 tablespoon of the remaining whipped topping, and 2 reserved raspberries. Cover and refrigerate until pudding is set, at least 30 minutes.

EACH SERVING PROVIDES: ½ MILK; 1 FRUIT; 50 OPTIONAL CALORIES
PER SERVING: 144 CALORIES; 5 G PROTEIN; 3 G FAT; 27 G CARBOHYDRATE; 166 MG CALCIUM; 404 MG SODIUM; 2 MG CHOLESTEROL; 3 G DIETARY FIBER
REDUCED CHOLESTEROL AND FAT

BRANDY ALEXANDER MOUSSE

MAKES 4 SERVINGS

1½ teaspoons unflavored gelatin
½ cup evaporated skimmed milk
2 tablespoons brandy
1 tablespoon crème de cacao
¼ teaspoon vanilla extract
¼ teaspoon imitation brandy
     extract

½ teaspoon ground nutmeg,
     divided
2 egg whites (at room
     temperature)
1 tablespoon granulated sugar
½ cup thawed frozen dairy
     whipped topping

1 In 1-quart saucepan sprinkle gelatin over milk and let stand 1 minute to soften; cook over low heat, stirring constantly, until gelatin is completely dissolved, about 1 minute. Remove from heat; stir in brandy, crème de cacao, extracts, and ¼ teaspoon nutmeg. Transfer to medium mixing bowl.

2 Fill large mixing bowl with ice water. Set bowl of gelatin-brandy mixture in ice water and let stand, stirring frequently with a rubber scraper, until mixture is the consistency of egg whites, about 2 minutes. Remove bowl from ice water and set aside.

3 Using a mixer on high speed, in medium mixing bowl beat egg whites and sugar until soft peaks form; set aside.

4 Using a rubber scraper, stir half of the whipped topping into gelatin-brandy mixture; fold in remaining whipped topping. Fold in beaten whites, ⅓ at a time.

5 Into each of four 10-ounce dessert dishes spoon ¼ of the mousse mixture. Sprinkle each portion with an equal amount of remaining nutmeg. Cover and refrigerate until set, at least 2 hours.

EACH SERVING PROVIDES: ¼ MILK; 80 OPTIONAL CALORIES
PER SERVING: 104 CALORIES; 5 G PROTEIN; 2 G FAT; 10 G CARBOHYDRATE; 94 MG CALCIUM; 75 MG SODIUM; 1 MG CHOLESTEROL; 0 G DIETARY FIBER
REDUCED CHOLESTEROL, FAT AND SODIUM

BAKED BANANAS IN PHYLLO

MAKES 4 SERVINGS

3 frozen phyllo dough sheets
    (12 × 17 inches each),
    thawed*
1 tablespoon plus 1 teaspoon
    reduced-calorie margarine
    (tub), melted
1 teaspoon granulated sugar
¼ teaspoon ground cinnamon

2 medium bananas (about 6
    ounces each), peeled and cut
    lengthwise into halves
¼ cup thawed frozen dairy
    whipped topping
2 tablespoons light sour cream
½ cup strawberries, pureed
¼ cup raspberries

1 Preheat oven to 400°F. Spray clean work surface with nonstick cooking spray. Unroll 1 sheet of phyllo dough and arrange on prepared work surface. Spray surface of phyllo dough sheet with nonstick cooking spray; top with second sheet of phyllo dough. Repeat procedure, using remaining sheet of phyllo dough and spraying with nonstick cooking spray. Using a paring knife, starting from wide side, cut stacked phyllo dough sheets into 4 equal pieces.

2 In small bowl combine margarine, sugar, and cinnamon. Onto each piece of phyllo dough arrange 1 banana half; drizzle an equal amount of margarine mixture over each banana. Fold narrow sides of phyllo dough over each banana. Starting from wide sides, roll phyllo dough to enclose bananas.

3 Spray nonstick baking sheet with nonstick cooking spray. Arrange phyllo dough–covered bananas, seam-side down, on baking sheet. Bake in middle of center oven rack until phyllo dough is golden, 5 to 8 minutes.

4 In small bowl combine whipped topping and sour cream. In a separate small mixing bowl combine strawberry puree and raspberries.

5 To serve, arrange 1 baked banana onto each of 4 individual serving plates; top each with an equal amount of berry mixture and whipped topping mixture.

EACH SERVING PROVIDES: ½ FAT; ½ BREAD; 1 FRUIT; 45 OPTIONAL CALORIES
PER SERVING: 155 CALORIES; 3 G PROTEIN; 4 G FAT; 28 G CARBOHYDRATE; 9 MG CALCIUM; 105 MG SODIUM; 3 MG CHOLESTEROL; 2 G DIETARY FIBER (THIS FIGURE DOES NOT INCLUDE PHYLLO DOUGH; NUTRITION ANALYSIS NOT AVAILABLE)
REDUCED CHOLESTEROL, FAT AND SODIUM

* Phyllo dough must be thawed in the refrigerator for at least 8 hours, or overnight.

BAKLAVA

MAKES 8 SERVINGS

1 cup golden raisins, plumped and drained
¼ pound walnuts, finely chopped
2 tablespoons granulated sugar
½ teaspoon ground cinnamon

12 frozen phyllo dough sheets (12 × 17 inches each), thawed*
2 tablespoons lemon juice
2 tablespoons honey

1 Preheat oven to 400°F. In medium mixing bowl combine raisins, walnuts, sugar, and cinnamon; stir to combine and set aside.

2 Spray an 8 × 8 × 2-inch baking dish with nonstick cooking spray. On clean work surface unroll 1 sheet of phyllo dough. Cover remaining sheets with plastic wrap or a slightly damp towel and set aside.

3 Spray surface of phyllo dough sheet with nonstick cooking spray. Fold in half crosswise, forming a rectangle. Repeat with a second sheet of dough. Fit dough into prepared baking dish, covering bottom of pan and folding dough when necessary.

4 Sprinkle ⅕ of the raisin-nut mixture over phyllo dough in baking dish.

5 Repeat, using remaining prepared phyllo dough and raisin-nut mixture, making 5 more layers and ending with phyllo dough.

6 Using a serrated knife, score surface of stacked phyllo dough sheets, making four 4 × 4-inch squares. Score each square in half diagonally, making 8 triangles. Bake for 15 minutes.

7 While Baklava is baking, in small saucepan combine lemon juice and honey and cook over low heat, stirring frequently, until honey is melted, about 1 minute. Remove Baklava from oven and cut at scored lines, making 8 triangles. Pour lemon-honey mixture evenly over Baklava. Return Baklava to oven and bake for 5 minutes. Cool in pan on wire rack.

EACH SERVING PROVIDES: 1 FAT; ½ PROTEIN; 1 BREAD; 1 FRUIT; 30 OPTIONAL CALORIES

PER SERVING: 270 CALORIES; 6 G PROTEIN; 9 G FAT; 45 G CARBOHYDRATE; 25 MG CALCIUM; 131 MG SODIUM; 0 MG CHOLESTEROL; 2 G DIETARY FIBER (THIS FIGURE DOES NOT INCLUDE PHYLLO DOUGH; NUTRITION ANALYSIS NOT AVAILABLE)

REDUCED CHOLESTEROL, FAT AND SODIUM

* Phyllo dough must be thawed in the refrigerator for at least 8 hours, or overnight.

PHYLLO PIROUETTE COOKIES

MAKES 4 SERVINGS, 3 COOKIES EACH
(SHOWN ON BACK JACKET WITH ORANGE LACE COOKIES AND ICED
JAMAICAN COFFEE; SEE PAGES 257 AND 278)

1 tablespoon margarine, melted	1 ounce semisweet chocolate
¼ teaspoon grated orange peel	chips
3 frozen phyllo dough sheets (12	
× 17 inches each), thawed*	

1 Preheat oven to 350°F. In small mixing bowl combine margarine and orange peel; set aside.

2 On clean work surface unroll 1 sheet of phyllo dough. Cover remaining sheets of dough with plastic wrap or a slightly damp towel and set aside.

3 Using pastry brush, brush ⅓ of the margarine mixture over unrolled sheet of phyllo dough. Using a paring knife and starting at wide side, cut phyllo dough sheet into 4 equal pieces. Starting from the narrow side of each piece of phyllo dough, roll each jelly-roll fashion. Repeat procedure, using remaining margarine mixture and phyllo dough sheets, making 8 more cookies.

4 Spray nonstick baking sheet with nonstick cooking spray and arrange cookies, seam-side down, on baking sheet. Bake in middle of center oven rack until cookies are golden, about 10 minutes. Transfer cookies to wire rack and let cool.

5 Place chocolate chips in 1-cup heat-resistant glass liquid measure and microwave on High (100%) for 15 seconds, until chocolate begins to melt; stir to combine. Microwave on High for 15 seconds, until chocolate is completely melted and smooth; stir to combine.

6 Arrange sheet of wax paper on baking sheet. Dip both ends of each cookie in melted chocolate and arrange on prepared baking sheet. Refrigerate cookies until chocolate is set, about 30 minutes.

EACH SERVING PROVIDES: ¾ FAT; ½ BREAD; 40 OPTIONAL CALORIES
PER SERVING: 110 CALORIES; 2 G PROTEIN; 5 G FAT; 15 G CARBOHYDRATE; 1 MG CALCIUM; 96 MG SODIUM; 0.1 MG CHOLESTEROL; DIETARY FIBER DATA NOT AVAILABLE
REDUCED CHOLESTEROL AND SODIUM

* Phyllo dough must be thawed in the refrigerator for at least 8 hours, or overnight.

ORANGE LACE COOKIES

MAKES 4 SERVINGS, 2 COOKIES EACH
(SHOWN ON BACK JACKET WITH PHYLLO PIROUETTE COOKIES AND
ICED JAMAICAN COFFEE; SEE PAGES 256 AND 278)

2 tablespoons firmly packed
    light brown sugar
2 tablespoons margarine
2 tablespoons light corn syrup
1½ teaspoons thawed frozen
    concentrated orange juice
    (no sugar added)

¼ cup all-purpose flour
½ teaspoon grated orange peel
    Dash ground mace

1 Preheat oven to 350°F. Using a spoon, in medium mixing bowl cream
sugar and margarine until light and fluffy. Stir in corn syrup. Add orange
juice concentrate and stir until thoroughly combined; stir in flour, orange
peel, and mace.

2 Onto nonstick baking sheet drop 4 heaping teaspoonsful of batter, leaving a space of about 6 inches between each.

3 Bake in middle of center oven rack until edges of cookies are lightly
browned, 6 to 8 minutes. Set baking sheet on wire rack and let cool
slightly, about 2 minutes. Using plastic pancake turner, carefully transfer
cookies to wire rack and let cool completely.

4 Repeat procedure using remaining batter to make 4 more cookies.

EACH SERVING PROVIDES: 1½ FATS; ¼ BREAD; 70 OPTIONAL CALORIES
PER SERVING: 139 CALORIES; 1 G PROTEIN; 6 G FAT; 21 G CARBOHYDRATE; 10 MG
CALCIUM; 84 MG SODIUM; 0 MG CHOLESTEROL; 0.2 G DIETARY FIBER
REDUCED CHOLESTEROL AND SODIUM

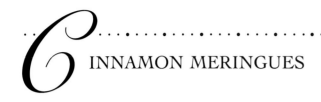

CINNAMON MERINGUES

Meringues can be stored in an airtight container for up to three weeks. When it comes time to serve, top them with fresh berries or ice milk.

MAKES 8 SERVINGS, 1 MERINGUE EACH

3 egg whites (at room temperature)
Dash cream of tartar

½ cup plus 1 tablespoon confectioners' sugar, sifted
⅛ teaspoon ground cinnamon

1 Preheat oven to 200°F. Line baking sheet with parchment paper; set aside.

2 Using mixer on high speed, in medium mixing bowl beat egg whites until foamy, about 1 minute. Add cream of tartar and beat until combined, about 1 minute. Gradually beat in sugar and cinnamon; continue beating until peaks are stiff but not dry, about 3 minutes.

3 Spoon mixture onto baking sheet, forming 8 equal mounds. Bake in middle of center oven rack until golden and crisp, about 55 minutes. Turn oven off and open oven door slightly; let meringues stand in oven for 4 to 6 hours to dry. Set baking sheet on wire rack and let cool completely.

EACH SERVING PROVIDES: 75 OPTIONAL CALORIES
PER SERVING: 39 CALORIES; 1 G PROTEIN; 0 G FAT; 9 G CARBOHYDRATE; 1 MG CALCIUM; 21 MG SODIUM; 0 MG CHOLESTEROL; 0 G DIETARY FIBER
REDUCED CHOLESTEROL, FAT AND SODIUM

APPLE MERINGUE

MAKES 4 SERVINGS

½ pound Golden Delicious *or*
    Granny Smith apples, cored,
    pared, and sliced
1 tablespoon honey
1 teaspoon lemon juice
½ teaspoon grated lemon peel,
    divided

¼ teaspoon cornstarch
3 egg whites (at room
    temperature)
    Dash cream of tartar
1 tablespoon granulated sugar

1 Preheat oven to 300°F. In 2-quart saucepan combine apples, honey, *1 tablespoon water,* the lemon juice, and ¼ teaspoon lemon peel and cook over medium heat, stirring occasionally, until apples are tender-crisp, about 5 minutes. Stir in cornstarch and cook until mixture thickens slightly, about 1 minute.

2 Spray 1-quart casserole with nonstick cooking spray and arrange apple mixture in casserole; set aside.

3 Using mixer on high speed, in large mixing bowl beat together egg whites and cream of tartar until frothy. Gradually beat in sugar, ½ teaspoon at a time. Add remaining lemon peel and continue beating until whites are stiff but not dry.

4 Spread beaten whites over apple mixture. Place casserole in middle of center oven rack; reduce oven temperature to 275°F and bake for 20 minutes, or until meringue is golden.

EACH SERVING PROVIDES: ¼ PROTEIN; ½ FRUIT; 30 OPTIONAL CALORIES
PER SERVING: 70 CALORIES; 3 G PROTEIN; 0.2 G FAT; 15 G CARBOHYDRATE; 4 MG CALCIUM; 42 MG SODIUM; 0 MG CHOLESTEROL; 1 G DIETARY FIBER
REDUCED CHOLESTEROL, FAT AND SODIUM

HOLIDAY FRUIT CAKE

MAKES 12 SERVINGS

2¼ cups all-purpose flour, divided
1 tablespoon double-acting baking powder
½ teaspoon baking soda
⅓ cup granulated sugar
¼ cup margarine, softened
3 eggs
1 cup low-fat buttermilk (1% milk fat)

¾ cup golden raisins, plumped and drained
1½ ounces walnuts, chopped
2 tablespoons candied mixed fruit
2 tablespoons confectioners' sugar, sifted

1 Preheat oven to 325°F. Spray 8-cup fluted tube pan with nonstick cooking spray; sprinkle with 2 teaspoons flour, tilting pan so flour coats bottom and sides. Remove excess flour to sheet of wax paper; set aside.

2 On same sheet of wax paper sift all remaining flour, the baking powder, and baking soda; set aside.

3 Using mixer on high speed, in medium mixing bowl beat together granulated sugar and margarine until light and fluffy, about 3 minutes. Add eggs, 1 at a time, beating after each addition until blended. Alternately stir in buttermilk and flour mixture. Stir in raisins, walnuts, and candied fruit.

4 Transfer batter to prepared pan and bake in middle of center oven rack for 40 to 45 minutes (until golden and a toothpick inserted in center comes out dry).

5 Let cake cool in pan for 5 minutes. Remove cake from pan and set on wire rack to cool.

6 In small bowl combine confectioners' sugar and *1 teaspoon warm water,* stirring to combine. Drizzle sugar mixture evenly over cake.

EACH SERVING PROVIDES: 1¼ FATS; ¼ PROTEIN; 1 BREAD; ½ FRUIT; 60 OPTIONAL CALORIES

PER SERVING: 231 CALORIES; 5 G PROTEIN; 8 G FAT; 36 G CARBOHYDRATE; 98 MG CALCIUM; 232 MG SODIUM; 54 MG CHOLESTEROL; 1 G DIETARY FIBER (THIS FIGURE DOES NOT INCLUDE CAKE FLOUR; NUTRITION ANALYSIS NOT AVAILABLE)

REDUCED FAT

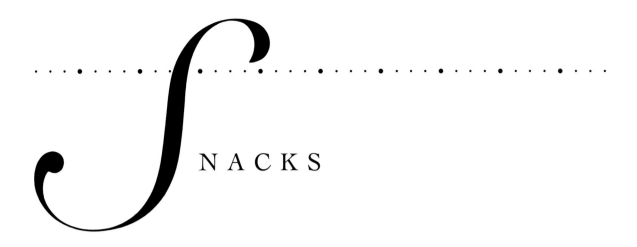

SNACKS

THE WORD *SNACK* HAS GENERATED SOME MIXED MEANINGS. But snacking is as healthy as what you choose to snack on, and even some foods we thought were taboo can be fine snacks—in moderation. "Mexican" Party Snack, made in the microwave, combines corn chips, peanuts, and cereal with a spicy Mexican flavor. This mix can be stored in a sealed container for up to two weeks, so make a lot to keep on hand. Crave popcorn? Bring your own bag of Buttery Szechwan Popcorn to the movies. For trail mix enthusiasts, Dried Fruit and Nut Mix does the trick. Freeze Granola Bars to bring to work. They'll thaw by munch time! For a more significant snack, try a Walnut-Cheese Sandwich on cinnamon raisin bread. The gang coming over? Impress them with an Elegant Fruit-and-Cheese Platter. It serves eight and the cheese is baked in phyllo for a surprising twist. Summer calls for cool and refreshing snacks, and Orange Thick Shake or Gazpacho Cooler with freeze-ahead vegetable cubes are ready when you are. Pair these with some snacks above or go solo. Island Iced Tea and Iced Jamaican Coffee with whipped topping both feature rum—a delicious way to imbibe, perhaps poolside!

ONION STRIPS

Save preparation time by using your food processor to shred the cheese for this irresistible snack.

MAKES 10 SERVINGS, 2 STRIPS EACH

5 cups thinly sliced onions
1 package refrigerated ready-to-bake pizza-crust dough (10 ounces)

7½ ounces reduced-fat Swiss cheese, shredded

1 Preheat oven to 425°F. Spray 10-inch nonstick skillet with nonstick cooking spray and heat; add onions and cook over medium heat, stirring occasionally, until translucent, about 2 minutes. Cover and let cook until softened, about 5 minutes; set aside.

2 Spread pizza crust dough over bottom of a 13 × 9 × 2-inch baking pan. Spread onions over dough and top with cheese.

3 Bake until dough is golden and cheese is melted, about 15 minutes. Transfer pan to wire rack and let cool.

4 Cut dough in half lengthwise; cut each half into 10 equal strips.

EACH SERVING PROVIDES: 1 PROTEIN; 1 VEGETABLE; 1 BREAD
PER SERVING: 167 CALORIES; 11 G PROTEIN; 5 G FAT; 19 G CARBOHYDRATE; 283 MG CALCIUM; 171 MG SODIUM; 15 MG CHOLESTEROL; 1 G DIETARY FIBER
REDUCED CHOLESTEROL, FAT AND SODIUM

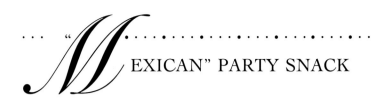

"MEXICAN" PARTY SNACK

Store this snack mixture in an airtight container for up to 2 weeks.

MAKES 4 SERVINGS

2 teaspoons margarine
¾ teaspoon Mexican seasoning
1 ounce corn chips
1 ounce shelled unsalted roasted
    peanuts

¾ ounce bite-sized crispy wheat
    or rice squares cereal

1 In medium microwavable mixing bowl microwave margarine on High (100%) for 30 seconds, until melted.

2 Add Mexican seasoning to margarine. Add remaining ingredients and toss to coat thoroughly. Microwave on Low (30%) for 1½ minutes, stirring every 30 seconds.

3 Spread party snack mixture on baking sheet; set aside and let cool.

EACH SERVING PROVIDES: 1 FAT; ¼ PROTEIN; ½ BREAD; 20 OPTIONAL CALORIES
PER SERVING: 119 CALORIES; 3 G PROTEIN; 8 G FAT; 10 G CARBOHYDRATE; 12 MG CALCIUM; 137 MG SODIUM; 0 MG CHOLESTEROL; 1 G DIETARY FIBER
REDUCED CHOLESTEROL AND SODIUM

BUTTERY SZECHUAN POPCORN

Keep this crunchy snack stored in an airtight container. To reheat, transfer popcorn mixture to medium microwavable mixing bowl and microwave on Medium (50%) for 2 minutes, stirring once halfway through cooking.

MAKES 2 SERVINGS, ABOUT 2 CUPS EACH

1 tablespoon sweet whipped butter

2 teaspoons sweet margarine

1 teaspoon reduced-sodium soy sauce

4 cups plain prepared popcorn (oil-popped)

¾ ounce toasted whole grain oat cereal

½ ounce shelled dry-roasted peanuts

¼ teaspoon garlic powder

¼ teaspoon onion powder

⅛ teaspoon ground red pepper

1 In small microwavable bowl combine butter and margarine. Microwave on High (100%) for 40 seconds, until butter and margarine are melted; stir in soy sauce.

2 In medium mixing bowl combine popcorn and cereal; add butter-margarine mixture and toss to coat.

3 Add remaining ingredients and toss to combine. Serve immediately.

EACH SERVING PROVIDES: 1½ FATS; ¼ PROTEIN; 1½ BREADS; 25 OPTIONAL CALORIES

PER SERVING: 262 CALORIES; 5 G PROTEIN; 19 G FAT; 19 G CARBOHYDRATE; 23 MG CALCIUM; 217 MG SODIUM; 10 MG CHOLESTEROL; 3 G DIETARY FIBER

Variation: Szechuan Popcorn—Omit whipped butter. In Serving Information omit Optional Calories.

PER SERVING: 228 CALORIES; 5 G PROTEIN; 16 G FAT; 19 G CARBOHYDRATE; 22 MG CALCIUM; 216 MG SODIUM; 0 MG CHOLESTEROL; 3 G DIETARY FIBER

REDUCED CHOLESTEROL

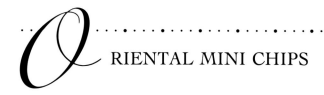

ORIENTAL MINI CHIPS

MAKES 2 SERVINGS, 20 CHIPS EACH

1 teaspoon teriyaki sauce
½ teaspoon vegetable *or* peanut
   oil
½ teaspoon Chinese sesame oil

10 wonton skins (wrappers),
   3 × 3-inch squares
1 teaspoon sesame seed

1   Preheat oven to 400°F. In small bowl combine teriyaki sauce and oils. Cut each wonton skin into quarters. Using a pastry brush, brush both sides of wonton-skin quarters with an equal amount of teriyaki mixture and arrange on nonstick baking sheet. Sprinkle wonton-skin quarters evenly with sesame seed.

2   Bake until golden, 6 to 8 minutes. Let chips cool on baking sheet. Store in an airtight container.

EACH SERVING PROVIDES: ½ FAT; 1 BREAD; 10 OPTIONAL CALORIES

PER SERVING: 118 CALORIES; 4 G PROTEIN; 3 G FAT; 18 G CARBOHYDRATE; 15 MG CALCIUM; 124 MG SODIUM; 0 MG CHOLESTEROL; DIETARY FIBER DATA NOT AVAILABLE

REDUCED CHOLESTEROL, FAT AND SODIUM

GRANOLA BARS

For easy storage, wrap each bar in plastic freezer wrap and freeze. Allow to thaw at room temperature for several hours or overnight in the refrigerator.

MAKES 8 SERVINGS, 1 BAR EACH

1 cup plus 2 tablespoons buttermilk baking mix
¼ cup dark raisins, divided
1½ ounces uncooked quick-cooking oats, divided
1½ ounces sliced almonds, divided
3 tablespoons firmly packed dark brown sugar, divided

½ cup skim *or* nonfat milk
¼ cup thawed frozen egg substitute
1 tablespoon plus 2 teaspoons margarine, melted
1 tablespoon toasted wheat germ
1 tablespoon shredded coconut

1 Preheat oven to 350°F. In medium mixing bowl combine baking mix, 2 tablespoons raisins, ¾ ounce oats, ¾ ounce almonds, and 1 tablespoon sugar, stirring to combine. Stir in milk and egg substitute.

2 Spray an 8 × 8 × 2-inch nonstick baking pan with nonstick cooking spray. Spread oat mixture in pan and set aside.

3 In medium mixing bowl combine remaining raisins, oats, almonds, sugar, the margarine, wheat germ, and coconut. Sprinkle evenly over oat mixture in pan.

4 Bake for 20 to 25 minutes (until a toothpick inserted in center comes out dry). Set pan on wire rack and let cool. Cut into 8 equal bars.

EACH SERVING PROVIDES: 1 FAT; ¼ PROTEIN; 1 BREAD; ¼ FRUIT; 55 OPTIONAL CALORIES
PER SERVING: 185 CALORIES; 5 G PROTEIN; 8 G FAT; 25 G CARBOHYDRATE; 69 MG CALCIUM; 246 MG SODIUM; 0.3 MG CHOLESTEROL; 1 G DIETARY FIBER
REDUCED CHOLESTEROL

DRIED FRUIT AND NUT MIX

MAKES 2 SERVINGS, ABOUT ½ CUP EACH

1½ ounces slivered almonds
1½ teaspoons shelled sunflower seed
1½ teaspoons shredded coconut
¾ ounce ready-to-eat crunchy nutlike cereal nuggets

6 dried apricot halves, chopped
2 tablespoons dark raisins
⅛ teaspoon ground nutmeg
⅛ teaspoon ground cinnamon

1 Heat 9-inch nonstick skillet; add almonds and sunflower seed and cook over medium heat, stirring constantly, until almonds begin to turn golden, about 2 minutes. Add coconut and, continuing to stir, cook for 30 seconds (*being careful not to burn*). Transfer to medium mixing bowl.

2 Add remaining ingredients to almond mixture and toss to combine. Set aside and let cool. Serve immediately or transfer to airtight container until ready to serve.

EACH SERVING PROVIDES: 1½ FATS; ¾ PROTEIN; ½ BREAD; 1 FRUIT; 25 OPTIONAL CALORIES

PER SERVING: 236 CALORIES; 7 G PROTEIN; 13 G FAT; 28 G CARBOHYDRATE; 74 MG CALCIUM; 70 MG SODIUM; 0 MG CHOLESTEROL; 3 G DIETARY FIBER (THIS FIGURE DOES NOT INCLUDE SUNFLOWER SEED; NUTRITIONAL ANALYSIS NOT AVAILABLE)

REDUCED CHOLESTEROL AND SODIUM

BANANA PUDDING SPLITS

MAKES 4 SERVINGS

1 cup plain low-fat yogurt
1 envelope (four ½-cup servings)
    reduced-calorie instant
    chocolate pudding mix (30
    calories per serving as
    packaged)
2 medium bananas (6 ounces
    each), peeled

½ teaspoon lemon juice
½ ounce pistachios, coarsely
    chopped
¼ cup thawed frozen dairy
    whipped topping
4 fresh bing cherries*

1 In blender process yogurt on high speed for 30 seconds; add pudding mix and process for 1 minute, scraping down sides of container as necessary.

2 Cut each banana into 6 diagonal slices and sprinkle with lemon juice.

3 Arrange 2 banana quarters into each of 4 goblets or dessert dishes; top with ¼ of the pudding mixture. Sprinkle each portion with ¼ of the pistachios; then top each with 1 tablespoon whipped topping and 1 cherry.

EACH SERVING PROVIDES: ¼ MILK; ¼ FAT; 1 FRUIT; 60 OPTIONAL CALORIES
PER SERVING: 161 CALORIES; 4 G PROTEIN; 5 G FAT; 28 G CARBOHYDRATE; 115 MG CALCIUM; 296 MG SODIUM; 3 MG CHOLESTEROL; 1 G DIETARY FIBER
REDUCED CHOLESTEROL AND FAT

* If bing cherries are not available, use 4 maraschino cherries; add 10 Optional Calories per serving.

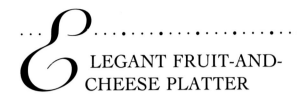

ELEGANT FRUIT-AND-CHEESE PLATTER

MAKES 8 SERVINGS

6 frozen phyllo dough sheets
    (12 × 17 inches each),
    thawed*
9 ounces Brie cheese, rind
    removed
½ small cantaloupe (about 1
    pound), seeded, pared, and
    cut into 8 equal wedges

24 large green *or* red seedless
    grapes
 2 cups strawberries
¾ cup raspberries
¾ cup blueberries

1   Preheat oven to 375°F. Spray clean work surface with nonstick cooking
    spray. Arrange 1 sheet of phyllo dough on prepared work surface. Spray
    surface of phyllo dough sheet with nonstick cooking spray; repeat lay-
    ering, spraying each sheet with nonstick cooking spray, making a stack
    of 6 sheets.

2   Set cheese in center of stacked phyllo dough sheets. Gather corners of
    phyllo dough sheets and twist to seal.

3   Spray nonstick baking sheet with nonstick cooking spray and set phyllo-
    covered cheese in center. Bake for 15 minutes (until phyllo dough is
    golden brown). Transfer baking sheet to wire rack and let cool slightly.

4   To serve, on serving platter decoratively arrange phyllo-covered cheese
    and fruit.

EACH SERVING PROVIDES: 1½ PROTEINS; ½ BREAD; 1 FRUIT

PER SERVING: 220 CALORIES; 9 G PROTEIN; 9 G FAT; 21 G CARBOHYDRATE; 72 MG
CALCIUM; 268 MG SODIUM; 32 MG CHOLESTEROL; 2 G DIETARY FIBER (THIS FIGURE
DOES NOT INCLUDE PHYLLO DOUGH; NUTRITION ANALYSIS NOT AVAILABLE)

*Phyllo dough must be thawed in the refrigerator for at least 8 hours, or overnight.

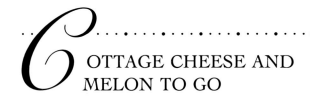

COTTAGE CHEESE AND MELON TO GO

MAKES 1 SERVING

1 cup cantaloupe chunks, divided
½ teaspoon lime juice (no sugar added)
⅓ cup low-fat cottage cheese (1% milk fat)

2 lettuce leaves
Dash ground nutmeg

1 In blender combine ⅓ cup cantaloupe chunks and the lime juice and process on high speed until pureed. Transfer to resealable plastic container. Cover and refrigerate until ready to pack.

2 In small mixing bowl combine remaining cantaloupe chunks with the cottage cheese and stir to combine.

3 Line a separate resealable plastic container with lettuce; top with cantaloupe–cottage cheese mixture and sprinkle with nutmeg. Cover and refrigerate until ready to pack.

4 To serve, pour pureed cantaloupe mixture over cantaloupe–cottage cheese mixture.

EACH SERVING PROVIDES: 1 PROTEIN; ½ VEGETABLE; 1 FRUIT
PER SERVING: 114 CALORIES; 11 G PROTEIN; 1 G FAT; 16 G CARBOHYDRATE; 75 MG CALCIUM; 319 MG SODIUM; 3 MG CHOLESTEROL; 1 G DIETARY FIBER

REDUCED CHOLESTEROL AND FAT

WALNUT-CHEESE SANDWICH

MAKES 1 SERVING

2 tablespoons Yogurt Cheese (see page 24)
1 tablespoon light cream cheese
2 slices cinnamon-raisin bread, toasted

½ ounce walnuts, chopped
1 teaspoon raspberry jam

1   In small mixing bowl blend Yogurt Cheese and cream cheese.

2   Onto 1 slice of bread spread cheese mixture; top with walnuts. Onto remaining slice of bread spread jam and set bread slice, jam-side down, over walnuts. Cut in half.

EACH SERVING (INCLUDING YOGURT CHEESE) PROVIDES: 1 FAT; ½ PROTEIN; 2 BREADS; 65 OPTIONAL CALORIES
PER SERVING: 295 CALORIES; 10 G PROTEIN; 13 G FAT; 36 G CARBOHYDRATE; 130 MG CALCIUM; 283 MG SODIUM; 10 MG CHOLESTEROL; 1 G DIETARY FIBER (THIS FIGURE DOES NOT INCLUDE RAISIN BREAD; NUTRITION ANALYSIS NOT AVAILABLE)
REDUCED CHOLESTEROL

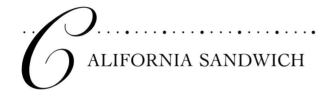

CALIFORNIA SANDWICH

MAKES 1 SERVING

1 tablespoon alfalfa sprouts
1 tablespoon dark raisins
1 tablespoon shredded carrot
½ teaspoon sunflower seed
2 slices reduced-calorie rye bread
    (40 calories per slice)
1 tablespoon plus 2 teaspoons
    light cream cheese

2 thin tomato slices
2 thin red onion slices
⅛ medium avocado (about 1
    ounce), pared and thinly
    sliced
2 lettuce leaves

1 In small mixing bowl combine sprouts, raisins, carrot, and sunflower seed; set aside.

2 Spread 1 slice of bread with cream cheese; top with sprout mixture, tomato, onion, avocado, lettuce, and remaining bread slice. Secure with toothpicks and cut sandwich in half.

EACH SERVING PROVIDES: 1 FAT; 1¾ VEGETABLES; 1 BREAD; ½ FRUIT; 65 OPTIONAL CALORIES
PER SERVING: 220 CALORIES; 8 G PROTEIN; 9 G FAT; 33 G CARBOHYDRATE; 104 MG CALCIUM; 334 MG SODIUM; 13 MG CHOLESTEROL; 5 G DIETARY FIBER (THIS FIGURE DOES NOT INCLUDE SUNFLOWER SEED; NUTRITION ANALYSIS NOT AVAILABLE)
REDUCED CHOLESTEROL

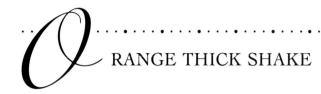

ORANGE THICK SHAKE

MAKES 1 SERVING, ABOUT ¾ CUP

1 packet reduced-calorie vanilla-
    flavored milk beverage
½ cup orange juice (no sugar
    added)

4 ice cubes
  Mint sprigs for garnish

1 In blender combine milk beverage and orange juice and process on high until smooth. Remove insert from center of blender cover and, with blender running on high, add ice cubes 1 at a time, processing after each addition, until ice is dissolved (mixture will be thick).

2 To serve, pour shake into chilled 8-ounce glass and garnish with mint.

EACH SERVING PROVIDES: 1 MILK; 1 FRUIT
PER SERVING: 126 CALORIES; 7 G PROTEIN; 0.1 G FAT; 24 G CARBOHYDRATE; 161 MG CALCIUM; 1 MG SODIUM; 0 MG CHOLESTEROL; 0.2 G DIETARY FIBER
REDUCED CHOLESTEROL, FAT AND SODIUM

SPICY TOMATO JUICE COOLER

MAKES 2 SERVINGS, ABOUT 1 CUP EACH

2 cups tomato juice, chilled
1 garlic clove, minced
1 teaspoon minced onion
1 teaspoon minced fresh parsley
1 teaspoon lemon juice
1 teaspoon apple cider vinegar
1 teaspoon reduced-sodium soy
    sauce

1 teaspoon prepared horseradish
1 teaspoon light corn syrup
  Dash hot sauce
  Dash pepper
6 ice cubes
2 medium celery ribs

1. In blender combine all ingredients, except ice cubes and celery ribs, and process on high speed until combined, about 30 seconds.

2. In each of 2 chilled 16-ounce glasses place 3 ice cubes and 1 celery rib. Pour half of the juice mixture into each glass.

EACH SERVING PROVIDES: 1½ VEGETABLES; 10 OPTIONAL CALORIES
PER SERVING: 64 CALORIES; 2 G PROTEIN; 0.2 G FAT; 16 G CARBOHYDRATE; 43 MG CALCIUM; 1,029 MG SODIUM; 0 MG CHOLESTEROL; 1 G DIETARY FIBER
REDUCED CHOLESTEROL AND FAT

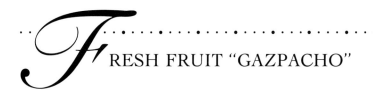

FRESH FRUIT "GAZPACHO"

This recipe calls for sliced fresh peaches. You can prepare the peaches in advance if you sprinkle them with lemon juice to prevent browning. Store in refrigerator until ready to use.

MAKES 8 SERVINGS, ABOUT ½ CUP EACH

2 cups watermelon chunks, pureed
¾ pound peaches, blanched, peeled, pitted, and sliced
½ pound kiwi fruit, pared and cut into chunks
¾ cup blueberries

20 small green *or* red seedless grapes
2 tablespoons freshly squeezed lime juice
2 teaspoons grated pared gingerroot

In medium serving bowl place all ingredients, stirring to combine. Cover and refrigerate until flavors blend, about 30 minutes. Stir again just before serving.

EACH SERVING PROVIDES: 1 FRUIT
PER SERVING: 56 CALORIES; 1 G PROTEIN; 0.4 G FAT; 14 G CARBOHYDRATE; 13 MG CALCIUM; 3 MG SODIUM; 0 MG CHOLESTEROL; 2 G DIETARY FIBER
REDUCED CHOLESTEROL, FAT AND SODIUM

GAZPACHO COOLER

Prepare the special ice cubes for this satisfying beverage the night before you plan to use them.

MAKES 2 SERVINGS

1 cup mixed vegetable juice *or* tomato juice
1 medium cucumber
1 cup chopped green bell pepper
¼ cup chopped onion
3 tablespoons freshly squeezed lime *or* lemon juice

2 teaspoons red wine vinegar
1 garlic clove
1 to 2 drops hot sauce
½ cup seltzer

1 Pour vegetable juice into an ice cube tray, making 10 cubes, and freeze until solid.

2 Cut 2 slices from cucumber and reserve for garnish. Pare and seed remaining cucumber, then cut into pieces.

3 In blender combine cucumber, pepper, onion, lime juice, vinegar, garlic, and hot sauce and process on medium speed until smooth. Stir in seltzer.

4 Into each of two 12-ounce glasses place half of the vegetable juice ice cubes; add half of the cucumber mixture. Garnish each serving with a reserved cucumber slice.

EACH SERVING PROVIDES: 2¾ VEGETABLES
PER SERVING: 62 CALORIES; 2 G PROTEIN; 1 G FAT; 15 G CARBOHYDRATE; 38 MG CALCIUM; 448 MG SODIUM; 0 MG CHOLESTEROL; 2 G DIETARY FIBER
REDUCED CHOLESTEROL AND FAT

ISLAND ICED TEA

MAKES 2 SERVINGS, ABOUT 1 CUP EACH

1 cup brewed tea
⅓ cup apricot nectar
⅓ cup pineapple juice (no sugar added)

2 tablespoons dark rum
6 ice cubes
2 lime *or* lemon slices for garnish

1 In small saucepan combine tea, apricot nectar, and pineapple juice and cook over medium-high heat until thoroughly heated, 1 to 2 minutes. Remove from heat; stir in rum.

2 Transfer to small pitcher or small mixing bowl and refrigerate until chilled, about 30 minutes.

3 Place 3 ice cubes in each of two 8-ounce glasses. Pour half of the tea mixture into each glass. Garnish each portion with a lime slice.

EACH SERVING PROVIDES: 1 FRUIT; 40 OPTIONAL CALORIES
PER SERVING: 80 CALORIES; 0.3 G PROTEIN; 0.1 G FAT; 12 G CARBOHYDRATE; 10 MG CALCIUM; 5 MG SODIUM; 0 MG CHOLESTEROL; 0.3 G DIETARY FIBER
REDUCED CHOLESTEROL, FAT AND SODIUM

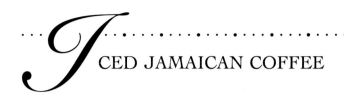CED JAMAICAN COFFEE

MAKES 1 SERVING
(SHOWN ON BACK JACKET WITH PHYLLO PIROUETTE AND ORANGE
LACE COOKIES; SEE PAGES 256 AND 257)

1 cup cold brewed coffee
2 tablespoons low-fat milk (1%
   milk fat)
1 tablespoon dark rum
¼ teaspoon ground cinnamon

⅛ teaspoon ground allspice
3 ice cubes
1 tablespoon thawed frozen dairy
   whipped topping

In chilled 12-ounce glass combine coffee, milk, rum, cinnamon, and allspice.
Add ice cubes and top with whipped topping.

EACH SERVING PROVIDES: 60 OPTIONAL CALORIES
PER SERVING: 64 CALORIES; 1 G PROTEIN; 1 G FAT; 4 G CARBOHYDRATE; 51 MG
CALCIUM; 25 MG SODIUM; 1 MG CHOLESTEROL; 0 G DIETARY FIBER
REDUCED CHOLESTEROL AND SODIUM

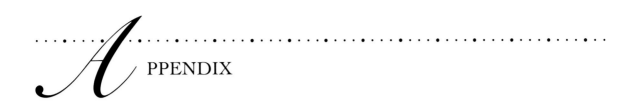

APPENDIX

GLOSSARY

Bake: To place food in a container and cook in an oven.

Baste: To moisten food while it cooks in order to add flavor and prevent the surface from drying out by coating with a liquid such as melted fat, a sauce, or meat drippings.

Beat: To make a mixture smooth by mixing ingredients vigorously with a spoon or electric mixer.

Blanch: To cook a food for a few minutes in boiling water to preserve the color, texture, or nutritional value or to loosen the skin from the food for easy removal.

Blend: To mix two or more ingredients thoroughly until smooth.

Boil: To cook in water or a liquid consisting mostly of water in which bubbles rise continually and break on the surface. A rolling boil is when the bubbles form rapidly.

Braise: To cook meat or poultry in a small amount of liquid in a covered container in the oven or over low heat on the range.

Broil: To cook by direct dry heat.

Brown: To cook a food, usually in a small amount of fat, on the range until the surface of the food changes color.

Chill: To refrigerate food or let it stand in ice or iced water until cold.

Chop: To cut into small pieces.

Combine: To mix together two or more ingredients.

Cool: To let a hot food come to room temperature.

Crimp: To press or pinch together.

Cube: To cut food into ½-inch squares.

Dash: Less than ⅛ teaspoon of an ingredient.

Dice: To cut a food into small squares, less than ½ inch in size.

Dredge: To cover a food with flour or a fine crumb mixture.

Fold: To combine ingredients lightly using a rubber scraper and cutting vertically through the mixture and then sliding the spatula across the bottom of the bowl, turning mixture over.

Fry: To cook, uncovered, in a small amount of fat.

Grate: To cut food into tiny particles using the small holes of a grater.

Grill: To cook over direct heat.

Julienne: To cut into slivers that resemble matchstick pieces.

Marinate: To let food stand in a mixture that will tenderize it or add flavor.

Mince: To cut or chop into very small pieces.

Mix: To combine ingredients so they are evenly distributed.

Pare: To cut off the outer covering of a food using a knife or vegetable peeler.

Peel: To remove the outer covering of a food using hands rather than a knife or vegetable peeler.

Pierce: A term applied to microwave cooking. To puncture a cover, thick skin, or membrane to allow steam to escape and prevent bursting.

Poach: To cook a food in a hot liquid.

Puree: To press food through a food mill or to process in a blender or food processor into a smooth, thick mixture.

Rearrange: A term applied to microwave cooking. To move food in its dish to another position for even cooking when the food cannot be stirred.

Reduce: To boil a liquid in an uncovered container until it cooks down, resulting in a specific consistency and flavor.

Roast: To cook foods on a rack, uncovered, in an oven.

Rotate: A term applied to microwave cooking. To turn a dish in a microwave oven one-quarter or one-half turn in order for the food to cook more evenly when it cannot be stirred.

Sauté: To brown or cook in a small amount of fat.

Shred: To cut food into long thin pieces using the large holes of a grater or shredding blade of a food processor.

Simmer: To cook in liquid just below the boiling point.

Slice: To cut a food into thin flat pieces.

Soften: To let cold butter or margarine stand at room temperature until it has a softer consistency.

Standing time: A term applied to microwave cooking. A period of time, after microwaving, which allows foods to complete heating or cooking in the center or in the thicker areas, without overcooking on the thin areas or edges.

Steam: To cook food on a rack or in a colander in a covered pan over steaming hot water.

Stir: To use a utensil in a circular motion to combine portions of a food.

Strain: To separate solid food from liquid by pouring the mixture through a strainer or sieve.

Whip: To beat a mixture rapidly with a whisk or electric mixer to incorporate air and increase volume.

METRIC CONVERSIONS

If you are converting the recipes in this book to metric measurements, use the following chart as a guide.

VOLUME			WEIGHT			OVEN TEMPERATURES	
¼ teaspoon	1 milliliter		1 ounce	30 grams		250°F	120°C
½ teaspoon	2 milliliters		¼ pound	120 grams		275°F	140°C
1 teaspoon	5 milliliters		½ pound	240 grams		300°F	150°C
1 tablespoon	15 milliliters		¾ pound	360 grams		325°F	160°C
2 tablespoons	30 milliliters		1 pound	480 grams		350°F	180°C
3 tablespoons	45 milliliters					375°F	190°C
¼ cup	50 milliliters					400°F	200°C
⅓ cup	75 milliliters					425°F	220°C
½ cup	125 milliliters					450°F	230°C
⅔ cup	150 milliliters		LENGTH			475°F	250°C
¾ cup	175 milliliters		1 inch	25 millimeters		500°F	260°C
1 cup	250 milliliters		1 inch	2.5 centimeters		525°F	270°C
1 quart	1 liter						

Dry and Liquid Measure Equivalents

TEASPOONS	TABLESPOONS	CUPS	FLUID OUNCES
3 teaspoons	1 tablespoon		½ fluid ounce
6 teaspoons	2 tablespoons	⅛ cup	1 fluid ounce
8 teaspoons	2 tablespoons plus 2 teaspoons	⅙ cup	
12 teaspoons	4 tablespoons	¼ cup	2 fluid ounces
15 teaspoons	5 tablespoons	⅓ cup less 1 teaspoon	
16 teaspoons	5 tablespoons plus 1 teaspoon	⅓ cup	
18 teaspoons	6 tablespoons	⅓ cup plus 2 teaspoons	3 fluid ounces
24 teaspoons	8 tablespoons	½ cup	4 fluid ounces
30 teaspoons	10 tablespoons	½ cup plus 2 tablespoons	5 fluid ounces
32 teaspoons	10 tablespoons plus 2 teaspoons	⅔ cup	
36 teaspoons	12 tablespoons	¾ cup	6 fluid ounces
42 teaspoons	14 tablespoons	1 cup less 2 tablespoons	7 fluid ounces
45 teaspoons	15 tablespoons	1 cup less 1 tablespoon	
48 teaspoons	16 tablespoons	1 cup	8 fluid ounces

Note: Measurement of less than ⅛ teaspoon is considered a dash or a pinch.

ACKNOWLEDGMENTS

Creating a top-notch cookbook takes many months of dedication and hard work. For this, we must thank many special people: Susan Astre, Patricia Barnett, Isabel Cohen, Christy Foley-McHale, Lee Haiken, Elizabeth Healy, Jackie Hines, Liz Marzulli, Susan Piscopo, Eileen Pregosin, Nina Procaccini, Judi Rettmer, Linda Rosensweig, Melonie Rothman, April Rozea, and Connie Welch for bringing their special skills and enthusiasm to this book.

INDEX

REDUCED-CHOLESTEROL RECIPES INDEX

$\mathcal{I}$NDEX FOR RECIPES WITH 30 PERCENT OR LESS OF THEIR CALORIES COMING FROM FAT

REDUCED-SODIUM RECIPES INDEX